WAR IN THE WOODS

WAR IN THE WOODS

Estonia's Struggle for Survival
1944–1956

by Mart Laar
Translation by Tiina Ets

Foreword by
Tõnu Parming

THE COMPASS PRESS
WASHINGTON, DC

Edited by Solon J. Candage
Book and Cover designed by Anne Meagher-Cook
Typesetting by Right Angle Graphics
Printed (alk paper) and bound by Edwards Brothers,
Ann Arbor, Michigan, USA

Library of Congress Cataloguing-in-Publication Data
Laar, M.
    [Sõda Metsas]
    War in the woods: Estonia's struggle for survival, 1944–1956 /
    by Mart Laar; translation by Tiina Ets; foreword by Tõnu Parming.
        p.   cm.
    Translation of: Sõda Metsas.
    Includes bibliographical references and index.
    ISBN 0-929590-08-2 (cloth). — ISBN 0-929590-09-0 (pbk.)
    1. Estonia — History — Autonomy and independence movements.
    2. Estonia — History — 1944–1991. I. Title.
    DK503.75.L3413 1992
    947'.410842 — dc20   92-14355
                                                             CIP

The Compass Press is an imprint of Howells House
Box 9546, Washington, DC 20016

"...The Finno-Ugric peoples are the children of neither the sea nor the hills, the steppes nor the deserts, the plateau nor the tundra, but of the forests of the North. The forests and the Spirit of the North — it is these that have shaped the character of the Finno-Ugric peoples through the millennia, it is these which define not only our character, but our inner strength."

— Oskar Loorits

Eestluse elujõud
Stockholm, 1951

This book is dedicated to the Forest Brothers, living and dead, and to all those who took the first steps toward the liberation of Estonia.

ESTONIA IN EUROPE 1945

ESTONIA 1945

This map depicts the 11 counties recognized by Estonians. Dashed line represents Estonian border which Soviets shortened.

BALTIC SEA

GULF OF FINLAND

GULF OF RIGA

SAAREMAA

HIIUMAA

Kärdla

Kuressaare

LÄÄNEMAA

Haapsalu

Nõmme
Paldiski
Tallinn
Keila

HARJUMAA

PÄRNUMAA

Mõisaküla
Kilingi-Nõmme
Sindi
Pärnu

LATVIA

VILJANDIMAA

Suure-Jaani
Viljandi
Mustla

Türi
Paide

JÄRVAMAA

Põltsamaa

Võrts
järv

VALGAMAA

Valga
Tõrva

Elva

Antsla

VÕRUMAA

Võru

TARTUMAA

Tartu

Jõgeva

Mustvee
Kallaste

Lake
Peipsi

Rakvere

VIRUMAA

Jõhvi

Narva

U.S.S.R.

TABLE OF CONTENTS

List of Illustrations

Photos:

I The Preview

1. General Serov, director of 1941 deportations
2–3. Trains for deportations
4. Early forest shelters
5. Early bunker
6–7. Forest Brothers, 1941
8–9. Soviet victims, Tartu, 1941
10–11. Basement of Tallinn's "Kave" building, 1941
12-13. Maps of Battle Sites and Resistance Activity

II Reoccupation and Resistance

14. Return of the "Finland Boys," 1944
15–16. Evacuees flee to Sweden by boat
17–24. Forest Brothers and activities, 1944
25–28. Scenes of resistance
29. Resistance note distributed by Forest Brothers
30–33. Jaan Roots and the "Orion" group

III The Antagonists

34–39. The enemy . . .
40–41. Equipment taken from alleged CIA agents
42–48. . . . and the Forest Brothers
49–53. August Sabe, the last free man

Photo credits:

1–11, 15, 16: Courtesy of Olaf Tammark
14, 42: Courtesy of the Estonian Archives in the US, Inc.
17–41, 43–53: Author's files

Figures 1–3: Bunker site plan, floor plan, and longitudinal section
Appendix A

Foreword

Guerrilla or partisan warfare has been a form of national resistance to foreign aggression since time immemorial. In Estonia, such resistance has traditionally been waged from the forests. Even the term for partisan warfare is derived from this, namely *metsavendlus*, or brotherhood of the forest. In modern Estonian history, the tactics of *metsavendlus* were widely used during the Soviet occupation of the country from mid–1940 to mid–1941, and once again after the Soviet reoccupation of Estonia in the fall of 1944.

While partisan resistance to Soviet rule is the stuff of legends and national pride for Estonians, the rest of the world has heard little of the tale to date. One reason is that during the Soviet occupation of Estonia, which lasted until August 1991, history was forced into the service of the state, and of the Communist Party which controlled the state. The Communist Party replaced factual history with fiction in order to advance its own ideologically predetermined view that "the working masses of Estonia, oppressed by bourgeois nationalists, yearned for socialism and Soviet rule." From this perspective of distorted history, Estonia was not occupied at all by the Soviet Union in 1940, but rather underwent "a progressive socialist revolution, the result of which was a voluntary union with the USSR." And, thus, from the viewpoint of the Communists, there was no postwar national resistance in Estonia, only "banditry."

Yet the historical record proves otherwise. The Communist Party of Estonia was politically irrelevant after the mid-1920s. So weak was its popular base in June 1940 that it had fewer than 150 members. Had Soviet troops not arrived in Estonia in the fall of 1939 as a result of a coercively imposed treaty of "mutual assistance," which followed the infamous Molotov–Ribbentrop Pact between Hitler and Stalin, the Republic of Estonia would not have been joined to the Soviet Union nine months later. The pivotal month was June 1940, when Stalin demanded that additional troops be stationed in Estonia. The result of this was that, in a country of 1,134,000 people with a standing army of 16,000 men, there were suddenly some 115,000 Soviet troops.

The military occupation allowed Moscow to dictate political terms which included the formation of a Communist-dominated cabinet hand-picked by Stalin's notorious henchman Andrei Zhdanov. This was followed by constitutionally illegal changes to the electoral law and Soviet-style one-party elections: There was only one candidate on the ballot in every electoral district, and this sole candidate was either a member of the Communist Party or screened by it. The farcical nature of the July 1940 elections is reflected in the fact that 99.8 percent of the legally valid votes were cast for these solo candidates. The new, bogus lower chamber of Estonia's parliament thus formed "asked" Moscow to admit Estonia to the Soviet Union.

The events of the first period of partisan resistance, 1940–1941, are better known than those of the second, postwar period. The Soviet occupiers were displaced in the summer of 1941 by German forces, which allowed enough of a respite to record the developments of the preceding year. Perhaps more important, many of those in the resistance during this first year of Soviet occupation fled to the West in the late summer of 1944, recording their experience there. Little of this information is available to date in English, however, and the definitive work is yet to be done.

Nevertheless, the English-language reader may acquire some insight into partisan warfare in Estonia from several historically realistic novels. Indeed, *Ristideta hauad* (1952), by the prominent Estonian novelist and poet Arved Viirlaid, has been translated into at least seven languages. The English translation, *Graves Without Crosses*, was issued in 1972 by the prominent Canadian publisher Clarke, Irwin & Company Ltd. Another work in a similar vein is Freed Kraav's *The Partisans* (New York: Vantage Press, 1952).

That any significant national resistance could be sustained at all after the Soviet occupation began in the summer of 1940 is remarkable. A large part of the Estonian standing army was transferred to the Soviet Red army. Most senior officers were separated from their units and staffs, and they were either executed soon after or they perished in the Norilsk region of Siberia. About 21,000 people disappeared or were murdered or deported during this first year of Soviet rule. And the fact that the German advance stopped in the middle of Estonia enabled Soviet authorities to conscript more than 33,000 young men in the northern half of the country. They were shipped to camps in Russia, where many of them perished in the harsh conditions of deprivation and forced labor. Thus, from the standpoint of manpower available for resistance, Estonia had suffered a devastating blow. Most important, the leaders of Estonian society in all sectors of life were by and large wiped out as a result of Soviet action. As it is, civil society was quickly destroyed through Sovietization, the movement of people was highly restricted, and even private communications were subjected to party and state control.

Although the organization of a patriotic resistance in these circumstances was by no means easy, it did occur. By the time the German invasion began in June 1941, the partisan movement had gained enough strength to engage sizable Soviet units, inflicting severe casualties upon them. Indeed, significant parts of Estonia were liberated from Soviet control in the summer of 1941 by Estonian partisans rather than by the German army.

The ensuing German occupation placed the Estonians in a rather difficult political position. Because of historical reasons there had been little popular sympathy for Germans until the brutal experience of Soviet rule. Yet the Germans would not allow Estonian national military units to be formed. And even when the Eastern Front was collapsing in 1944, and Estonian men agreed to serve in the defense of their own homeland in the German army, the command structure remained German. The important demographic point is that a large number of young Estonian men perished in the German army as well.

The tenacity of Estonian soldiers in the fight against the new Soviet onslaught provided a possibility for tens of thousands of their countrymen to escape westward in the late summer of 1944. Yet the Red tide could not be stemmed. By early 1945, all of Estonia was once again in the Stalinist grip, and the circumstances for national resistance became even more difficult now. By January 1945 Estonia had lost about 25 percent of its prewar population through deportations, military and civilian fatalities, political executions, flight, and territorial transfer. Almost all those societal leaders who had miraculously survived the first year of Soviet rule had by now fled or were dead or deported.

An important role in the postwar resistance was at first played by men who had served in German uniform in one form or another, and who had been cut off from retreat or withdrawal. Yet resistance was fueled primarily by the brutality of Soviet rule itself. The years 1940 and 1941 were fresh in everyone's memory, and as the full fury of postwar Stalinism befell Estonia, the ranks of the brotherhood of the forest swelled. It is this period of armed national resistance which is the subject of *War in the Woods*.

This is a story which could not until now have been readily told by historians. Few of the partisans ever made it to the West, and the Communist system simply would not allow anything to be published about the topic at home except in support of the Party's own dogmatic line. Thus, the true historical record of Estonian national resistance survived primarily in the memory of individuals, in a clandestine oral tradition, and in part in official archives which were inaccessible.

The Gorbachevian policies of *perestroika* and *glasnost* facilitated a change in the treatment of history. By 1987, there were strong demands in Estonia for the recordation of the historical truth. An important role in this regard was played by the Estonian Heritage Society (*Eesti Muinsuskaitse Selts*), founded toward the end of 1987. Mart Laar, a historian by training, was a founding member and a prominent leader in the society. Indeed, a student group organized by Laar in the early 1980s at the University of Tartu was already active in redefining the approaches to Estonian history before the Heritage Society was formed.

One of the major contributions of the Heritage Society was the restoration of monuments and historical sites, in particular the monuments erected mostly in the early 1920s in memory of those who made the supreme sacrifice in the Estonian War of Independence (1918–1920). These statues had been either destroyed by the Soviets or, in some cases, hidden by patriots. The Heritage Society's Historical Commission, headed by Mart Laar, began to collect surviving diaries and documents and, most important, it launched an ambitious program for recording the personal experiences of survivors.

The methodology of oral history has found wide applicability. It is an especially important technique in circumstances where the written record is lost, inaccurate, or nonexistent. Postwar Estonia is one such place. Without the systematic debriefing of individuals, the historical record of postwar Estonia could not possibly be set straight. We know, of course, that individual memory fails and may contain factual inaccuracies, but there is no alternative to the sifting and collation of information on this basis. It is the task of the historian to sort out the wheat from the chaff.

In any case, the legacy of five decades of Soviet occupation has been simply too destructive to allow history to be corrected on the basis of documentary evidence alone. Soviet archives have been selective in the documents which have been preserved. And even if unlimited access to Communist Party, governmental, and KGB archival collections were possible, it would at best yield useful insight into the official reaction to *metsavendlus* rather than into the motivation, organization, and activities of *metsavendlus*. In other words, the recreation of the historical record from the viewpoint of the Estonian national resistance to Soviet rule necessitates precisely the historiographic approach which Mart Laar has chosen and very skillfully presented in this book. He has listened to the tales of survivors —

participants as well as those in the partisan support networks — and combined this information with insight garnished from official documents.

The result of Mart Laar's effort is exciting history, a story of a woods alive with the struggle for freedom and independence. To be sure, gaps remain in this tale of national valor, but a monumental first step has been taken.

* * * * * *

Guerrilla warfare is a struggle by irregular forces and means against a stronger conventional force. Not all guerrilla movements are as successful as that in Afghanistan. The outcome depends greatly on the territorial and demographic base of the resistance, as well as on the scope and efficacy of external support. The eastern littoral of the Baltic Sea was not of important concern to the Western allies until well after the Second World War. While British, American, and West German intelligence maintained some contacts with Estonian partisans, the available evidence does not allow a conclusion that the degree of external support was significant. In the end, *metsavendlus* was an Estonian struggle against monumental odds.

It could hardly be expected that a small, decimated people on a small territory could succeed militarily against the might of a highly militarized totalitarian state. Yet the Soviet system for years could not crush the Estonian national resistance. The fateful blow to *metsavendlus* was delivered in March 1949 with the coercive collectivization of agriculture, and the concurrent massive deportation of the rural population. Collectivization in effect paralyzed the partisans' support networks, without which guerrilla warfare is difficult to wage. The brotherhood of the forest was not yet wiped out, but the most active phase of Estonian armed national resistance to Soviet rule came to an end.

Metsavendlus had clearly not achieved military victory. But the true value of guerrilla resistance has often been political and even moral. That the active period of armed struggle lasted as long as it did implies with certainty that a very sizable proportion of the Estonian people supported it or were otherwise sympathetic to it. And therein lies the essence of the political and moral victory of the Estonian national resistance. Namely, the resistance proved that the Estonians were a conquered people and the Republic of Estonia an occupied country. The Soviets could be said to have won the armed struggle, but *metsavendlus* denied them a political victory. In the end, the lack of such a victory helped to undermine the very legitimacy of Soviet rule over Estonia, a critical historical fact in the rebirth of Estonian independence in August 1991.

— Tönu Parming, Ph.D.
Toronto, Canada

Translator's Note

The Forest Brothers, called *Metsavennad* in Estonian, had a number of names — partisans, members of the Green Battalion, guerrillas, men of the Green army, and woodsmen. The Soviet authorities called them "bandits." These names are used interchangeably throughout the text, but refer to the same group of people resisting Soviet rule.

Another group known by many names is the Soviet state security apparatus, whose roots reach back to the Cheka (established by the Council of People's Commissars in 1917 to serve as the Bolshevik political police) and which underwent several metamorphoses and name changes between the years 1922 and 1954, being known as the GPU, NKVD (People's Commissariat of Internal Affairs), OGPU, GUGB, NKGB, MGB, and MVD, until it adopted its present name, the KGB, in March 1954. To avoid unnecessary confusion, the Soviet security establishment is referred to in this book as the NKVD until 1954, and as the KGB thereafter. When the author refers to the security apparatus it is important to keep in mind that the local KGB administration in Estonia was directly subordinate to the central KGB in Moscow, and thus the "security apparatus" operating in Estonia was no more than an obedient local arm of the central Soviet state security organization. Although the forerunner of the NKVD and KGB, the Cheka, changed its name as early as 1922, Soviet security workers were popularly referred to as "chekists" throughout the Soviet occupation of Estonia.

During its independence, the Republic of Estonia was divided into eleven administrative areas, which are referred to in this text as counties (*maakond*). Each county was subdivided into a number of districts (*vald*), the borders of which approximated the borders of traditional church and civil parishes (*kihelkond*) established over centuries. Although the Soviet authorities redrew the boundaries of the counties to form thirty-nine "raions" in 1950, diminishing their number to fifteen "raions" in 1964, the people continued to refer to their occupied homeland by the traditional and familiar terms of *maakond*, *vald*, and *kihelkond*.

Several Russian and Soviet terms that were inevitably injected in everyday speech during the occupation include *kulak*, which in Soviet usage represented a derogatory term for persons owning a more prosperous or larger farm and who were subsequently targeted for persecution. *Komsomol* refers to the Communist Youth League.

Quite often, the author refers to "destruction battalions" as groups of Soviet sympathizers organized to intimidate the population of Estonia. These battalions were formed in 1941 to carry out a scorched-earth campaign in Estonia during the first Soviet occupation, when it became evident that the German invasion would soon succeed. The destruction battalions were re-formed in 1944 with the onset of the second Soviet occupation and renamed People's Defense Units (whose "official" job it was to protect the local populace from hostile elements). The new name, however, never caught on in popular usage, since the battalions' tactics of destruction and intimidation remained unchanged.

Another group of men introduced in the text is the "Finland Boys." This term refers to the approximately 2,300 Estonian volunteers serving in the Finnish army and navy during World War II. For the most part, these men had fled German-occupied Estonia to join the Finnish armed forces, where they received military training and took part in action on the Finnish fronts. However, the threat of a new invasion of Estonia by the Red army prompted these men to return to their homeland to help in its defense. After the war, a number of the Finland Boys fought alongside the Forest Brothers.

—T. E.

Preface

Every nation looks upon its freedom fighters, its men and women who have fallen in defense of their land and people, as heroes. Estonia, lying at the crossroads of Eastern and Western interests, has paid dearly for its freedom. After centuries of foreign rule, the Estonians succeeded in creating an independent state in 1918, struggling desperately to defend it against all aggressors, and proving its vitality and potential for development to the whole world during the following decades. During its years of independence, Estonia changed beyond recognition.

Estonia's dynamic progress ground to a halt in 1940, when Stalinist Russia, acting in accordance with the Molotov–Ribbentrop Pact's secret additional protocols, occupied the Republic of Estonia and annexed it to the Union as the Estonian SSR. Estonia was swept by a wave of brutal terror that shattered its economic and social structures and suppressed its national culture and religion.

And yet, the Estonian people never lost hope for the rebirth of freedom. For several decades, a desperate struggle against the occupation authorities raged in the forests of Estonia. It was here that the "Forest Brothers," as the partisans were called, carried on the struggle for independence. The last Estonian partisan perished in 1978, 33 years after the end of World War II. Such fierce resistance and such painful losses are rarely found in the annals of history. Estonia lost nearly one-third of its population as a consequence of the occupation. Even in 1992, the number of Estonians in Estonia was less that it was in 1939.

For so long, it seemed that the bloodshed and sacrifices had been to no avail. Men, women, and children died in the forests of Estonia, but no one in the world heard this captive nation's cry for freedom. And yet, the concept of partisan war was a natural and commonly known phenomenon in the post-World War II era. Everyone knows of the partisan wars in Asia that peaked in the Indo-Chinese jungles. More recently, the Afghan partisans forced the Soviet occupation army to leave their land. Partisan war tactics are an inseparable part of the military doctrine of many countries.

Partisans also have a defined legal status. The Hague Convention regards partisans as regular combatants, guaranteeing them the same rights that soldiers have. Article 4 of the Third Geneva Convention of August 12, 1949 addresses the issue in more detail. It states that if the population of an occupied state takes up arms spontaneously, it should be dealt with as an equal party in the conflict.

Despite all this, very little attention has been devoted to the partisan wars in Eastern Europe, including Estonia. Some literature on this subject has been published in the West, written almost entirely by participants in the resistance movement or individuals indirectly involved with it. Among actual research works, some of Rein Taagepera's writings should be noted, as well as Tom Bower's book *The Red Web*, published in England.

More works have been published on this subject in the Soviet Union. These publications, however, rarely give an honest account of events, usually depicting resistance fighters as "bandits" who lacked popular support. Soviet archives, in this case the archives of the Communist Party of Estonia (CPE) and the archives of the Estonian Committee for State Security, now represent a valuable resource for the investigator of the postwar resistance movement. Both these archives were sealed to researchers for nearly all of the Soviet occupation era, but I was able to gain access to these materials shortly before Soviet rule in Estonia came to an end.

The CPE archives do, indeed, contain County Party Committee reports on Forest Brother activities and accounts of battles with Forest Brothers, but the files are all too obviously incomplete. It is not that the archival materials have been destroyed, but rather that they are the victims of the intense secrecy that pervaded the establishments of the occupying regime, including the Communist Party. The CPE archives could not possibly contain original copies of many important documents and decrees because all directives of any importance emanating from Moscow were sent out as secret letters, which were to be read and then returned to the central authorities. Instead, the CPE archives contain entire volumes of signatures indicating the receipt and return of these secret documents, but not the documents themselves. Fortunately for researchers, however, the Soviet bureaucratic system was not airtight, and some of these secret missives remained in the hands of district Party Committees, who ultimately filed them in the archives. That discussions conducted at the most important Party meetings were not recorded in writing also reflects the intensity of the Soviet desire for secrecy.

Although the situation in the archives of the Committee for State Security is a bit more encouraging, even their materials fail to give an exhaustive picture of the Forest Brothers movement. The security archives are divided into three separate levels of classification: first, the ultrasecret operations archives; second, the slightly less secret operations report records; third, the court files, which were opened to researchers in 1991. These court files do, indeed, provide some valuable source material, but their revelations are limited to the fate of those Forest Brothers who were captured alive by the security apparatus and made their way through the Soviet court system. The files on those Forest Brothers who fell in battle or died of their wounds have not been released, perhaps in deference to the axiom put forth by Stalin: "No person, no problem."

Although Soviet archives are obviously very important to the researcher of the resistance movement, the primary source of information remains the recollections of those who lived in the era of the Forest Brothers.

Estonia's first major opposition movement — the Estonian Heritage Society — took the lead in gathering this information. Realizing that most written historical accounts had been destroyed, the Heritage Society sought out the people who had experienced the postwar era in order to record their recollections of events. Under the society's sponsorship, I recorded the first stories in the summer of 1985. In 1986, I worked with a large group of young people collecting personal accounts in southern Estonia. We rode from village to town on bicycles and wrote down old people's narratives. By the summer of 1987, a large number of similar youth groups were working in Estonia. Naturally, the KGB took a great deal of interest in our operations. We were harassed and our work was disrupted.

At the end of 1987, an opposition magazine published my first in-depth survey of the terror that the Soviet occupation had wrought upon Estonia. The KGB initiated criminal proceedings against me. I was accused of "slandering the Soviet regime." Since these charges were pressed while I was abroad for the first time, they seemed to hope that I would ask for political asylum abroad and not return to Estonia. I proved to be more pigheaded than the KGB expected, and soon I was at the mercy of the investigative apparatus. A wave of protest rolled through Estonia; defense committees were formed in New York, Toronto, and Paris. At this, the startled authorities rushed to assure everyone that this had all been a "mistake."

After that, our work could continue. To date, the archives of the Estonian Heritage Society have collected more than 30,000 pages of recollections, original documents, photographs, etc. The past, left for dead by the aggressors, lives again. The Heritage Society archives, preserving a nation's history as told by its own people, are awe-inspiring.

This book draws from the recollections of the Forest Brothers themselves as well as from documents unearthed in Soviet archives, and represents the first volume to draw from a number of sources in an attempt to describe Estonia's desperate struggle for freedom in the years 1944 to 1956.

May it be a memorial to those Forest Brothers still living, as well as to those who fell in battle and those who endured torture and death in Siberian slave camps.

Many people have helped and contributed to this book, but I owe special thanks to Olaf Tammark for his valuable advice and his description of his bunker in the appendix, Tönu Parming for his comments and foreword, and Tiina Ets for her excellent translation.

I wish also to thank Agu Ets and Peeter Luksep for their invaluable help in bridging the gap between Tallinn and Washington.

—Mart Laar
Tallinn, March, 1992

(this page intentionally blank)

ESTONIAN PARISHES

Naissaare

Iru
Harku Tallinn Jõelähtme
Pakri Kuusalu Kolga
Rae Raasiku Kõnnu
Keila Anija
Saue Tõdva Peningi
Nõva Padise Kernu Kohila
Riguldi Nissi Kuivajõe Ravila
Noarootsi Hageri Kõue
Vormsi Oru Piirsalu Juuru
Kõrgessare Pühalepa Taebla Varbola Rapla
Käina Asuküla Raikküla Kuimetsa
Emmaste Kullamaa Märjamaa Kehtna
Ridala Martna Märjamaa
Kirbla Velise Lelle
Lihula Vigala
Muhu Kaisma
Leisi Pöide Karuse Halinga Vändra
Mustjala Pärsamaa Soontaga Are
Kihelkonna Kaarma Valjala Laimjala Varbla Tori
Lümanda Kärla Pihtla Audru Sauga
Kuressaare Tõstamaa Paikuse
Salme Seliste
Torgu Tahkuranna Tihemetsa
Saarde Abja
Kihnu Häädemeeste Rajangu
Laiksaare Tali
Orajõe

Chapter 1

The Tradition: Guerrillas, Partisans, and Mõrtsuks

Estonia is a small land of forests and swamps on the shores of the Baltic Sea. Its geographical location has made it a frequent theater of war. Along with its northern neighbor Finland and its southern neighbors Latvia and Lithuania, Estonia comprises a unique buffer zone between Western civilization and Eastern barbarianism. Estonians have had to repel attacks from east, west, north, and south on this small tract of land squeezed between larger powers. And yet, Estonia has been better known for its skilled farmers and brave seamen than for its courageous fighting men. These talents have made the nation prosper, but have also enticed new invaders to enter the land.

The Estonians and Finns belong to the Finno-Ugric family of nations. Setting out on their westward trek from the Ural mountains during the great migration, they reached their current territory about 5,000 years ago. While the nomadic peoples accustomed to the open steppes feared the mystic silence of the forest, the Finno-Ugrians, having migrated mostly by way of forests and swamps, felt a warm kinship with the forest. They saw the forests as friendly and protective, rather than dark and evil. Since these people were usually vastly outnumbered by their invaders, they relied on their characteristically Finno-Ugric affinity with the forest to withdraw into the mazes of the woods and swamps where no enemy dared to go. The Finno-Ugric peoples preferred ambush from the depths of the forest over a bold attack across an open field. In 1132, the Estonians destroyed the army of Russian ruler Izyaslav in the swamps of central Estonia; in 1210, they dealt a crushing blow to the German crusaders on a narrow forest path in Ümera, Livonia.

The ancient years of freedom ended all too quickly. The Estonians were unable to continue resisting the enemies who invaded from every direction. Estonia, one of the last Northern European pagan

1

strongholds, surrendered to invading forces in the 13th century and submitted to Christianization. After several wars, Estonia came under the rule of the Livonian Order, which represented the German crusaders. The land was renamed *Maarjamaa* — the Land of Mary, Mother of God. Churches and mighty fortresses rose throughout the land. The cities of Tallinn (then Reval) and Tartu (then Dorpat) were well known throughout medieval Europe as centers for Eastern trade. Through these contacts, Estonia basked in the influences of Western culture, although the invaders soon stripped the Estonians of most of their basic rights and forced them into bondage as serfs. In 1507, the Estonian peasants lost the free man's right to bear arms. The core of the Livonian Order's army was now made up of mercenaries instead of free peasants. This proved disastrous for the land's defense capability. Old Livonia was now easy prey for neighboring Russia, whose czar Ivan the Terrible felt the time was right to expand his empire into Europe in the mid-sixteenth century.

In 1558, the huge armies of Russia with their Tatar horsemen invaded Estonia and ravaged the land. The Livonian War was to last for decades. The German manor lords abandoned the Estonian peasants to their fate. Hundreds of defenseless peasants locked outside the city walls of Tartu by fearful city dwellers were killed by the Tatar cavalry. News of Russia's success lured other great powers to the area, and soon Estonia had become a battleground where the Russians, Poles, Swedes, and Danes waged war against each other.

The Estonians had no choice but to take up arms, band into guerrilla units, and take action in defense of their homes and their lives. Women and children were sent into the depths of the forest when danger threatened, while the men lay in ambush to surprise the enemy. While the peasants' early resistance was random and spontaneous, most began serving in the Swedish army before long, since Sweden guaranteed greater rights for the peasantry. Estonian guerrilla units attacked Russian squads and convoys, ambushed messengers, and reclaimed livestock taken by the enemy. During the Livonian War, the most famous of these units were the peasant troops led by Ivo Schenkenberg. Called the "Livonian Hannibal" by his adversaries, Schenkenberg armed his unit well and proved to be a worthy opponent for the Russians. Schenkenberg's peasants played a noteworthy role in the defense of Tallinn in 1577, subsequently working together with other peasant troops in larger operations. Peasant guerrillas, known as mõrtsuks, achieved fame and notoriety during the Livonian war. Indeed, the peasants were instrumental in helping bring Estonia under Swedish rule in 1627.

The Swedish king, however, did not give the Estonian peasants the freedom they had anticipated. And yet, the period of Swedish rule remains in popular memory as "the good Swedish years." The land was rebuilt. In the final decades of the seventeenth century, the central Swedish government began limiting the rights of the manor lords and expanding the freedoms of the peasants. One of the most valuable contributions of the Swedish kings was their emphasis on general education in Estonia. With the creation of a network of Estonian-language rural schools, written Estonian flourished and the number of Estonian-language publications grew. In 1632, King Gustavus IV Adolphus founded the University of Tartu.

The peaceful period of Swedish rule was brief. In 1700, the young Russian czar Peter I, opening a window to Europe, invaded Estonia once more and turned the country into a battleground. Again, the peasants hid in the forests and swamps and fought for their lives. In Iisaku, one of these guerrilla units operated under the leadership of the local minister Christian Kelch, who found enough time during his guerrilla activity to write the Livonian Chronicles. The small partisan units, however, proved to be no match for the invading armies. Tatar units scoured the forests with bloodhounds. Under brutal torture, people were forced to reveal secret paths and hideouts. The resistance was suppressed. Many Estonians were killed; many were deported to Russia as slaves. So much of the population was destroyed that a person finding another human footprint would weep for joy. In 1721, Estonia fell under Russian rule. The Russians restored the rights of the manor lords; the Estonian people were thrust into an era of cruel oppression.

In retrospect, the fact that Estonians were able to endure in such conditions is a miracle. And yet, they did. The roots growing deep into their homeland's soil over thousands of years proved to be stronger than the death and destruction wrought by their enemies. The Estonians replanted fallow fields and restored their ravaged farms. Moreover, despite the centuries of efforts by the Germans and Russians to crush the national identity of the Estonian people, the Estonians retained their unique language and culture. During the period of national awakening that blossomed in Eastern and Northern Europe in the nineteenth century, the Estonians began demanding the right to use their native language and the right of ownership in their ancestral land. The voices of Estonians and Finns harmonized in these demands. Over a period of two decades, the socially undifferentiated "country folk" made the transition to a modern European people. The economy prospered, a local intelligentsia emerged, national culture flourished, and a variety of organizations and unions sprang up throughout the land. The first political parties were formed early in the nineteenth century. Following the example of the Finns, Estonian demands for autonomy within the Russian Empire grew more insistent.

World War I broke out in 1914. Within a few years, the forces of the German Empire stood at the Estonian border. Imposition of German rule would have dealt a serious blow to the Estonians who were trying to eliminate the privileges of the German manor lords, but the tottering Russian Empire was no longer able to preserve control of its borderlands, and in 1917, it collapsed. Drawing from their traditions of self-government, the Estonians quickly established the institutions necessary for realizing their right to self-determination. The Estonian soldiers and officers who had fought in the czarist army during the World War played an instrumental role in these endeavors.

By the fall of 1917, Estonian political figures realized that no matter which government emerged victorious in Russia — left-wing or right-wing — both had the common desire to wipe out the national identity of the nations on the borders of its empire. Since only full independence could guarantee Estonia's survival, the people set their sights on this goal. On February 24, 1918, the establishment of the independent and democratic Republic of Estonia was proclaimed in the capital city of Tallinn. The young state had to defend its sovereignty against the onslaught of Bolshevik Russia as well as the German Empire. German forces were the first to occupy Estonia, but were forced to leave as the German Empire collapsed. Then, the Red army invaded the land under instructions from Lenin to push westward and light the flame of revolution in Europe.

The newly independent states on the frontiers of the empire had no resources with which to resist the Red army except the resolute desire to defend their freedom. This helped little against the heavily armed Red army units, who easily pushed back the weak "White" front. By early January, 1919, only one-fourth of Estonia's territory was under the control of the Estonian Republic, and the Red army stood within forty kilometers of the capital. To the south, the Red Latvian Riflemen prepared to join forces with the East Prussian workers' brigades. There seemed to be no escape. Reason would dictate that the struggle of these small nations against the Russian colossus could end only in absolute defeat.

Although they had their backs to the wall, the Estonian people had undergone an irreversible transformation. The new generation of Estonians, raised in a nationalistic spirit, refused to accept defeat. In the absence of an alternative, the Estonians brought an ancient tactic into play. They activated partisan units behind the Red army's front lines to harass the enemy's rear, jam his communications, and carry out diversionary tactics. The Red units on the front lines were suddenly cut off from the rear. In addition, volunteers from Finland and Denmark arrived in Tallinn to help the Estonians.

The resistance threw the Red front off balance. The hit-and-run tactics of partisans from the forest struck panic into the enemy's ranks and helped in shifting the advantage to the Estonians. One of the most well-known units formed in the enemy rear was young Lieutenant Julius Kuperjanov's partisan battalion, whose bold attacks on the communications and transport lines of the enemy allowed the Estonians' "armored trains," improvised from common wagons and sandbags, to retake Estonia's second-largest city, Tartu. By February 24, 1919, Estonia had driven out the enemy. Now they rushed to help their southern neighbors, the Latvians.

The Estonians' successes disrupted the plans of the Soviet military command. The Russians broke off their strike toward Germany on March 3, 1918 in accordance with the newly concluded Treaty of Brest Litovsk, and concentrated their forces against the Estonians, whose military prowess had become the greatest in the region. The effort proved futile. The Estonians, driven by nationalistic enthusiasm, repulsed all Soviet attacks, also fighting fiercely in Latvia to drive out the Reds, and helping a Latvian national government come to power. Lenin's plan to "export the revolution" into Western Europe had failed. On February 2, 1920, a peace treaty was concluded in Tartu between the Republic of Estonia and Soviet Russia, which unconditionally recognized Estonia's independence. In 1921, Estonia was admitted to the League of Nations. Economic and cultural reconstruction went into full swing. An independent Estonian state, no more than a dream several years before, had become a reality.

The greatest challenges lay ahead. The land was ravaged, the economy stood in ruins, and the country lacked the experience and specialized talents it needed for reconstruction. The traditional work ethic of the Estonian people came to the rescue. In 1919, the democratically elected *Asutav Kogu* (Constituent Assembly) passed the Estonian Constitution and a number of laws. The most significant of these was the land reform law, which returned land rights to the peasants. This law dissolved the power of the manor lords and paved the way for the establishment of an effective agrarian economy.

Naturally, the young state faced a number of difficulties in its early years. Heavy industry, which up to now had been oriented toward the Russian market, had to be reconstructed to fit the needs of a small independent state. A large number of factories had to be closed or redesigned. The worldwide economic crisis of the 1920s and 1930s struck Estonia as well, but national growth was all the greater after that. In the latter half of the 1930s, the rate of Estonia's economic growth was among the six highest in the world. Estonia's high-quality agricultural products found a solid market in Europe. The chemical industry based on the mining of oil shale thrived.

Above all, Estonia managed to preserve a parliamentary system of government, despite an inclination toward governmental authoritarianism. In contrast to a number of European countries, not one person was put to death in Estonia for political reasons. The law on cultural autonomy passed in 1925 was one of the most progressive in the world, and it demonstrated the Estonian government's faith in its citizens. A totally unprecedented action in Europe during that period was Estonia's 1938 amnesty for all political prisoners, including left-wing as well as right-wing extremists. Although problems persisted in 1938, Estonia's fortunes were on the rise.

Estonia's standard of living equaled that of Finland, falling slightly behind that of Sweden and Denmark. The gap narrowed with every year. Further progress was destined to remain no more than a fond wish, since the winds of war that swept over the world during the next several years would smash the aspirations of small nations.

On August 23, 1939, the representatives of the dictators Hitler and Stalin, Joachim von Ribbentrop and Vyacheslav Molotov, signed a so-called non-aggression treaty, in whose secret additional protocols, the Soviet Union and Nazi Germany divided Europe between themselves, whereby part of Poland, Finland, Estonia, Latvia, and later Lithuania were allocated to the Soviet sphere of influence. In late September 1939, the Soviet Union began exercising the liberties it had been granted, extending an ultimatum to Estonia to sign a treaty allowing deployment of Soviet military troops on Estonian soil.

The Estonian army was placed on alert. In the event of war, the voluntary military organization *Kaitseliit* (Defense League) was to play the leading role in coordinating the partisan war. General Johan Laidoner named Defense League Commander General Orasmaa as his successor in the event of his death, saying that by the time he was replaced, Estonia would be engulfed in a partisan war. Although most of the population and some of the military supported the rejection of Soviet demands, Estonian political leaders decided in favor of the only peaceful solution. Indeed, the Soviet Union had repeatedly assured Estonia that the treaty in question would in no way dictate or change the economic or governmental system of Estonia. After the signing of the treaty in October 1939, the Red army marched into the bases allotted to it. The Soviet Union signed analogous pacts with Lithuania and Latvia.

Finland, however, resolutely rebuffed similar Soviet demands, and defended its decision heroically in the Winter War. Although Estonia officially had to maintain a neutral stance in this conflict, Estonia assisted the Finns in every way it could. Hundreds of young Estonian men crossed the icy gulf into Finland, where they joined Finnish forces on the front under assumed names. In the spring of 1940, these units planned a joint invasion of Soviet bases in Estonia. Unfortunately, Finland's resources had been exhausted by this time. Despite its heavy material, territorial, and human losses, Finland succeeded in retaining its most cherished treasure — its national independence. Across the gulf, the fate of the Baltic States had already been sealed.

In June 1940, the Soviet Union extended another ultimatum to the Baltic States demanding agreement to the deployment of "supplemental military units" on their territories. With this, the Baltic States fell under total occupation. Under Soviet orchestration, legally elected local governments were replaced by Soviet-style "people's governments" manipulated by Soviet deputies and defended by Soviet tanks. These "people's governments" disbanded the former government establishments and organized new elections according to the Soviet model, which permitted only one candidate for each post, and which guaranteed that Soviet-minded representatives of the "working class" won all seats. Estonia was now declared a Soviet state which asked to be admitted into the "friendly family of Soviet nations," a request that was granted in August 1940. No one asked the Estonian population for its opinion. Western analyses of such "revolutions" justify the fact that most major Western states never recognized the legality of the annexation and incorporation of the Baltic States into the Soviet Union.

Nothing, however, would save the Estonians from Red terror, the worst of all nightmares. By first arresting Estonia's military and political leaders, the new regime hoped to nip potential resistance in the bud. The occupying regime's order to disarm and disband the Defense League attests to its fear of popular resistance.

Even before the Soviet Union officially annexed Estonia, the President of the Republic of Estonia Konstantin Päts and his family, and Supreme Commander Johan Laidoner and his wife were deported to Russia. This was only the beginning. In the fall of 1940, most of Estonia's public figures, government leaders, and military leaders were arrested. Mass murders began in the spring of 1941. In 1940 and 1941, Soviet authorities arrested more than 7,000 people in Estonia.

Along with the onslaught of terror, the new authorities began dismantling the country itself. The Bolshevik "land reform" disrupted the work of efficient private farms and eventually (in 1949) replaced them with a large number of unviable collective farms, resulting in a catastrophic decline of agricultural production. Industry and trade collapsed soon after they were nationalized. Within one year, this thriving country became a poor and miserable shadow of its former self. Estonia's standard of living declined markedly, in spite of the promises of the new regime.

The Soviet wrecking ball did not spare cultural life. As a start, all organizations including even cooking clubs and athletic leagues were closed, not to mention such "anti-Soviet" organizations as the Boy Scouts and the Y.M.C.A. The organizations' properties were confiscated and subsequently misused by the Komsomol and the Communist Party. Libraries suffered a thorough "housecleaning." In the first year of the occupation, more than a million volumes were sorted out and destroyed. The church was also subjected to brutal pressure. Soviet authorities declared all clergy to be outlaws and ordered military forces to desecrate houses of worship. Many clergy members were arrested, and a number of them were tortured to death. Furthermore, the authorities tried to strip the people of their national conscience and memory by destroying valued memorials and desecrating national symbols.

The tragedy that struck the Estonian people on June 14, 1941, was the final blow. On that day, over ten thousand people were forcibly removed from their homes and deported to Siberia in long trains of cattle cars. Two-thirds of the deportees were women and children. The nature of their "crime" will likely be a mystery forever. The archives of the Estonian Heritage Society contain unsettling documentation of this tragic event: a diary kept painstakingly by a young boy sent to Siberia; a scrap of paper with a husband's and father's final message to his family, before he was shot in prison camp; an Estonian identity document on which a child describes the final days of his mother's life as she starves to death. This final document, carefully hidden and preserved, later helped the child preserve his language and nationality after being placed in a Russian orphanage. Of more than 10,000 Estonian citizens deported to Siberia, less than one-third returned alive.

The first wave of deportation was meant to be only a modest introduction of things to come. Soviet authorities planned to deport nearly twenty-five percent of the population of Estonia to Siberia in 1941. The second wave of deportations, which started on the islands of Hiiumaa and Saaremaa, was cut short because of the rapid advance of German forces on the mainland. Already, Estonia had lost 60,000 of its people to execution, deportations, and exile in just one year. Estonia had its back against a wall. The nation had only two choices — to submit to slaughter or to take up arms and resist. Most of the people chose the latter.

Resistance reared its head as soon as the land was occupied. As early as the summer of 1940, secret underground organizations formed in Estonia for the purpose of rising against the occupiers in armed struggle, in which the now-underground *Kaitseliit* (Defense League) played an essential role. Although the occupation authorities had confiscated the League's arsenal in the summer of 1940, League members succeeded in hiding some of the weapons. They came in handy in the following summer. Resistance groups worked at disseminating political information, as well as gathering and relaying news about current events. On Estonian Independence Day, February 24, 1941, leaflets were distributed throughout Estonia, and the outlawed blue-black-and-white national flags were hoisted onto posts, tall trees, and radio towers.

A nationwide resistance organization — the *Päästekomitee* (a three-member underground committee to establish Estonia's independence) — was formed in the fall of 1940 and led by Ülo Maramaa, son of the former mayor of Viljandi City. Its objective was to gather weapons, establish communications with the West, contact Estonian soldiers who had fled to Finland, and prepare groups for action when war broke out. Unfortunately, the NKVD soon succeeded in discovering, arresting, and ultimately executing the leaders of the *Päästekomitee*.

In the aftermath of the mass deportations of June 14, 1941, the numbers of fugitives in the woods increased sharply, now including women and children. Although some fled to Finland with the help of resistance groups and some hid in safe houses with friends, the forests offered them shelter in the summer. The first sporadic battles erupted between the fugitives and the Soviet security troops. A new war was the only hope for salvation for the people hiding in the forests, since only all-out war could curb the Red terror.

Full-scale battles broke out only after Nazi Germany attacked its former ally, the Soviet Union, on June 22, 1941. Germany had never been a very popular nation among the Estonians, who had lived under the yoke of German manor lords for 700 years. One year of Soviet occupation, however, had left such a mark on the population that they cared little whose forces entered their country, so long as they threw out the Reds. Estonia hoped that the Germans might help to restore its independence, and many localities welcomed the Germans as liberators.

A new wave of terror in Estonia accompanied the outbreak of war. As the Soviet army retreated from the blows of the Germans in late June of 1941, Stalin ordered the Soviets to carry out a scorched earth policy. Special "destruction battalions" formed for this purpose ostensibly were to fight against saboteurs and traitors; hence their official name of "People's Defense" units. The formation of these battalions in Estonia began on June 27, 1941. Officially, these units were voluntary; in actuality, many people were forcibly recruited. A large number of characters with a shady past, a criminal record, or a streak of Communist fanaticism joined the destruction battalions voluntarily. Thanks to the broad mandate given to the destruction battalion troops, including the right to execute summarily any "suspicious" person, they unleashed a massacre in Estonia. They burned dozens of villages, schools, and public buildings to the ground and blew up factories.

Thousands of people, among them large numbers of women and children, fell as victims to the barbaric destruction battalions and their cohort, the NKVD. When Tullio Lindsaar, a schoolboy from Urvaste (in southeastern Estonia), hoisted a national flag in his farmyard to celebrate the departure of the Reds, these battalions broke the bones in his hands and fingers and punctured him with bayonets. They doused Mauricius Parts, son of the War of Independence hero Karl Parts, with acid. The wife of Forest Brother Captain Rätsep was raped and then tortured to death. In many parts of Estonia, the battalions burned people alive. In the August 1941 massacre at Viru-Kabala (in northeastern Estonia), they killed all the residents they captured, including a two-year-old child and a six-day-old infant in his mother's arms. Sadly enough, this was not an isolated incident in the summer of 1941. It seemed that hell had ascended to earth.

In response to the atrocities of the destruction battalions, a partisan war broke out in Estonia, where tens of thousands of men had congregated in the forests. The partisans, popularly called "Forest Brothers," attacked Soviet military units as well as destruction battalions, protecting the local populations from Red army brutality. They repeatedly ambushed destruction battalion transport columns. In

Tartumaa County on July 6, 1941, the Forest Brothers blew up a stretch of railway track and derailed a destruction battalion train.

It is hard to say exactly how many men found shelter in the forests of Estonia. In northern Estonia, their numbers were estimated at 15,000, and there is no reason to believe that there were any fewer in southern Estonia. They were plagued by a chronic shortage of weapons, but they compensated for it with courage and a keen familiarity with the terrain.

An excerpt from recollections of that time illustrates the events of that summer of war. The first tells of a Forest Brothers' attack on northern Estonia's vital industrial center of Kiviõli. A Forest Brother who fled to the Free World in 1944 explains:

> Soon after midnight on July 1, (1941) thousands of residents of Kiviõli awoke to shouts and the rattle of gunfire. The shooting was most intense south of the railroad near the railway station. Sporadic waves of machine gun fire and shouts and screams filled the night. And yet the residents, aroused from their sleep, remained calm and felt some satisfaction in knowing that something was finally happening.
>
> What was happening was the Forest Brothers' first attack against the new regime. The Forest Brothers had emerged from their hideout in the village forest of Aru in Maidla Parish, where their cache of trucks, motorcycles, radios, ammunition, and Estonian flags was located. Ensigns Lauri and Nurk led the partisans' offensive. A large number of Kiviõli's workers, farmers, and officials took part in the action. At twilight, their formations approached Kiviõli from the south. The assault served two purposes: to destroy Communist establishments and to capture new weapons. In a vicious and heroic battle, they captured the railway station, wrecking all the equipment. Next they invaded the post office building, destroying the lines of the central telephone exchange. They smashed several of Kiviõli's strategic military points. Although the Soviet police resisted fiercely at first, they were finally forced to retreat. Their casualties included eight dead and eight wounded. The Forest Brothers lost member Jaan Tiib, who sustained stomach wounds and died some time later. After their victorious strike, the Forest Brothers withdrew to the

woods. The Kiviõli Communists had managed to call for
reinforcements, and trucks containing auxiliary troops
rolled toward Kiviõli. But help arrived too late; the
Forest Brothers' "housecleaning" had already proved
successful.

The Forest Brothers were particularly active in southern
Pärnumaa County. A resident of the town of Kilingi-Nõmme wishing
to remain anonymous relates his recollections of events:

At Kilingi-Nõmme, the last days before the Reds
withdrew were very tense. A lot of the city's population
had been deported on June 14, (1941) but that wasn't
enough to suit the local Reds. They quickly compiled
new lists of "anti-Soviet" elements, but their plans were
foiled when the war broke out on June 22. They were
unable to order trucks from Pärnu to haul away the
deportees, so they "had no other choice" but to dig a
huge ditch behind the city to use as a mass grave. The
purpose of the ditch was not lost on the local residents.
    In the fierce uprising that followed, the Forest Broth-
ers took control and arrested the Reds. News of the
uprising spread fast, and Forest Brothers units from the
city outskirts rushed to the city. The local Reds who had
ordered the deportations were put on trial, and those
sentenced to death by firing squad were taken to the
same ditch they had just finished digging. Before the
fatal volley, the execution commando chief recited the
old proverb: "He who digs a pit for another will fall into
it himself."
    On July 4, a report about the approach of powerful
Red army and destruction battalions reached the city of
Kilingi-Nõmme. Despite their meager armaments, the
Forest Brothers decided to face the battle, setting up an
ambush at Liivamäed (Sand Hills) near the city. The Forest Brothers let the Reds' advance scouts go by and then
tossed a homemade grenade at the first bus. The bus
veered into a ditch, blocking the entire column.
Although the Reds suffered grave casualties, their numbers were overwhelming. The Mõisaküla Forest Brothers
arrived in the nick of time, attacking the Reds from the
rear. Panic ensued, and the entire Red squad was wiped

out in the battle. Of the several hundred Soviet soldiers who had left Pärnu, only seven returned.

On July 5, Soviet tanks and a regular army battalion rolled against the city of Kilingi-Nõmme. The Forest Brothers retreated, letting the tanks pass and preparing to attack the following infantry. The tanks, however, did not dare stay in the city. They burned several dozen buildings, arrested some of the remaining people, and murdered the injured. After that, they returned to Pärnu. A few days later, German advance units reached Kilingi-Nõmme.

The situation proved much more complex in northern Estonia, since German forces did not arrive in this part of the country until two weeks after they had entered the south. The Soviet military command had time to use their best forces against the Forest Brothers, forcing them to withdraw into the forests.

The Estonian reconnaissance and diversion group "Erna" sent from Finland was a key player in the battles of northern Estonia. This unit was made up of Estonian volunteers who had fled to Finland and wanted to make their contribution to the liberation of Estonia. Since 1940, Finland had watched the destruction of Estonia with concern, and provided not only shelter, but also a forum for action by Estonian political refugees. The former Estonian "newspaper king" Harald Vellner was particularly effective. His close relations with Finnish newspapers provided him with access to leading Finnish politicians. At Vellner's suggestion, Finnish intelligence provided military training to Estonians in Finland and assembled them into a special unit which was to return to Estonia at the outbreak of war, organize a resistance movement, and engage in reconnaissance work. Soon Germany, then an ally of Finland, joined the endeavor.

In July 1941, the members of this "Erna" group landed in several parts of Estonia, some coming by sea on speedboats, some from the air with parachutes. The group was equipped with radio transmitters. They were assigned to send reconnaissance data on troop movements to the Finns. The optimistic and well-armed men in Finnish uniforms who joined the guerrilla units already in the forest buoyed the fighting spirit and became the impetus for the formation of many new partisan groups. The Kõrvemaa district in northern Estonia was proclaimed a "partisan republic," in which Soviet power was declared overthrown. Farms sported national flags; independence-era laws were reinstated. As weapons arrived from Finland, the Forest Brothers planned to form a regiment that would liberate the capital city of Tallinn with a surprise attack. The German command, however, did not like the idea of sharing power, and the shipment of weapons was stopped at their insistence. This dealt a serious blow to the Forest Brothers.

By this time, the Soviet authorities had recovered from their initial shock, and the encirclement of the "partisan republic" tightened. Numerous destruction battalions and NKVD units were concentrated in that area to oppose the partisans. On July 31, 1941, Soviet destruction battalion, border patrol, and NKVD units launched their biggest raid of all times in Estonia, disregarding the fact that the forests also sheltered unarmed men, women, and children. The attack, coming from three sides, was supposed to press the partisans into a central point and destroy them. The partisans themselves could have easily escaped the siege, but they were concerned about the defenseless civilians. A detachment of parachutists had arrived from Finland the day before under the leadership of Lieutenant Oleg Marnot. Colonel Henn A. Kurg sent this detachment to keep the civilians' escape route clear. A witness, Heino Lossmann, explains:

> Nearing the anticipated combat area, Lieutenant Marnot gathered his men and asked if they should copy the German tactic of executing a direct punch, i.e., carrying out a surprise attack and using the resulting panic and confusion to our advantage. All the men agreed wholeheartedly, since the long-awaited moment had finally arrived to vent their rage on their most hated enemy. At that instant, the roar of transport motors sounded from the edge of the swamp near the forest. The entire unit charged the roar as one man. From about twenty meters, they lobbed hand grenades at the transport column. Sixteen machine guns directed their deadly fire toward the enemy. The partisans were unaware of how many Russians and destruction battalion units they were up against until they ran from the forest and faced the enemy on the road. But there was no longer time to think twice. The viciousness of this hornets' nest caught the Russians and destruction battalions by surprise, and their immediate casualties were extensive. As the partisans stormed onto the road, Lieutenant Marnot sustained fatal wounds and died with the words, "Let 'em have it, boys!" on his lips. Sergeant Rosin fell along with him, mowed down by heavy artillery fire.

The battle intensified. Hand-to-hand combat alternated with exchange of gunfire as the men ran between the cars. When other ammunition ran out, pistols were drawn. Only a few men in the Soviet transport escaped with their lives. After a thirty-five-minute battle, the "Erna" parachutists suddenly found themselves victorious amid the rubble of vehicles.

The lull in fighting lasted only a few minutes. The roar of approaching transports sounded once more. At a distance of about 150 meters from the "Erna" men, the transports stopped and the Russians charged out toward our men. At the same instant, the transports opened a blaze of heavy artillery fire. Surrounded on three sides, Sergeant Parts gave the order to retreat and returned the men to our camp.

Bowing before their fate, the column of refugees organized and defended by Major Hindpere began the solemn trek through the swamp toward the west to escape the siege that threatened to destroy them. It was heart wrenching to watch this defenseless ribbon of gray forest refugees, numbering nearly a thousand, stepping forward into an uncertain future with heads bowed and hearts filled with bitterness.

The "Erna" unit succeeded in breaking through the siege and taking the refugees with it. The disappointed destruction battalions brutally murdered dozens of the local residents they happened to capture and burned down scores of farms within the area of siege. They did not succeed, however, in dampening the Forest Brothers movement.

The partisans intensified their activity with the approach of German forces. In many areas, the Forest Brothers seized power from the Reds before the Germans arrived. Republic-era parish administrations reopened their offices, and blue-black-and-white national flags flew from the buildings. In some areas, the "Republic of Estonia" was declared officially restored. On July 10, 1941, a group of Forest Brothers, including several Estonian Army officers who had escaped deportation, took over the southern part of Estonia's second-largest city, Tartu, in an offensive led by Major Friedrich Kurg. Shortly before that, the Reds had murdered 192 civilians in Tartu Prison in one night; the resistance offered by the Forest Brothers prevented the massacre from spreading.

Under the protection of the Estonian partisans, a council of Estonian political leaders led by Jüri Uluots met in Tartu and sent the German military command an official request to restore the Republic of Estonia. Since this idea did not conform to the Germans' plans, they set about disarming and disbanding the partisan units. Most of the partisans then joined the *Omakaitse* (Self-Defense) military organization which replaced the *Kaitseliit*.

Although Estonia had initially greeted the Germans as liberators, the people soon realized that it was a matter of one occupation succeeding another. However, an anti-German armed resistance movement never materialized, because the Estonian national leadership felt it was wiser not to weaken the German eastern front further. Although it was clear that Germany would lose the war sooner or later, a new Soviet occupation would be the end of all hope.

During the German occupation, the Communists did their best to restore the breath of life to partisan movements, hoping the guerrillas would oppose the Germans. As the Reds withdrew from Estonia, they left behind a substantial network of agents to organize resistance to the Germans, along with preformulated secret documents and caches of weapons and supplies. They managed to forget, however, that a partisan war can be waged only with the support of the local population. Since support for Communist-inspired partisans never materialized, the Red "partisans" remaining in Estonia were arrested and jailed within a few months. Those few who remained alive lacked the resources to carry out operations.

In order to bring the guerrilla movement to life against the Germans, Soviet "partisans" from Leningrad and Pihkva Oblast were shipped into Estonia. The fate of these "partisans" is described in the recollections of Elmar Veersalu:

> In 1943, we were taken to partisan training at a
> school building in Ivanovo. We stayed there until the
> autumn of 1943. We were taught everything that bandits
> could be taught: how to deliver fatal stabs, how to break
> hands, how to kick and box. Training went on constantly.
> We had to set mines and detonate explosives. And then
> we were called to Moscow! First, (Party functionary)
> Karotamm showed up and administered our oath: "I
> swear to be such and such, I will strangle and shoot and
> have no mercy. . ." A few days later we were taken to a
> liberated region near Velikiye Luki. We pitched our tents
> at the airport and waited for a transport. The winter of

1943 was warm. First, a ton of supplies was tossed down
on ten parachutes, and we followed. In Estonia it was
hard for us to live, much less operate. The poorest person
would give us a piece of bread only after we coerced him.
One time I threatened someone by saying: "You'd better
give me something to eat. We can wipe out everything."
But of course, no one gave us anything.

At partisan training, they told us that the people
were waiting for us to drive out the Germans. And so
we had to drive out the Germans. But we were never
told that we'd be assaulted by the Estonians themselves.
We were chased the whole time, with no chance to rest. I
was finally handcuffed in the middle of a yard and
taken to the prison camp at Viljandi.

The Estonian *Omakaitse* units demonstrated remarkable effectiveness in their fight against the Soviet "partisans," usually
rounding up such groups within a few days. In 1944, several "partisan brigades" were sent across the ice to the Estonian shores of Lake
Peipsi. These brigades became notorious for their acts of violence
against the local population. However, they enjoyed only a brief
existence.

The partisan movement did indeed undergo a revitalization in
Estonia, but not as a Soviet-inspired movement. The universal German
mobilization announced in February 1944 provided the new impetus
for the restoration of the woodland partisan units, since many conscripts wished to evade military service. Draft evaders and deserters
numbered several thousands. Each man had his own reason for taking
to the forests, but the primary motivation for most of them was the
refusal to serve in a foreign army, be it German or Russian. Thus, the
partisan movement's initial purpose was not the formation of an active
resistance movement, but the evasion of foreign military service.

While winter made it difficult to find a hideout, the summertime
forests provided shelter for anyone who wanted it. Few people bothered to build bunkers, since they could sleep in haylofts or farm
buildings. In most regions, the local Self-Defense units shut their eyes
to the draft evaders, occasionally even warning them of approaching
raids. In some places, however, armed conflicts raged, causing casualties on both sides. One of Võrumaa County's legendary Forest
Brothers Johannes Heeska earned his fame in an encounter with a
German patrol commando.

I had a falling out with the Germans during the German occupation. They wanted to mow down all the Communists in the parish, but that didn't sit well with me. Then came the German mobilization, but how could I sign up if I'd already been on the outs with them for two years. There were three of us hiding out.

We happened to go home one night, and then we found out that a patrol commando had come to Sulbi. At dawn we went back to our hideout, but the patrols were waiting in the valley. We were playing cards and out of the shadows came six or seven men in German uniforms. I yelled, "Let's get 'em!", but the boys were so scared they started running. This left me there all alone, so I followed them. We ran along the ditch, but the commando men in the field were yelling, "You're surrounded. Throw down your weapons!" I dropped into a hole and thought, "Damn them." So I came up over the edge and opened fire. This forced them down and the firing stopped. I ran like the devil to the next thicket and crawled under a dense fir tree. Their line caught up. I put my hands together and said, "Dear God, I'll get out of this only if you help me." And He helped me.

I heard automatic weapons fire behind me and thought, "Now they've shot my friends." But I found out that one of our boys had been firing at the ones who were shooting at me. That held them up. They started to comb the woods, and four of them went right past me, but they didn't find me.

The situation on the front continued to worsen. For half a year, the Estonians fighting in the German army managed to keep the Red army outside Estonia's borders, but the Reds seized southern Estonia in 1944. Estonian national leaders now appealed to those hiding in the forests, calling on them to form battalions to fight for the restoration of the Republic of Estonia when the opportunity presented itself. The War of Independence hero Admiral Jaan Pitka initiated the plan. Pitka's plan was to form a single battalion, supplying it with German armaments. The battalion was to cross the front into southern Estonia, start a partisan war against the Reds, and return with the necessary armaments for a second battalion.

Sensing Germany's imminent collapse, Estonian nationalists swung into action. An organization based on several resistance groups, the National Committee of the Republic of Estonia (EVRK), was formed in March 1944. The organization succeeded in establishing an adequate communications network with Estonian diplomats in Finland and Sweden, and through them with the rest of the West. In April 1944, the Germans destroyed the central figures of the EVRK, but by June, the extent and influence of the EVRK's activities had broadened even more. It worked closely with the last legal prime minister Jüri Uluots and his cabinet, the bearers of the continuity of the Republic of Estonia.

Estonian-manned reconnaissance groups, ostensibly working for the Germans but in reality controlled by the National Committee, played an important role in the resistance movement. At the core were the "Erna" men, many of whom had fled to Finland to escape the German mobilization.

> During leave, Talgre was in Helsinki, and then he and Vellner came up with the idea of forming a new twenty-five-member group. The official purpose of this group was to establish an information network for the Finns in the event the Russians invaded Estonia. As young and naive as I was, I didn't believe that would happen. The actual purpose, which was not the same as the official one, was to find out what the Germans were doing and transmit the information to the West. The underground government that was already being formed in Estonia needed communications lines. We planned to send our radio operators into some border patrol regiments manned by Estonians in German uniform, so that all our forces could be called up easily if necessary.
>
> Our central command was in Haukka, Finland, and training took place on Sööppo Island. I got to be a real veteran. I went to Estonia, did my job, and came back. I managed to go back and forth quite a few times in that short period. We had a powerful boat with a Rolls-Royce motor and a nice quiet stroke. The first time, we landed somewhere near Salmistu (on the northern coast). That was in late autumn, and an awful storm was raging.
>
> Officially, these preparations were a kind of smokescreen for the Germans, to make our operation look like we were collaborating with them. Actually, the Finns were interested in what the Germans were doing

and wanted to find out whether they were preparing to
evacuate Estonia. We were interested in that too, but our
main job was maintaining communications with the
West. We had lots of our men in the German police apparatus. Of course there were government stooges there
too, but no one ever bothered us. We also had a station-
ary radio transmitter on site in the Technical School
under Toomi and Talgre's control, and that's where we
communicated with Sweden. In Finland our central command was in Haukka, where Simmo picked up our
transmissions from Estonia.

The Germans never caught any of our communications men, but they did apprehend and shoot a couple of
our boatmen. The Germans never found out whom we
were really working for. Officially, everything was in
order. The Haukka group as a whole did not communi-
cate directly with the National Committee. Our interme-
diaries were Toomas Hellat and Leo Talgre; our job was
to relay information. Still, helping the National Committee was our utmost desire. Haukka was actually an
Estonian reconnaissance mission.

The Finns wanted us to watch Tallinn roadstead to
find out whether the Germans were planning a landing
into Finland. In the meantime, we made several transmissions daily. We were in service to the Finnish army
while working for the interests of Estonia.

Of course, the Germans were less than enthusiastic about such
activities, and in the summer of 1944 they decided to end the operations
of the Haukka group. Most of its members were transferred to the
Tümmler platoon which operated under German control and was to
be linked up with the men and women being trained at Königsberg.
In reality, many of the Haukka men continued to take their orders from
the National Committee and persisted in transmitting information to
Finland. The EVRK itself recruited men into these groups, emphasizing the political importance of their mission. Jüri Hanko recalls:

In the spring of 1943, I was mobilized into the German army after graduating from secondary school. I
evaded conscription and hid out with a relative in
Järvamaa County. When things got tougher there in the
fall, I returned to Tartu. Of course it was impossible for

I. PREVIEW:

It is the spring of 1941. The Soviet Union had liberated Estonia from its independence the year before, following the Molotov-Ribbentrop Pact of 1939, and Estonians are being introduced to Soviet customs. The deportation and forced conscription of over 50,000 Estonians in 1941 provided the impetus for the first phase of the Forest Brothers' movement.

1. Moscow appoints General Serov to oversee the deportation of Estonians not compatible with the new Communist regime.

2. Freight trains are used for the deportations, and Soviet shipping documents list deportees as freight, not passengers.

3. On the night of June 14, 1941, over 10,000 Estonians leave for the Soviet Union in these cattle cars; 40 to 50 deportees were jammed into each car, sometimes waiting for several days without food or water.

4. Some of those not arrested or conscripted, take refuge in the forests in primitive, temporary shelters because they thought the occupation would not last long.

5. Early bunkers were barely concealed because the Soviets did not pursue evaders in the forests. When the Germans drove out the Soviets later in the year, Forest Brothers returned home with such photographs as souvenirs.

6. This Forest Brother has one of the few weapons available in the early phase; since firearms had been registered in the Republic of Estonia, the Soviets had easily confiscated them on arrival.

7. This Forest Brother, wearing an Estonian policeman's cap, poses in front of his temporary shelter in the summer of 1941.

8. & 9. After German forces had driven the Soviets from Estonia, the bodies of victims are found on premises occupied by Soviet authorities– in this case, a building in Tartu occupied by the GPU.

10 & 11. The basement of Tallinn's "Kave" building still retains marks of the first Soviet occupation–bullet holes (above) and the drain (below) used to wash away the effects of torture and execution.

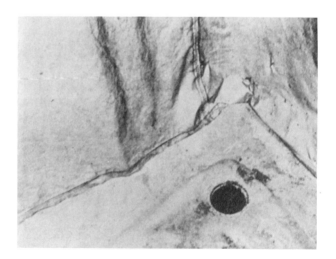

Fig. 12 **SITES OF BATTLES AND KILLINGS**

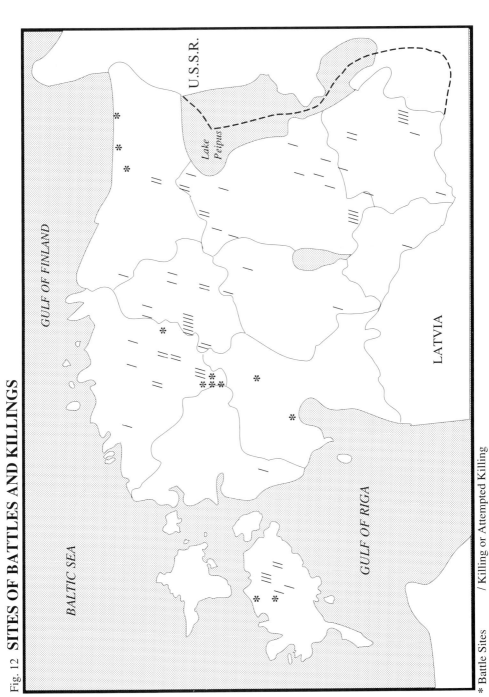

* Battle Sites   / Killing or Attempted Killing

Fig. 13 **INTENSITY OF RESISTANCE BY REGION**

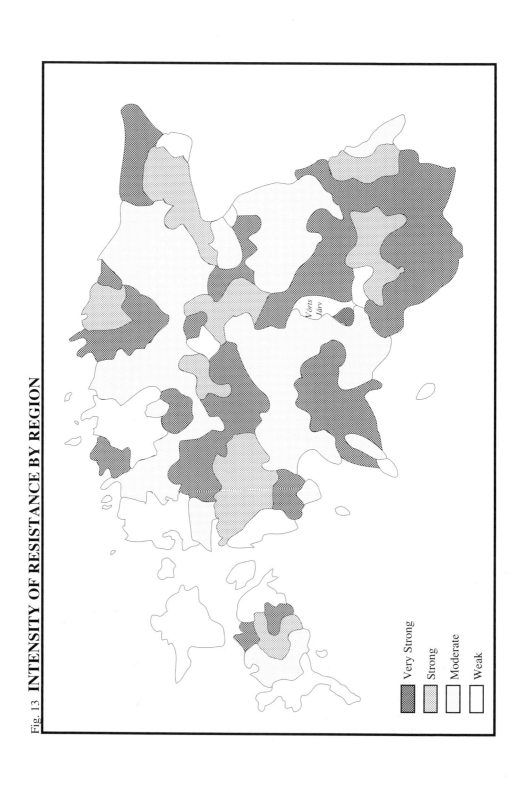

Võrts järv

Very Strong

Strong

Moderate

Weak

me to live at home, because the *Feldgendarmerie* had come looking for me several times and I knew for sure they'd come again. I found myself a hideout with a schoolmate on Lepik Street. From there, I made repeated trips to Tallinn, where I forged ties with the so-called "transport offices to Finland." Through them, I helped people from southern Estonia escape to Finland, and I transported leaflets issued in Finland by the government-in-exile of the Republic of Estonia to Tartu and to southern Estonia.

Since everyone needed special permits to ride the railways during the German occupation, and since I was on the lam, I got most of these special permits through Ensign Olev Reinthal, who worked for the *Abwehr Meldestelle* (Counter-Espionage Recruiting Office) in Tartu. My father knew him, and I had hidden out at his place for a while. I think he was arrested by the Germans for nationalist activities, but he was freed some time later. He was the one who suggested early in 1944 that I go to Riga for training. The *Abwehr* instructors would give me full training in radio communications, along with courses in reconnaissance, blowing up railroads, and other such skills. After completing the course, I was to live quietly somewhere in Estonia as a serviceman in the German army and to wait for the war to end. If it became necessary, i.e., if the Russians occupied Estonia, I would be ready for action. Reinthal explained that my training would not be for the Germans' benefit, but for eventual service as communications man with the Estonian government-in-exile. I agreed without thinking about it any further, because I knew that Stalin and his cronies were set on destroying the most talented and able portion of the Estonian people and consolidating Soviet power on the shores of the Baltic.

And so I rode to Riga with my guide Tiiu Oinas-Mikiver, and went into training. Tiiu Oinas was the daughter of former government minister and famous social democrat Aino Ostra-Oinas. She was one of the most remarkable figures among the university students at Tartu during that time. I completed the course at a reconnaissance training camp near Königsberg just shortly before the Germans left Estonia.

Using the Haukka-Tümmler radio operators, the Germans planned to leave a large number of groups in Estonia with mutual communications ties and radio transmitters. The Germans believed that these men would transmit information to them, not realizing that in reality they were taking orders from the National Committee and seeking to maintain communications with Sweden. In Sweden as well as Estonia, the second Soviet occupation that began in the autumn of 1944 was seen as a temporary phenomenon, during which it was essential to maintain communications with the West and prepare for the country's liberation. It was especially important that persons under immediate threat from the Soviet regime be removed to a foreign country. Operations of that nature required communications networks.

The orders of the National Committee, particularly "Order No. 2" included instructions to continue the resistance. This document recognized the courageous activity of the Forest Brothers in battles with the Red army in southern Estonia and gave instructions for future operations.

> Those of you unable to evacuate, conceal yourselves
> from the Bolsheviks! Organize Forest Brothers units
> behind the Bolsheviks' backs and establish communica-
> tions with Estonian Self-Defense and military units.
> When evacuating, take along all important lists and
> other valuable documents; if this is not possible, hide
> them or destroy them so that they will not fall into
> enemy hands.

Unfortunately, real preparations were in their early stages when on September 16, 1944, Hitler's central command approved plan "Aster," according to which German forces would withdraw from Estonia. Estonian units fighting on the front lines were sacrificed to cover the retreat. In Tallinn, Uluots succeeded in reestablishing the government of the Republic of Estonia for three days, before the invading Red army drowned all efforts for freedom in blood. Before the slaughter, Leo Talgre was able to transmit information to the West about the establishment of Uluots's government and the names of its members, thus carrying out the final orders of the short-lived government. Very few of its members were fortunate enough to escape the country. The Red army swept over the entire land. The Soviet occupation swallowed Estonia once more.

Chapter 2

The Soviets Return

In 1944 and 1945, the Red army descended once again on the territories allotted to the Soviet Union by the secret additional protocols of the Molotov–Ribbentrop Pact. The people of the territories, however, holding fast to the principles of the Atlantic Charter, continued their fight for freedom. The tenets of the Atlantic Charter, approved by Franklin D. Roosevelt and Winston Churchill at Placentia Bay, Newfoundland in August 1941, were well known in Estonia. The Charter affirmed "the right to restore self-government to nations who have been forcibly deprived thereof" as an important premise for victory in World War II. It was the Atlantic Charter that provided moral justification and encouragement for the Forest Brothers to persist in their struggle. In the name of freedom and justice, the flame of partisan war flared up on the western borders of the Soviet Empire.

In Latvia, preparations for a partisan war in the event of the country's occupation had already begun during the German occupation, but the Germans arrested the Latvian national units formed for this purpose by the end of 1944. The leaders of the resistance organization were shot; a large number of the rank and file were sent to concentration camps. For this reason, Latvia lacked a central command structure to organize the resistance movement when the occupation swallowed the land. Of course, partisan and Forest Brother units reemerged in Latvia despite the setback, but for the most part, their operation remained spontaneous and their movements scattered. Some groups reportedly had ties with German forces stationed in Kurland, where they obtained some supplies and even a bit of training.

If the partisan movement had been an exclusively German-organized movement, it would have died a natural death in the spring of 1945 after Germany surrendered. The opposite proved to be true. Until this time, the partisans had avoided stepping into action, anticipating a clash between the Western alliance and the Soviet Union after Germany's collapse, but they soon realized that they had no one to rely on but themselves. The resistance movement gained new vitality.

Soldiers of the Latvian Legion remaining in their homeland made up the core of the Latvian partisan movement, which was later joined by peasants, intellectuals, and workers, all hiding from Red terror. The total number of Latvian Forest Brothers over the entire period is estimated at 40,000; the number of active combatants during the peak of the movement reached 10,000 to 15,000. At first, the Forest Brothers were armed with German weapons; in time, these were exchanged for Russian weapons.

The Latvian Forest Brothers maintained contacts in the West. The eastern regions had ties with the Estonian resistance movement, and the western regions with the Lithuanians. Soviet sources list a number of all-Latvian resistance organizations, whose Central Command resided on Matisa Street in Riga until 1947. No information is available on how many Forest Brother groups were led by the Central Command.

And yet, the Latvian Forest Brothers remained a persistent thorn in the side of Soviet occupation authorities. The battles in the forests of Latvia raged until the mid-1950s. The Forest Brothers were most active in the heavily wooded and swampy areas near the Latvian borders. They operated in 135 parishes, with the largest centers being Dundaga, Taurkalne, Lubna, Aloja, and Livni. The partisans were most interested in hiding themselves while defending the local population against violence. They kept the Soviet power centers in a state of constant uncertainty by attacking government establishments and killing those who collaborated with the new regime. Local peasants supplied the Forest Brothers with goods and kept the partisans well informed of the movements and plans of the NKVD punitive troops. From time to time, the Forest Brothers derailed trains, attacked shops, and ambushed money shipments. Many groups did not hesitate to attack small military units to replenish their own supply of weapons.

The NKVD was forced to devote a remarkable number of units to their fight against the partisans. And still, the resistance movement enjoyed actual control of many regions of Latvia for a number of years. All too often, the partisans knew of the arrival of punitive troops and dealt the NKVD some painful setbacks.

Since the Latvian partisans worked in close cooperation with the Estonian side in the Estonian-Latvian border areas, recollections about Latvian Forest Brothers have been recorded in Estonia. A farmer arrested in 1945 and sent to a Valga city prison writes in his recollections:

> One time, a whole wedding party was brought into prison. Into our cell they brought the groom and four musicians, one with a wooden leg. And there was the chairman of the parish Executive Committee, a Latvian with a real long mustache. He slept next to me in the cell and he spoke very good Russian. This is what he told me.
>
> He's in the town hall late at night when a group of hundreds of bandits ride up. And they demand that he get five horses for them from the livery stables because they have to go to a wedding. The horses are brought around, although the bandits have several dozen horses already. They take off and take the chairman with them. He thinks, "Well, they're going to kill me anyway."
>
> The wedding is at a farm deep in the woods. They ride out there. The partisans operate according to rules of military discipline, taking turns sleeping and standing guard. Some go to guard duty, the others to the wedding. The wedding table is lavishly set. The chief of the bandits makes the first speech. He says, "We are sitting at a lavishly set wedding table, which is a legacy of the free Latvian republic, but the black night of Communist slavery stands before us with hunger and misery." And he raises a toast to free Latvia. And then he asks my cellmate, the parish Executive Committee chairman, to speak. This fellow feels like he's been struck by lightning and thinks, "What am I supposed to say now?" So he says, "Our people have suffered a lot and made many sacrifices. Here we have a worldly-wise groom taking a young wife so that our nation may endure." He raises a toast to free Latvia and to the bandits. The bandits are wearing German uniforms, Russian uniforms and several other kinds of uniforms and civilian clothes.
>
> The next day, a battalion of soldiers comes by and a battle breaks out. There are casualties on both sides. None of the wounded bandits let themselves be captured; they blow themselves to bits with grenades. And the whole wedding party is brought to Valga jail. The Executive Committee chairman was put on trial. He was

accused of treason against the fatherland, banditry, and
lots of other laws they said he broke.

In the early 1950s, the partisan movement suffered serious setbacks. Arrests and deportations diminished the potential reserves of
the resistance movement. No one was left to replace the departed
partisans. Taking advantage of the weakening of the Forest Brothers
movement, the NKVD succeeded in infiltrating some Forest Brothers
groups and using them for espionage games with Western intelligence agencies. The crushing of the 1956 popular uprising in Hungary, however, dealt the final blow to the resistance movement by
finally rendering armed resistance hopeless. The last Latvian partisan
groups emerged from the forests in 1956 and 1957.

In Lithuania the partisan movement was much more widespread
than in Latvia. It was built upon a well-structured and centrally
commanded partisan army of tens of thousands of men, organized in
the forests during the German occupation. This permitted the immediate start of armed resistance when the second Soviet occupation
began. The awful terror that swept through the land in 1944 swelled
the ranks of the partisans even more.

The Lithuanian partisans who had fought against the German
occupation now turned their weapons against the Red army.
Although the Lithuanian Central Command formed in 1944 was
crushed by the NKVD the following year, it was soon reestablished
under the name of the United Resistance Movement, which included
armed units, political organizations, and passive resistance groups. In
1949, the partisans separated from the organization and created their
own Lithuanian Freedom Fighters Movement. Nine independent
partisan regions were united into three military regions with a common military and political leadership. In addition to attacks on Soviet
establishments, the partisans dealt in political education. The movement had its own newspaper and printing presses, which produced
leaflets as well as forged documents. It conducted nationwide officers'
training courses. In 1948, some NKVD punitive troops stumbled on
the location of one of these courses, and lost half their members in the
resulting battle. A total of nearly 100,000 Lithuanian partisans, indeed
a remarkable number, fought during the years of resistance. The
largest groups comprised 800 combatants; the smallest, two or three
fugitives.

The Lithuanian Forest Brothers maintained contacts with the
West. The prominent partisan leader Juozas Luksa-Daumantas managed to escape from Lithuania in 1948, hoping to obtain substantial

Western support for the Lithuanian resistance movement. Sadly, these hopes were destined to remain unfulfilled, and in 1949 Luksa returned to Lithuania, where he was killed a few months later.

Lithuania's strong and militarily organized resistance movement caused the Soviet regime some serious problems. For a long time, the resistance held almost complete control over rural territories. The partisans thwarted elections and land reform, killed large numbers of those collaborating with the occupying powers, and oversaw the coordination of local affairs in many areas, including the fight against the distillation of moonshine.

There are reports of a partisan movement in Byelorussia as well. Partisan activity flourished in the western Ukraine, where national resistance movements had developed in the 1920s and 1930s, going into full swing with the onset of the German occupation, which succeeded in destroying Soviet power without establishing true control over the Ukraine. The political organization OUN (Organizatsia Ukrainiskikh Nationalistiv — Ukrainian Nationalist Organization) founded by Stepan Bandera provided the political foundation for the Ukrainian resistance movement. In 1941, this organization lay the groundwork for the Ukrainian government formed in Lvov but later disbanded by the Germans.

Since OUN did not support active armed resistance to the German occupation, a military-style organization, UPA, was formed under General Roman Shukevich-Khruprinka. The purpose of the UPA, which drew its resources from the western Ukraine, was to gain control of that region and subsequently expand its control over the whole country. The UPA perceived both the Germans and the Russians as enemies.

The UPA succeeded in carrying out an effective mobilization in the western Ukraine. In 1944, its armed forces numbered nearly 200,000 men, a group the Germans were unable to handle. The situation changed in 1944, when the Soviet army forced its way into the Ukraine. Although the UPA carried out many successful anti-Soviet operations (such as the killing of Marshal Nikolai Vatutin), the UPA groups were soon forced back into the Carpathians. In 1944 and 1945, the Red army carried out its first major operation against the UPA after surrounding a number of areas under partisan control. The UPA suffered serious casualties and was forced to abandon its system of military battalions and to split into smaller groups. Despite the setback, the struggle wore on for a long time.

The resistance movement thriving in the borderlands of the Russian Empire proved to be a serious problem for Soviet authorities.

Initially, they had hoped that the "national" puppet governments made up of local Communists would render the population more sympathetic toward the occupation. Unfortunately, such hopes were built on sand, and the local populations showed little true support for the occupation authorities. This forced the Soviet occupiers to resort to harsher measures. The occupying regime had to expend tremendous energy in its effort to stifle or at least curb the partisan movement. In 1944, a meeting was held in Paneveys, Lithuania, between the leaders of the Soviet armed forces, the security apparatus, the interior ministry, and local Communist organizations. NKVD General Kruglov, Lavrenti Beria's special envoy, reported on Stalin's extreme dissatisfaction with the situation that had developed in the Baltics. The resistance movement was to be crushed as soon as possible. Kruglov demanded an end to "liberal attitudes" and called for the use of terror and intimidation. Since the military destruction of the Forest Brothers had proved to be a complex undertaking, the main thrust was to be directed against their potential supporters. The families of individuals involved in the resistance movement were to be arrested or deported; farmsteads suspected of supporting the Forest Brothers were to be razed.

Estonia had already experienced the brutality of the Red army in the first months of 1944. A special Soviet army unit that landed near Narva on February 14 had been instructed to eliminate all the civilians it encountered as potential enemies. Before their attack was stopped, this unit succeeded in murdering a large number of civilians, including a young woman and her infant. Although the Red army units sweeping into Estonia in the summer and fall of 1944 had no such instructions, they unleashed acts of unspeakable terror on the local population in many areas. Pillaging and looting were common, as well as the rape of captured women. In some parts of the country, they murdered entire families simply to crush any resistance before it had a chance to take root. In Süvahavva, Võrumaa County, Red soldiers killed about ten people whose corpses were then tossed into a farmyard well. Estonians captured alive by the Soviet side fared little better. In one incident on September 21, 1944, the commander of a Soviet tank unit that had just taken the northeastern Estonian town of Kadrina ordered the murder of about twenty young Estonian men who had just surrendered without resistance. The troops lined up the bodies along the road and drove their tanks over them repeatedly, until there was little left of the young men. In some areas, Red army units annoyed by the resistance gathered all the male residents of some villages, regardless of age, and shot them on the spot. One such incident took place in the northern Estonian town of Kose on September 22, 1944.

Naturally, these acts of terror brought the authorities no closer to achieving their stated goal of winning popular support. Popular reaction took the opposite track. The brutality of the Soviet army and the new Soviet authorities heightened the nation's spirit of opposition, clearly indicating that popular attitude toward Soviet domination would not shift in a favorable direction. When local Communist leaders finally realized the futility of brutality, they tried to restrain the army's penchant for violence, but without success. Without the backing of the Red army, they themselves would have had no hope of remaining in power. The new authorities desperately needed the Red army and the security apparatus to suppress the national resistance movement which threatened their own hold on power. Inevitably, the interests of the Red army and the local Communist authorities converged, and overwhelming forces were assembled in Estonia to eliminate the Estonian national resistance movement.

The first NKVD units reached Tallinn even before the city fell to the Red army. As they took control of all *Abwehr* offices in Tallinn, they were met by a pleasant surprise. Although the Germans had had sufficient time to evacuate their archives, they had somehow neglected to remove the part dealing with the national resistance movement in Estonia. German intelligence had not succeeded in eliminating Estonian nationalists; therefore, it decided to let its Soviet counterparts finish the job, surrendering all the files it had gathered over the years including names and addresses of the resistance movement leaders, their friends, and relatives. These were extremely valuable materials which helped make the elimination of resistance organizations no more than a matter of time.

First of all, the authorities had to ensure that no more people could escape the grasp of the NKVD. They placed the coastline under heavy army patrol, wrecking or confiscating the boats they found. And yet, the escapes continued. A number of daring men transported people to freedom by piloting speedboats from Sweden, and initially also from Finland, to Estonia and rescuing refugees waiting on the shore. In response, the Soviets were forced to set up ambushes at sea. They met with little success until Soviet naval intelligence managed to infiltrate its own agents into the refugee groups. Although the security apparatus never fully succeeded in putting an end to the daring dashes for freedom, it did manage to complicate plans for escape.

A frenzied manhunt was launched for Estonian public figures. The first targets were the members of the National Committee and the members of Otto Tief's government appointed by Jüri Uluots. One after another, Arnold Susi, Otto Tief, Felix Pärtelpoeg, and other activists in the resistance movement during the German occupation were arrested. The only one who escaped arrest was Professor Karl Liidak, who lived secretly in southern Estonia under an assumed name until his death.

The Soviets made quick work of another target: the Keila-Joa reconnaissance school, established by the Germans for long-distance reconnaissance training. Soviet intelligence infiltrated one of their agents into the student body. The graduates of the Keila-Joa reconnaissance school had actively worked to restore the Republic of Estonia in Tallinn in September 1944, defended members of the Republic's government, and fought against the Germans. With the arrival of the Red army, it was decided to disband the group temporarily. A graduate of the reconnaissance school, returning to his home near Pärnu, recalls what happened next:

> I'd been at home a few days when one night there was a knock on the door. Not suspecting any harm, I went to open it. Several automatics stared me in the face. I could have tried to resist, since I had some grenades nearby, but I didn't want to endanger the others at home. I just raised my hands, and they searched me and confiscated my weapons.
>
> Then I was taken out in the courtyard, where several men, armed to the teeth, emerged from around the house and the gardens. It was a special unit of the NKVD. They put me in a car and took me to Tallinn. My entire group was there with the exception of a few men, but they were brought in soon. We found out that during the whole time at Keila-Joa, one of the most fervent patriots among us had worked as a Soviet informer. He had collected all our addresses, so the NKVD was able to catch us easily even after the group had disbanded.

The capture of the nationalist reconnaissance group led by Leo Talgre and Toomas Hellat proved to be a more formidable task, since it had managed to make secret plans and prepare for underground operations. The group lacked the necessary skills, however, for a struggle against the experienced and well-oiled Soviet intelligence apparatus. The network of bunkers and storerooms that they had planned to build in Estonia remained unbuilt, and the men sent to southern Estonia perished as they were caught in battles. The group lacked forged documents and safe houses, and money was tight. With the help of the files left by the Germans, the Soviet security apparatus staked out a large number of apartments of the friends of national activists. This made it even harder for the group members to find a place to hide. Moreover, the national activists lacked a detailed plan for long-term operations. During the German occupation, they had concentrated on preparing to reestablish the government of the Republic of Estonia; plans for all subsequent actions had received low priority. Only the fundamental goal remained well defined. Upon the Soviet reoccupation of Estonia, all reconnaissance groups remaining in Estonia had to be united under a common leadership and their operations coordinated according to the guidelines set forth by the national command center to be set up in Sweden.

During its October 1944 conference, the national reconnaissance group honed its plan of action, discussing the possibility of armed encounters and organizing acts of sabotage. At that time, however, they felt such action to be inexpedient, considering it wiser to sit tight and wait for better times. Their ties with Germany had been broken, but they continued sending reconnaissance data to Finland. At the conference, no one entertained any illusions about the future. Since the Soviet security apparatus was hot on the trail of the National Committee leadership, the national activists decided to spirit out of the country those men closely connected with the National Committee and targeted for capture, and to have another group take over operations in Estonia — the "Second Echelon," which was yet unknown to the security apparatus. They planned to set up permanent communications between radio stations, maintain communications with the West, and make ready to commence active operations at the signal from the West. By doing so, they constructed a framework on which a larger-scale resistance organization could be built. Their greatest problem was that of acquiring speedboats to transport individuals through the ever-tightening net of Soviet border guard patrols.

On their last refugee boat, which departed on November 21, 1944, the Haukka men had sent their wives, sweethearts, and children to Finland. None of them ever saw their loved ones again, but even in their final radiograms, the men in Estonia expressed concern about the fate and future of the families they had sent to a foreign land. As they suffered in the KGB torture chambers, their only consolation was the knowledge that their loved ones lay beyond the grasp of the KGB. They owed their thanks to the Finnish scouts who whisked several thousand Estonian refugees to Sweden, passing directly under the nose of the Soviet Control Commission. These men were later forced to flee Finland themselves.

By this time, the frenzied manhunt for the Haukka group had begun. The first men were captured incidentally as a result of routine checks. One such capture is described by Juhan Teder, a former EVRK communications man between Estonia and Finland, who at one time had been the target of a costly manhunt by the Gestapo. Because he had fought in the final battles for Estonia, he was forced to hide out with relatives, until he finally decided to establish contact with his former colleagues.

> After Estonia was occupied, I dug the forged docu-
> ments I'd gotten during the German occupation out of
> my hideout and went to Tallinn, where I registered for
> work. I looked for Talgre and the other radio men, but
> was unable to establish contact.
>
> I was staying at the Baltic Hotel when one day a
> Red army officer, an Estonian national, stumbled in and
> demanded a list of guests from the innkeeper. He looked
> it over and demanded to know who I was. I had all the
> proper documents. According to my papers, I had been
> in the Taagepera Sanatorium with tuberculosis all dur-
> ing the German occupation. When I showed them to
> him, he stuck them in his pocket and told me to come
> down to headquarters for a while. He started off in front
> of me. I had a Walther (gun) in my pocket; I could have
> laid him out right there, but there was no point in it. I
> didn't know then that the security forces were already
> looking for us. We got to headquarters, which turned
> out to be the ones on Pagari Street (NKVD headquar-
> ters). At first they treated me cordially, because they
> didn't know my real background or identity. Soon after
> that, they beat a confession out of a Public Health
> Museum man who had been in the resistance movement
> during the German occupation, and the whole endeavor
> collapsed.

The noose was tightening. Most of the men remaining in Estonia lacked safe houses and money. Only one bunker, out near Aegviidu, was stocked and ready for action. We get an idea of the nature of the group's supplies from a summary of its contents, as it appears in Soviet sources:

One notebook with red cover, fifty German reichs-
marks, worker's ID N-16380 in the name of Leonid Kaar,
one photo, the resolution of the Nov. 20, 1944 meeting,
one code table and two cipher tables, five notebooks,
two German radio transmitters Nos. 343 and 13, fifteen
self-loading semi-automatic rifles, four Russian rifles,
one double-barreled hunting rifle, three boxes rifle cartridges, one box grenades and two officers' grenades,
one box fuses, three German automatics, two suitcases
with supplies, two topographical maps, six sheets, two
ponchos, two flashlights.

It was certainly an unimpressive inventory for a group covering
a large part of Estonia.

The supplies and training of the reconnaissance groups entering
Estonia across the front line were not much better. They were no match
for the NKVD, who hunted them down quickly. Some were simply
unlucky. In September 1944, the Red army 193rd Engineers' Battalion
reconnaissance group happened upon a group of six persons near
Kanaküla Village in Pärnumaa County. Some responded immediately
to the order to raise their hands; others jumped into the roadside ditch
and opened fire. The resistance was stifled in short order and the
group was jailed. Weapons, radio transmitters, forged documents,
Soviet money, and medals were found in the area.

Only one man managed to escape: Ants Tamme. A few days later,
Tamme met with his former battalion chief Talliste in a forest behind
Pärnu City. With Tamme's radio set, they began transmitting informa-
tion on the movements of the Red army. The KGB soon succeeded in
locating the radio station and raided the area, capturing Major Talliste.
Tamme escaped again, continuing to evade the KGB for several years.

Most of those arrested at Kanaküla were sentenced to death.
Only one group member was coerced into collaboration: a woman,
Benita Arro. The KGB learned that she was to meet with the other
partisans in Viljandimaa County and work for them as a radio
operator. Security officers Sergei Printsev and former Narva resident
Sasha Kassatkin, impersonating an *Abwehr* agent, accompanied her
to the meeting. Their assignment was to infiltrate the group. The
meeting was set for Laane Robison's farm in Kõpu Village. The
farm's hayloft contained an arsenal and the forests nearby hid several
partisan bunkers and supply depots. The Soviet security officers
burst into the house where group leader Ain Pedanik and two
companions were hiding. The officers told the men to raise their

hands and searched them. As Capt. Printsev began writing up a report, Pedanik grabbed a knife from his boot and lunged for the officer. Only the quick reaction of the chekists (security officers) saved Capt. Printsev's life. Pedanik, who once worked with the "Erna" group, was now active with Haukka-Tümmler.

Soviet naval reconnaissance also succeeded in capturing another network of reconnaissance men left in Estonia by the Germans. This group commanded yet another network of radio transmitters and weapons depots. Their resident agent was 24-year-old Hans Käsper. He was recruited by German intelligence in 1944, trained near Königsberg, and sent back to Estonia along with other agents to "acclimatize" in the spring of 1944. Upon the occupation of Estonia by the Red army, the group was to transmit reconnaissance data to Königsberg and carry out diversionary operations wherever possible. Radio transmitters were located in the capital city of Tallinn, as well as the cities of Rakvere, Kuressaare, Paldiski, Pärnu, and on Hiiumaa Island. All the men were supplied with Soviet money and forged documents. Apparently, their group was never slated to engage in military operations, since their weapons were few. By the end of 1944, the Soviet security apparatus succeeded in crushing this German reconnaissance network. Only a few men remained free, like Vambola Orav, who proved to be an extremely valuable asset for the Forest Brothers at a later date.

Despite its successes, the Soviet security apparatus was dissatisfied. After all their efforts, they had not managed to destroy the leaders of Haukka-Tümmler. They ordered the security forces of each county to find these men, and instructed the border guard patrols to keep close watch over the coastline. Slowly, the ranks of Haukka-Tümmler thinned. In one instance, one of Haukka-Tümmler's communications men was shot while trying to escape from an apartment under surveillance by the NKVD. In two other incidents, both Leo Talgre and Toomas Hellat escaped entrapment thanks only to a warning from a friend, chess master Paul Keres. Talgre and Hellat continued to operate against all odds. The reconnaissance data, gathered mostly by Talgre, were usually transmitted by the radio station at the Technical University in Tallinn to Sweden and Finland. Communications between Estonia and Sweden became quite regular.

In early December, the NKVD came within a hair's breadth of the resistance movement's leadership. An accident put one Haukka-Tümmler radioman into a hospital, where he was easy prey for the agents, who took him to KGB headquarters. The Soviet security apparatus also succeeded in capturing Leo Talgre, who was taken to security headquarters for interrogation. Talgre's dull demeanor lulled the security men into slackening their vigilance. The security offices had not yet been secured against escape attempts. After waiting and finding the proper moment, Talgre pushed the interrogator aside and jumped from a second-floor window to the street. Thanks to his training as a parachutist, he landed softly on his feet and disappeared.

The situation, however, grew steadily more complicated. Although Finland received regular communications from the men, it denied their request to send a speedboat to Estonia to rescue them. Finally, Sweden agreed to attempt a rescue. Leo Talgre and Toomas Hellat selected a spot for the speedboat landing and prepared to transport most of the underground reconnaissance men out of Estonia, leaving behind only those who were living as "legals" by this time. They also planned to evacuate members of the National Committee targeted by the Soviet security forces. Several days before the evacuation, however, the KGB arrested a Haukka communications man on the coast, and the carefully laid plans collapsed.

On December 10, Toomas Hellat fell into a trap in a secret hideout. The KGB now used all the methods at its disposal to "work him over." In a few days, Hellat was ready to sign anything they wanted him to. A wave of arrests followed, and the noose tightened around those still free. Nearly every apartment that Hellat's partner Leo Talgre might visit was placed under surveillance. Then came Christmas Eve, 1944. Arved Vaisserik, a supporter of Haukka-Tümmler, recalls:

> Talgre had gone to visit friends to find out what they'd heard about the other men. When the doorbell rang, the door opened, and an armed soldier took aim at him and shouted, "Hands up!" Talgre had a gun in his pocket and he fired it straight from his coat pocket, hitting the soldier, who crumpled to the floor. Talgre drew out his pistol and tried to shoot again, but the cartridge jammed in the chamber. He started adjusting the pistol to get the cartridge into the chamber. In the seconds it took to do that, the soldier revived and showered Talgre with machine gun fire. Talgre fell down dead.

His last words had been: "Say hello to Meets." The attending NKVD officer who had stepped out for a minute only shrugged over Talgre's bloody corpse. The operation had failed; Talgre had not been taken alive. Security Lieutenant Sarkisyan, wounded by Talgre, died in the hospital. At the seizure of Talgre's companions, the operation's chief leader Captain Sergei Printsev was seriously wounded.

With these events, the core of the reconnaissance groups remaining in Estonia was destroyed. Most of the members of the National Committee were arrested, including its first leader Ernst Kull, who had also been imprisoned during the German occupation. Many men suffered the fate of being imprisoned for the same crime by two different occupation forces. Members of the Uluots government went on trial in Moscow. Minister of War Jaan Maide was sentenced to death; the rest to long terms of imprisonment. The members of the last government of the Republic conducted themselves bravely during the trial, calling the proceedings an illegal settling of accounts with the government of an independent state, and accusing the Soviet Union of occupying Estonia. Their spirit remained undaunted in the prison camps of Siberia, where the Minister of Education Arnold Susi became the barracks companion of and one of the greatest influences on a young Russian officer named Aleksandr Solzhenitsyn.

The Haukka-Tümmler radiomen were tried in Tallinn on Roosikrantsi Street. Some of the men "worked over" by security guards were so weak that they could hardly move on their own. Their apparent weakness deceived the guards, who became careless when escorting the prisoners, forgetting that the spirit of these men was unbreakable. What happened next is related in his memoirs by one of the accused, Arved Vaisserik:

> On the last day of the trial, before we were to be removed from Patarei Prison, I played doctor.
> (Voldemar) Särak had huge boils on both elbows, and his hands were swollen and painful. During interrogation, they always handcuffed his hands behind his back and beat his elbows with a steel rifle cleaning rod. Of course nobody disinfected those rods, so they beat all that putrefied blood back into his elbows. I squeezed the thick yellow pus out of both his elbows and it squirted in a large puddle on the floor. But Särak said his hands felt better. I looked at them. It's a miracle, but they still had life and strength. I ripped up a shirt and made bandages of the strips. Särak tried his hands and told me I was a pretty good doctor. He said his hands were as good as new.
> Before the final session of the tribunal, they took us to the courtroom, but today they didn't count us out one

by one. They opened the cell door and told us to go up. Särak, who was to sit in the third chair, first row in the courtroom, had to go third. He let some others go before him. Sepik and Leo did the same, staying in the middle of the group in front of me. Lääts was the first in line. He was in such miserable health that he was hardly one to rush. The group went up the stairs, crowding on the basement steps, the landing, and the stairway leading to the main entrance, and from there to the tribunal hall up two stairways. As I came up the basement steps to the landing with the door to the outside, the group in front of me swung into action. They'd realized that only one armed guard stood by the outside door.

As he passed the guard, one of the men swung and caught the guard's chin with a right hook. Sepik grabbed his gun and Särak grabbed him by the shirt and belt, lifted him over his head, and hurled him down the stairs in a heap. Sepik tossed the gun down after him. They pulled on the door. It wasn't locked. Särak and Sepik slipped out the door.

I looked out the window. Sepik ran to the left and vanished behind the corner of a house in the shadow of a stone wall. Särak chose a tougher route — directly across the yard toward the board fence, beyond which lay a stone house and the French Lyceum schoolhouse. By that route, he could reach Hariduse Street near the Tõnismäe Polyclinic. He ran slowly, zigzagging to avoid being hit. Pulling himself up with both arms, he jumped over the board fence. He had barely hit the ground when we heard automatic weapons fire from the downstairs door. But they were shooting blind. Särak didn't get hit, and he disappeared around the corner.

Events like these no longer had any great significance. Those who escaped, Särak and Sepik, operated in Estonia for several years, but were finally apprehended. Most of the men involved with Haukka-Tümmler were sentenced to long terms of forced labor in Siberian death camps. The core of national activists left behind to organize the resistance movement had been destroyed, and contact with the members of the National Committee who had fled to the West was cut off.

Chapter 3

Estonia Under Siege

By 1945, Estonia's destiny seemed to be irreversible. The land was once more under Red army control, and the Communist authorities who had fled the seat of government at Toompea in 1941 had returned to their positions. Officially, the power now belonged to the Supreme Soviet of the Estonian Soviet Socialist Republic (ESSR) and its Presidium, headed by Chairman Johannes Vares-Barbarus. In reality, the Communist Party of Estonia (with First Secretary Nikolai Karotamm), actually a subsidiary of the All-Union Communist Party and directly subservient to Moscow, was the one organization giving orders in the land.

The foreign authorities, however, found themselves in a difficult situation, because of their lack of any real support within Estonia itself. The independent Republic of Estonia had been a socially homogenous state, lacking marked differences and conflicts among the various levels of society. With the help of the land reform law, most rural dwellers had become small landowners. The relative importance of Estonia's rural proletariat was insignificant. In view of these facts, it is little wonder that the Communist movement in Estonia remained weak. As a matter of fact, since their movement was not considered a danger to this independent country, Estonia released all imprisoned Communists in the late 1930s. In the summer of 1940, the Communist Party of Estonia (CPE) counted fewer than 150 members.

Of course, after Estonia was reoccupied by Soviet forces, Party membership increased. Nationalist groups compiled lists and characterizations, currently preserved in the archives, of Estonians who had become Soviet activists and collaborators. The lists of collaborators included people from all social levels. Most of these were people who had been failures in the Republic of Estonia for one reason or another and now wanted to take advantage of the new situation to launch a successful career and gain influence. A few true, "idealistic" Communists were listed separately.

The Soviet regime remained an alien and hostile force to the people as a whole. The independence era was popularly referred to as the "Estonian era," while life under occupation was referred to as the "Russian (resp. German) era." In the early years, Soviet authorities sought to entice the lower classes by distributing land confiscated from large farms to small landowners or landless peasants. Logic would dictate that this class of new landowners should have thrown its full support behind the new authorities, but most of them remained loyal to their own nation. It was just as well. Soviet authorities launched their program of forced collectivization in the late 1940s, reconfiscating the land they had so ceremoniously given to the new landowners "for use in perpetuity." In summary, the occupation authorities never succeeded in establishing a solid footing in Estonian society. They could remain in power only with the help of intimidation and terror, forcing into collaboration those members of society least able to resist. The question of why, time and again, there are people willing to collaborate with foreign authorities occupying their homeland, is a painful one to all nations who have suffered through an occupation. The answers to this question remain complex and elusive, particularly when we are dealing with an occupation that lasts for decades.

The Soviet authorities were more than aware of the weakness of their foothold in Estonia. Moscow mistrusted the Estonian people as a whole, including the Estonian Communists. Stalin was suspicious of any person who had had any contact with Western culture and lifestyles. For this reason, a tight rein was kept on the Communist Parties in the Baltic States. A special Baltic Bureau was set up within the Communist Party of the Soviet Union to oversee the activities of the Communist Party of Estonia. The members of the Bureau had the power to block directives issued by Estonian Communist authorities and to replace the leaders of the Party leadership in Estonia when necessary, thereby exercising general control.

Actually, this two-tiered system of control over Estonia was redundant, because the CPE had no involvement with Estonian interests in the first place. The ethnic makeup of the CPE during the postwar period provides graphic proof of this fact. In 1944, the CPE had 7,400 members. The final battles of World War II diminished the ranks of the CPE, which then failed to attract any significant number of new members in Estonia. In 1946, the CPE comprised 7,139 members, of whom 52 percent were Russians, 27 percent local Estonians, and 21 percent Soviet Estonians brought into Estonia from Russia. This final category, derisively called "Yestonians" because of their heavily Russian-accented Estonian speech and Russian sympathies, played a significant role in postwar Estonia. Moscow distrusted the native Estonian Communists who had grown up during the Estonian independence era, and therefore gave preferential treatment to the imported "Yestonians." During the second half of the 1940s, a fierce power struggle raged between the local Communists and the "Yestonians," which ended with the victory of the latter in 1951. The Party was purged almost entirely of native Estonian Communists. Although CPE membership had reached 15,000 to 16,000 by this time, Russians made up 60 percent of this group. By 1952, all the upper echelons of the CPE were made up of either Russians or "Yestonians."

The "Yestonians" were also important in the Executive Committees, the local establishments of Soviet executive authority. Soviet authorities had decided upon the makeup of these as well as other official establishments (police, courts, procuracy) as early as 1943 or 1944. "Yestonians," as well as men and women who had left Estonia with the Red army, were subjected to a thorough security check and placed in training. In late 1944, these new authorities assumed their positions in Estonia. The fact that many a new Executive Committee chairman could hardly write his own name was not an issue. Other things were more important — namely, loyalty to the Soviet regime and complete submission to its directives. The conquerors needed underlings who were obedient rather than educated.

The Soviet destruction battalions (officially named *Rahvakaitse* — People's Defense Units) who resumed operations in the autumn of 1944 were to play an important role in securing Soviet power. These units, designed to crush resistance, comprised mostly volunteers, although new members were occasionally recruited with intimidation, the principle being: "Anyone who is not with us is against us."

As of January 1947, these destruction battalion units contained 7,889 members. In those days, destruction battalion troops drew fairly good pay for their "services." They were assigned to guard township halls, Executive Committee buildings, and other important targets, to carry out arrests and deportations, to requisition the property of "the *kulaks* (owners of larger and better managed farms and their families) and those collaborating with the Germans," and to take part in raids. Since the destruction battalions had only limited combat skills, they served only to fill out the numbers of real troops in operations of any importance.

Who joined these destruction battalions? Names and characterizations of destruction battalion members have been collected throughout Estonia. An example from Orava Parish in Võrumaa County:

> In 1944, when Bolshevik rule was restored in Estonia, the so-called People's Defense Units were formed. The Commies regarded the men who joined these units as Red patriots and entrusted them with weapons. But most of the People's Defense troops were thieves, opportunists, bandits, and all sorts of crude, toadying human trash who spat upon Lenin and the ideals of Communism. They craved the power that let them steal from and intimidate the population by threatening innocent citizens with deportation to Siberia and prosecution under cruel Soviet laws.
>
> I remember the first People's Defense men in Orava: Eduard Pettai, a hardened old Communist, who spoke of nothing else but seizing the property of the so-called *kulaks* and sending these people to Siberia. Then there was Paul Männipalu, nicknamed "Goggle-eyed Paul," an illiterate and emotionally stunted man whose only goal in life was to steal. There was Karl Orion of Linnamäe, a hardened crook, thief, and mean-spirited person, with a penchant for violence. Pjotr Leskin — also an unjust man, a drunkard, and an opportunist. Pjotr Rublov — an ethnic Russian and convinced Bolshevik who hated the prosperous farmers and everything else that wasn't to his liking. Then there were the lesser People's Defense types like Friedrich Haaviste, who had been tried in the township hall during the German occupation and released. There was Paul Pruus — a former War of Independence soldier who had received a homestead in Orava from the government during land reform and now joined up with the Communists to curry their favor. Another one was August Tamm, a man from our own village who had been a police brigadier in 1941 and had been released from detention during the German occupation at my intercession. Later, Tamm was arrested again. He served a year in Võru Prison and was released once more. I remember Gustav Pähn — a small homesteader from Rässa — a toady to the Communists. Another one was Herbert Sonne, a homesteader at Orava, who shot Mihkel Jallai to death without warning,

assuming Jallai was a partisan because the man was
making sauna switches in the forest. There were Eduard
Raud and Lord, whose first name I don't recall, from the
Orava homesteads. These men were real criminals, killing a man from Suuremetsa after stealing his cow. I
think they were imprisoned for a year or two.

This brief review clearly illustrates the nature of these "patriots
and people's defenders." The people had good reason to call them "a
bunch of no-good thieves." The People's Defense units all over
Estonia were similar in nature. They included few principled Communists; most of the troops were the dregs of society for whom the
door to social leadership was opened by the occupying regime.

Destruction battalion troops also worked at destroying books
and desecrating the family graveyards of the German nobility. Those
who do not respect the dead can hardly be expected to respect the
living.

Official reports preserved in the CPE archives provide us with an
assessment of these People's Defense Units as seen from a different
angle. For instance, a Võrumaa County record dated December 24,
1949 states:

> The battalion to destroy the bandits (under Cmdr.
> Comrade Polyakov, with political assistant Comrade
> Nikiforov) does not even remotely live up to expecta-
> tions. In many parishes, for instance Misso, Vastseliina,
> Laheda, and Haanja, the platoon commanders are drunk-
> ards and morally decadent individuals. Discipline is lax
> in the Võrumaa Office of State Security, as illustrated by
> the fact that personnel problems, all relating to drinking
> and moral decadence, have been addressed twelve times
> this year at the Party organization meetings.

The same archives contain a description of an incident on December 8, 1946, when the Tartumaa County, Kasepää Township People's
Defense platoon commander Melnikov, after drinking with his brother,
threw a hand grenade into his neighbor's window, killing the entire
Sarapuu family, including a mother and two children. Clearly, the
people were defenseless in the presence of the People's Defense units.

Of course, not all the individuals collaborating with the new
authorities were bums, drunks, or freeloaders. Quite a few young
people from the poorer classes were seduced by the beautiful and noble

slogans of Communism. Unfortunately, the hopes of such starry-eyed idealists were usually shattered at the first contact with reality. These individuals were left with two choices — to continue the game or to call it quits. Ambitious leftist intellectuals, who felt unappreciated in independent Estonia and threw their support behind the occupying powers in 1940, were destined to become sadly disillusioned. By 1945 and 1946 it was eminently clear to them that instead of leading their people to a bright future, they had set it on the path to total destruction. On November 29, 1946, the chairman of the ESSR Supreme Soviet Presidium Johannes Vares-Barbarus was found shot to death in his apartment. It has never been determined beyond a doubt whether he took his own life or was killed by security workers. At any rate, it was clear that Vares-Barbarus had called it quits.

Several honest local Communists met a similar fate. In Sõmerpalu Parish of Võrumaa County, there lived a man named August Pedras, who was known for his Communist sympathies during the independence period. In 1940, he played an active role in the Soviet seizure of power and fought in the ranks of the Red Estonian Rifle Corps during World War II. After the war, Pedras fell out of political favor for some reason, and was exiled to Sõmerpalu Parish to work as local Party secretary. His superiors hoped that the Forest Brothers would do him in. It didn't happen that way, because Pedras turned out to be an unusual Party secretary for his time. He kept his word, never made an effort to seize local private property for himself, and did not regard the deportation of large numbers of "people's enemies" to Siberia as his primary duty. Rather, he worked to protect his people from arbitrary violence. Instead of commending Pedras for his work, however, his superiors in Tallinn showered him with constant reprimands and abuse. Finally, Pedras could stand no more. In 1946, on his way to face another deluge of reprimands, he shot himself to death on the platform of the Valga train station. In a letter Pedras left behind for his wife, he declared that he'd dedicated his life to serving the ideals of Communism, but now he realized what kind of misery these ideals were inflicting on his country. His life had been a failure and he had no choice but to end it.

Estonia suffered greatly in the grip of the new regime. At Moscow's orders, local authorities began cultivating a typical colonial economy and stripping the land of all its natural resources. Under the guise of an "industrial revolution," they ruined Estonia's traditional branches of industry and built gigantic factories for the production of military goods. As a result of this massive reorganization, Estonia's economy was made dependent on that of the Soviet Union. Estonian products that had formerly been remarkable in their quality became unable to compete on the world market. The work ethic and general productivity declined sharply. One example is provided by the shale oil industry, which was producing 494 tons per worker annually in 1939, but only 482 tons per worker by 1950.

The ruin of Estonia's agriculture dealt an even harsher blow to the land. The Soviet authorities used the same tactics in Estonia as they had when collectivizing agriculture in the Soviet Union in the 1930s. First, private farms were burdened with heavy taxes, and when this failed to close them down, the authorities resorted to direct terror. In 1949, under the threat of deportation to Siberia, masses of peasants joined collective farms. Private ownership of property, a centuries-old tradition in Estonia, was abolished. As a result, agricultural production declined sharply. Within a few years, nearly half of all fields lay fallow. Everyone who could fled to the cities to escape famine. Urbanization increased rapidly, but urban areas lacked sufficient living space for the new residents. Consequently, the standard of living suffered a sudden drop, especially when compared to the prewar standard.

Soviet authorities cared little about the new state of chaos and the destruction of the independence-era way of life. Their goal was to sweep away all traces of the "former world," starting by destroying monuments and works of art, but also renaming streets and even a city. The actions of the Communists differed little from those of the Nazis.

Generalplan Ost, compiled years earlier at the instructions of Adolf Hitler, had called for the transfer of half a million German colonists to the Baltic over a period of twenty-five years. The Soviet powers colonized the same territory in the same period of time with more than a million of its citizens — more than twice the number the Nazis had planned. The Soviets' goal was eminently clear. The Estonian spirit of resistance and perseverance had to be crushed with deportations and terror; the indigenous population was to become a minority in its own homeland, finally to be assimilated. A frequent boast of Soviet propaganda: "the flourishing of national cultures," seems particularly cynical when viewed in this light. In Estonia, this "flourishing" entailed the transformation of the Estonian National Museum grounds into a Soviet military base, the arrest or ostracism of nearly all writers, composers, and scientists, the burning or "quartering" (i.e., chopping into fourths with an ax) of millions of books, and the destruction of works of art and national monuments.

As early as the first few years of the occupation, the Estonian people realized that they had to dedicate all their energies to resisting the thrust of the iron weight threatening to crush them, even if they had to hold it back with nothing more than their bare hands. Moreover, the people retained a resolute faith in the imminent arrival of assistance from the Western democracies and the victory of justice in the world. It was far more sensible to lie low and preserve oneself and one's family than to submit voluntarily to the terrorizers. No one was safe from the punitive grasp of the new authorities. The wave of arrests which engulfed Estonia at the end of 1944 and claimed about 10,000 people gives clear indication of the Soviets' long-term plans. People were crammed into jails; dozens of prisoners were forced to occupy cells a few square meters large.

In 1945, all ethnic Germans were sent out of Estonia. Members of religious organizations were the next to go. The Christian leaders who had assumed the duties of the Estonian archbishop (who had left the country) were arrested and sent to Siberia. Most of the rest of the clergy soon followed. As a result of all the arrests, deportations, and murders, Estonia lost nearly one-third of its population. The number of Estonians in Estonia even today is *less* than it was in 1939.

No one had foreseen such a tragedy for 1945. The younger generation, raised during the period of national independence, could not imagine living in a world without an independent Estonia. Their only feasible alternative was to fight for the restoration of independence. Moreover, most of them already had scores to settle with the occupation authorities. In postwar Estonia, brutality and injustice had reached such proportions that the mere pointing of a finger provided sufficient grounds for execution. The soldiers of the occupation army killed and plundered at will.

Materials preserved in the CPE archives give a fairly accurate picture of events, clearly indicating that acts of violence by the Soviet army killed more Estonians than the partisan war itself.

An example is provided by several excerpts of official reports by the Saaremaa Party Committee (1945):

> The situation is particularly serious in the villages
> of Kärla, Pihtla, and Kuressaare, where soldiers ride
> around at night in armed bands of six to eight men,
> taking whatever they want from the farmers. For
> instance, on January 20 in Upa Village of Kuressaare
> Parish, comrade Juhan Koov, age seventy-four, and his
> wife Elisaveta, age seventy-three (whose son serves in
> the Red army), were murdered with an ax, all their
> clothes stolen, and their property searched for money.
> The Upa villager who discovered the crime encountered

two singing soldiers on a sleigh; he saw the murdered man's shoe fall onto the road. The murderers were members of Colonel Kotik's unit.

On February 8, mother and son Mets were stabbed and shot to death with automatic weapons in Võrsna Village of Valjala. (The father and one son had been murdered by the Germans.) The motive was robbery. Col. Kotik's soldiers were found to be the murderers. On February 23, the first lieutenant of Unit VP 02567 killed citizen Loonurm in Torgu Parish by striking him on the head with a log while drunk.

There are numerous reports of soldiers assaulting isolated women in the country. Only last week, some soldiers raped a woman on her way to the hospital to give birth, inflicting serious injuries on her husband as well, so that the couple later died in the hospital. Because the incidence of robberies, murders, and thefts is so high, the people are dispirited and no longer dare to live on isolated farms.

The local governments were powerless to provide protection for the population. If a terrorizer did happen to face a tribunal, his punishment was minimal. A Sergeant Stradyevski, who had stabbed five women in Kuressaare City, was sentenced to only seven years. Small wonder, since the Red army officers regarded Estonia as their conquered land and the Estonians as second-rate citizens. The new local governments could do nothing, since this same Red army guaranteed their own hold on power. Their personal interests and practices varied little from those of the occupation army soldiers. As a reward for obedience, the Soviet authorities gave their local representatives free rein to steal from and intimidate the families of the "bandits." They hoped this would suppress resistance at its source. Salme Eomõis, the wife of a shopkeeper who was arrested in 1944 and disappeared without a trace, relates a sadly typical incident in postwar Estonia in her memoirs:

The time: the evening of January 21, 1949. The place: the settlement near Mõniste railway station; the house of Estonian-era shopkeeper Eomõis, where I, his wife, lived with our two small children. At that time, the house contained a shop and the apartment of shopkeeper Richard Toop. At the end of the workday, some

men of the Mõniste Executive Committee — local Party
Secretary Robert Lätt, Chairman Oskar Liiv, Alfred
Kripp, and Julius Henning — came by to drink at the
shopkeeper's apartment. A bit later, my cousin Arnold
Ruven arrived on horseback to invite me to his birthday
party. Arnold stayed at my place several hours and nod-
ded off because he'd had a bit to drink. Suddenly, Liiv
and Kripp, both drunk, crashed into my apartment and
attacked Arnold, shouting: "Let's take care of the bandit!" They pulled Arnold to the floor and started beating
him. I shouted for help, grabbed my children, and fled
into the corridor. Liiv stormed after me and punched my
face bloody. I couldn't protect my face since I was holding the children's hands. In my room, they kept beating
Arnold. I managed to escape with my children up the
stairs into the attic room where Leeni Kalliver lived with
her two children and her mother. From there, we took a
secret door to a hiding place in the attic. Leeni's old
mother stayed in the room alone. Meanwhile, the bloodied Arnold had been dragged from my room into the
shopkeeper's room, where they smashed him over the
head with a weight. We later found blood and hair all
over it. Liiv stumbled upstairs to "take care of us," but
we six sat quietly in the attic hideout and he didn't find
us. Arnold was dragged out of the house and thrown
into the road, where the cold air brought him back to
consciousness.

Of course, the Executive Committee men were not punished for
this crime, although Salme Eomõis was summoned to the
procurator's office and deported with her children in March 1949.

The NKVD punitive troops sent into the countryside in late 1944
left particularly painful scars on the nation's consciousness. The units
set up headquarters in schoolhouses and community halls and set
about conducting raids on local Forest Brothers. The punitive troops
seized large numbers of people, demanding information about "anti-
Soviet" elements. Anyone refusing to disclose the requested information was tortured. Not even women and children were spared their
beatings. In Mõniste Parish of Võrumaa County, a man named Enn
Luhtmaa was in hiding from the Soviet authorities. He could have left
the country in the fall of 1944, but he decided not to leave his young
wife and newborn son. He returned to southern Estonia and hid out

near his home. Although Enn Luhtmaa avoided any kind of resistance activity, he was hunted mercilessly. His home was ransacked and his wife taken to repeated interrogations. During one interrogation, an irritated security officer grabbed the crying child from Luhtmaa's wife and flung him headfirst against the wall. The child survived, but remained feebleminded for life.

Whenever anyone died under torture, a doctor was ordered to write out a death certificate attesting to "death from natural causes." Since the end of 1944, Edgar Ranniste had been in hiding in Undla Parish of Virumaa County. At first, his hideout was a secret cellar under the floor. However, as the raids intensified, he fled to the forest along with his wife. They were forced to leave behind his aunt and gravely ill mother. His aunt is the sole witness to what happened on August 4, 1945:

> That night, I slept at my sister's, because her legs had been bothering her lately and she wasn't able to move about on her own. I was making dinner when I heard the roar of a truck outside. By the time I got to the door, the yard was full of soldiers surrounding all the buildings. Their commanders stepped in and informed us in Estonian that all the property here was to be confiscated, and nothing belongs to us *kulaks* any longer. My sister demanded that they call the procurator. At that, they laughed and said that they were the ones who represented the law. They said, "You have hidden and fed your daughter and son-in-law; you've assisted the bandits." Then he called in his men and ordered them to empty all the rooms and haul all the contents onto the trucks. When they moved the big bed in the bedroom, they found a trapdoor in the floor beneath it. They demanded to know who had been hiding here. I said I didn't know. They'd found a German soldier's belt somewhere and they started beating me with it, ordering me to reveal who had been hiding here.
>
> Then they started on my sister, who was lying in bed. They shook her and beat her with the belt and demanded to know who had been hiding here. My sister screamed for help, "People, help me." Then they stopped and said, "We'll get you to talk."
>
> Then a Russian began torturing my sister and saying, "Old woman, where have you hidden your gold?

Give it to us." My sister was screaming and I begged
them to stop torturing a sick woman. They ordered me
to leave the room, and I fled the house in tears.

The next day a soldier came for me and ordered me
to get dressed and go with him. When we got to my
sister's place, an officer outside informed me that the
kulak had hanged herself last night. They told me to prepare the body for burial. I went inside and saw my sister looking oddly blue there in bed. I prayed. Then I
summoned my neighbor Kikerpill to help me. They
told me that the doctor had been by that morning.
When we undressed my sister's body, it was an awful
sight. Her upper body, chest, and arms were blotchy
blue, and she had the same blue blotches around her
neck. The neighbor and I looked at each other but we
were afraid to say anything. Finally, they ordered me
and Kikerpill into the other room, gave us some papers,
and demanded that we sign them. The papers said that
if we talked about what happened, we could only say
she had hanged herself; otherwise we'd be arrested for
spreading false information.

In 1945, a man named Davodov was commanding the punitive
troops operating in western Estonia's Märjamaa Township. The operations of this unit, designed to terrorize and kill people, are described
by a schoolboy of that time, Aksel Viisut:

In the late fall of 1945, a christening celebration was
being held at the Loigu farm in Ligeda Village of Velise
Parish. Artur Seelmann's baby boy was being christened
as Jaan. The whole village had been invited. They
laughed and danced and drank homemade beer. Suddenly, gunshots and the rattle of automatic weapons
sounded from outside. Splinters flew from the wooden
walls. Bullets whined through the house. Ado
Linkmann, who was sitting with his back against the
wall, suddenly grabbed his stomach and slowly collapsed, saying, "I'm done for." Then Ernst Liisalu
yanked open the door and called into the night, "Stop
being such pigs. Stop it!" In the dark, we could see a little blue flame heading toward the door in a wide arc.

Ernst shut the door just in time and the grenade hit the door and rolled into the yard, where it burst.

When the shooting subsided, Aadu Minna lay dead on the floor in a pool of blood. His daughters Ida and Emilie were tending to him. Maria Lansberg had a shell splinter in her lung. Erich Viisut crawled in with two bullet wounds.

We were all flat on the floor. We lay there quietly until it got light. We heard shouts from outside: "Surrender! You're surrounded! Resistance is useless." We went out and the soldiers drifted in. Their victory was complete. We had one killed and two wounded; one of their soldiers had been scratched by his own shell fragments. All our men were taken to Märjamaa prison. The troops took whatever bounty they could find, including the homemade brew for the christening celebration. One soldier took along an old wall clock. On the truck, he held it in his lap like a precious treasure. About half a kilometer from the prison, he jumped from the moving truck onto the road and fell, sliding along for several meters on his stomach with the clock under him. I saw its little gears and wheels scatter across the snowy road.

We were held in Märjamaa prison for three days and interrogated repeatedly. Then they let us go and I could go back to school.

Others were not as fortunate.

On June 5, 1945, a Security Forces unit conducted a raid in the Undriku-Männiku Village of Undla Parish in Virumaa County. They were directed there by Heino Maidla, who worked as a Soviet security informer. On the evening of June 5, several women were attending the birthday celebration of one's daughter. Their husbands, who were local men hiding in the forest, stopped by later in the evening. They all sat around the table and celebrated the birthday. One of the men went outside, then came back in and told Ardi Treial that there was some suspicious movement going on out there. As Treial went to the door, someone outside shouted: "Surrender! The house is surrounded!" Treial replied: "Let the women come out, but we men will not surrender." At that, automatic weapons fire rattled at the house. The men inside responded with the same. The gunfire went on for a long time. There were many dead and wounded. The men outside shot tracer bullets at the house, which set it on fire. The whole house was in flames, and whoever ran out was shot down. The women's screams were muted by the crackling of the fire and the rattle of gunfire. Only Treial and Soovik managed to crawl away from this battle, wounded, but all the others were burned, some alive, some already dead, in the ruins of the collapsed house.

When the fire had burned itself out, the soldiers collected the charred bodies, tossed them onto the truck, and drove them into Rakvere City. A few days later, some local people and relatives came by to clean the site where the house had stood and found two more women's bodies lying by the wall. The wall had collapsed onto them. They recognized Helga Treial and Ellen Tiikoja. The birthday girl, Valve Koitla, is buried nearby.

Fourteen people perished in the raid, including eight women.

Despite such acts of intimidation and terror, Soviet authorities failed to achieve their ultimate goals. The nation it had forced into a corner neither fought nor surrendered, but rather sought every opportunity to bare its teeth. More importantly, in their concentrated hunt for a handful of professionals, the NKVD had neglected to devote sufficient attention to the steadily growing and more formidable force gathering quietly in the forests of Estonia — the tens of thousands of yet unorganized and untrained men who believed that the war in Estonia was nowhere near its end.

Chapter 4

The Resistance Takes Form

Men, women, and children began hiding from the Soviet regime as early as the autumn of 1944. The occupying Soviet forces had conquered the capital city of Tallinn on September 22, 1944, and most of the rest of the mainland and the islands in October. Everyone knew that the return of Soviet occupation signified the return of terror and brutality. All those who could, left the country, doing so in the resolute faith that soon they would come home once more. Hardly anyone could conceive of the scope of the injustice that would erase three independent states from the world map at the end of the war. In 1944, the Estonians were certain that the collapse of Germany would be followed by a conflict between the Western Allies and Stalin, and that this conflict would restore freedom to the Baltic States and other captive nations. Until then, the people had to lie low and wait for the right moment to rise up for freedom.

The first men to congregate in the forests were those who had fought in the German army and later, in September 1944, under the national flag of the Estonian Republic. Most of them could have left the country along with the retreating German forces, but a majority preferred to continue the fight in Estonia. Estonian Legion Lieutenant Olaf Tammark describes the events of that time in his memoirs:

> On September 22, our battalion deviated from our planned route of retreat at Rimmu Fork, as agreed upon by the battalion officers, and headed west and then north, instead of southwest. That same night near Kõpu township hall, the battalion commander Major Friedrich Kurg assembled his men and informed them of his personal decision to remain in Estonia. "We now have the opportunity to join the Germans as they retreat. Anyone

following his best instincts in the present situation will
not be court-martialed. Whoever decides to stay with
me remains subject to Estonian army discipline. We are
Estonian soldiers, soon to be without uniforms, rank,
front and rear. The front line and the rear will soon be
one, and they will be everywhere."

Although some of the soldiers tried to flee across the sea to
Sweden to join their families, most stayed behind. At first, they lived
in large groups, which soon dispersed as men made their way back
to their home districts, where it was much easier to hide. The forests
of Estonia filled with soldiers on their homeward trek. The autumn of
1944 was unusually mild and sunny, as if Mother Nature herself had
set about protecting Estonia's sons.

The people held together with remarkable tenacity during those
difficult times. They offered the soldiers food and shelter. Kettles
bubbled day and night in the forest farms as the people dyed the
soldiers' uniforms to help the fugitives look more like typical farm
folk. Transporting heavier weaponry proved to be a serious problem
for the fugitive soldiers, and so they hid their artillery in well-planned
storage sites in anticipation of coming battles. Typical hiding spots
included hummocks or isolated forest farmsteads. In Pärnumaa
County, large quantities of military supplies were "laid to rest" in
Tõstamaa Cemetery. Olaf Tammark recalls the autumn of 1944:

Our reports said that Pärnu had fallen to the Russians on September 23, 1944. Those who came from the
area said the coast was still teeming with refugees,
although the last boats had already left.

Some men continued their westward trek, still hoping to make it to Sweden or the Estonian islands. Others
helped harvest potatoes at the farms of Öördi (in southwestern Estonia), exchanging their possessions and uniforms for civilian clothes. One forest farmer's wife said
that she could outfit an entire platoon of soldiers from
the supplies she had. Within six weeks, most of the men
and civilians had left the Öördi forest. The nights had
grown cold. In the mornings, the tents were white with
frost. The forest canopy thinned; the rain fell more frequently. The "Forest Ranger," a lone Russian reconnaissance plane, made its daily flight over the forest, noisy
as a tractor. No Russians had come into Öördi Village

yet, but there were plenty of them around nearby Viljandi City. The long arm of the newly empowered Communists reached these forests and swamps soon enough. It was no longer safe to move about in daylight. The Executive Committee had already summoned several local people and accused them of sheltering the bandits and fascists.

We started our long journey to Valgamaa County in the dark of night: Major Kurg, a few men, two horses, and one wagon with heavy weapons and ammunition hidden under the straw. "Is the fighting over now?" asked one of the men. "No," I said, "*our* battle is just beginning."

Of course, the Soviet army did not plan to stand by calmly. With the first swoop, it succeeded in taking 3,000 to 4,000 prisoners in battles and raids, but the number of men slipping through the Red army's grasp was much greater. To catch the fugitive soldiers, all roads throughout Estonia were placed under surveillance, with special attention focused on bridges. To reach their homes, men had to swim rivers or steal boats, hide in haystacks, or find other uniforms to wear.

Not everyone succeeded in evading the enemy. Long columns of prisoners were soon moving along Estonian roads. Some Estonian prisoners landed in Estonian camps (at Tallinn-Nõmme or Narva), but most were deported, mainly to Karelia. The trip across Estonia was hard for the prisoners. The men were prodded mercilessly; anyone lagging behind was threatened with execution. An Estonian Legionnaire captured in Pärnumaa recalls:

> I was seized because of my boots. The patrol was stopping men on the road. Most of us lacked identification papers, so they identified us by our boots. Those wearing German boots were taken for interrogation. There was nothing to deny; we admitted serving in the German army. At first we were held in a shed. After that, we were forced to march through southern Estonia toward Valga City. As soon as we reached southern Estonia, a lot of the men made a dash for freedom. They knew every thicket and ditch along the way, so the escape was easy. Sure, they were shot at, but how can you catch the wind? At any rate, no one dared follow the fugitives into the forest. The number of prisoners, however, had to agree with the numbers

on the lists; so the Russians seized some farmers by the roadside to replace the soldiers who had escaped. They just pressed their rifle against the farmer's chest and said, "*Davai*" ("Get going"). The local women shrieked and cried, but it was of no use. Those men were the first to give up the ghost at the Valga distribution camp. They were used to good country food and couldn't survive on starvation rations.

Going home was fraught with danger. Quite a few men met their fate at their own front gate; others escaped death by miracles. Aksel Mõttus, an Estonian volunteer who fought in the final battles in the defense of Tallinn, recalls:

On September 23, I happened to meet some men of the Estonian Corps. They told me to go home. A Russian army transport took me to Põltsamaa Parish. By nightfall, I reached a large marsh near Kolga-Jaani. The retreating Germans had blown up parts of the road through the marsh. The Russians had patched it with boards. I helped push out some of the mired cars. As we were struggling with one of them, I saw a motorcycle and a sidecar with three Russian soldiers. The sergeant sitting on it looked at me closely but drove on. Having finished my work, I continued on foot.

A half-kilometer ahead, the same motorcycle was waiting for me. They asked me for my papers. I gave them my occupation-era passport, but the men noticed my university I.D. with its red covers. They asked what it was. I replied in German: "*Studentenbilett.*" At that, one man grabbed my wallet and pulled out 400 German marks. "Why so much money?" they asked. I tried to explain in mixed Russian and Estonian that my father had given it to me. They asked where I was going and I replied "*Domoi*" ("Home"). They asked, "*Nemets?*" ("German?"); I answered, "*Estonets*" ("Estonian").

Then one of the men pointed to my university I.D. and shouted: "That's a German national socialist party card!" I denied it and got punched in the face. Blood flowed onto my shirt. They ordered me to sit. I sat. I got one, two, three kicks in my groin. I fell by the ditch. They stopped beating me to go through my wallet.

I saw a military car carrying some higher officer driving toward us. Now my captors pretended they were starting the motorcycle and ordered me to help. When the car had passed, they got to working on me again. They ordered me to sit with my feet in the ditch. They sat opposite me. My wallet had about thirty postage stamps with portraits of Hitler. The officer took one, shoved it in my face and asked: "Who's this?" I answered: "Hitler." He punched me in the face and both soldiers slugged me. He threw that stamp down and took the next one. Again the question, my answer, and the blows. After a few stamps, I refused to answer. But he asked again and they punched me again. They beat me until I answered, "Hitler."

Then the junior officer whispered something to the soldiers. They got up and took the submachine gun off the motorcycle. I was dazed and bloody. The junior officer hit me over the head with a long metal box. I fell into the ditch. The water at the bottom revived me and I sat up. I understood enough of the junior officer's words to know he wanted me to walk twenty paces. One soldier loaded a new round into the submachine gun. I knew that they were going to shoot me right here in this potato field. The junior officer said: "You know Russian, but won't speak it. You're acting, spy!"

I turned my back and started walking slowly through the potato field. I'd been on the front lines often enough to know these Russian machine guns. I knew how many seconds I had to reckon with. The soldier didn't seem to be rushing either, thinking I had been beaten into submission. Thirty or forty paces past the potato field there was a field of grain. About halfway across, I darted to the side, behind the haystacks. The machine gun rounds blazed through the haystacks, which hid me as I ran toward a protective thicket. I had escaped.

Most of the soldiers finally reached their homes. But a man's problems did not end there; actually, they were only beginning. First of all, he had to choose whether to go into hiding or to respond to the enticing calls of the new regime to emerge from the woods and "begin constructive work." This campaign became especially fervent in 1946, when each Party Committee had to make a monthly report on each "legalized" individual. CPE First Secretary Nikolai Karotamm was personally active in the campaign, sending his missives to the county Party Committees, "strongly suggesting" their publication. The following is an example of one of these appeals:

> Leave the forests immediately and without fear. Return to your homes and begin honest work. You have nothing to fear from the Soviet regime. Errors of judgment, such as service in police forces, will be forgiven by the Soviet regime.
>
> It has already been stated that all those who are guilty of killing Soviet people, all those whose hands are stained with Soviet blood, must be punished.
>
> But even to these people, the Soviet powers say: Your voluntary exit from the woods and surrender to the Soviet regime will guarantee you your life, which will certainly be in grave danger sooner or later.

Unfortunately, these seductive words were hollow, designed to entice the gullible from their hideouts. Some men emerging from the forests were arrested right away, some later, and thus all the amnesties and calls to leave the forest soon lost their effectiveness. The Soviet establishments themselves were forced to admit to the flaws in this process. At a meeting of Saaremaa Party activists, someone stated bluntly: "I think that the Saaremaa branch of our State Security Committee is partly to blame for these people taking to the forests, because it immediately arrests those who come out to be legalized." Similar complaints can be found in CPE archives of other counties. These complaints do not necessarily signify any sympathy with the arrested individuals. For instance, in a complaint filed by the Pärnumaa County Party Committee, the local Party Secretary worries above all about the "incorrectness" of the security units' actions. He felt that if they were going to arrest someone emerging from the forests, they had to do it more discreetly to avoid sending a warning to others planning to turn themselves in.

A shocking incident emerges from recollections recorded in Sadala Parish:

> When amnesty was declared for the Forest Brothers who left the forests voluntarily, a man from Veneküla Village in Sadala Parish was one who responded. He was family man August Saar, with a wife and three children.

His only crime was evading military service in 1941. He was placed in a cell at Sadala and interrogated. They wanted him to take some soldiers to the Forest Brothers' hideout in the woods. Since the Forest Brothers hid out in several places, each one according to his own instincts, there was no single spot where they could all be found together, so Saar did not know where to take the troops. He was tortured at the Executive Committee building for two days. On the third day, August Saar, who had come in search of amnesty, hanged himself in his cell. His body was given to his wife for burial. His face had been beaten black and blue, and his hair had turned gray. There were marks of torture on his hands and body.

Such acts of brutality served only to distance the authorities from their goal of achieving popular support or, at the least, submission. Their reign of terror drove men into the forest who otherwise would not have gone into hiding. With the passing of time, more and more partisans had personal scores to settle with the new regime. Many had lost their parents, siblings, sweetheart or wife. It was this group — those who had nothing to lose, those whose only wish was to take revenge and then die — that emerged as Estonia's bloodiest Forest Brothers. The story of Paul Randmaa, a well-known partisan from southern Estonia, is related by one of his comrades in arms:

Paul Randmaa was an easygoing guy. He started hiding out from the authorities with some other men in 1944, thereby targeting his family members for persecution. Because of a personal vendetta, the destruction battalion men treated his family with particular brutality. First, they stripped the farm completely bare, conducted repeated searches, and dragged Paul's father and sister to interrogations.

One time, the destruction battalion was lurking near the farm. It was late in the evening, and the old man came out to shut the granary door. The destruction battalion thought that perhaps Paul had come home and opened fire on old Randmaa, who took several bullets and died. When Paul heard of this, his face turned gray. We covered him when he secretly returned home to bid a final farewell to his father before the burial.

The Reds still weren't satisfied. Some time after the previous incident, a group of destruction battalion men returned to the farm. They were drunk and very aggressive. First they trashed the rooms; then they started on Paul's sister Ilse. They stripped, taunted, and beat the girl. Then the men went into the next room to make their plans, and their driver, who was guarding Ilse, said the men were planning to rape and then kill her. He let the girl escape through the window, and she ran naked across the frost-covered meadow to the neighboring farm, where she got some clothes and joined her brother in the woods.

In the events of those times, even love became entangled in the hate. Kalju Kirbits explains:

In the 1940s, the Rõuge Township Komsomol (Communist Youth Organization) leader was a woman named Õilme Teder. She had a red, blotchy face. She was as big and stupid as a cow. She was a real activist, walking around with an automatic slung over her shoulder. She was the one who put together the lists of those people to be arrested or deported. A boy named Auleid Toomsalu lived in Rõuge at that time; his home was nearby, across the valley. He was a handsome fellow who played in the firemen's band. Even though all the girls were after him, he wasn't a girl-chaser; he had one steady sweetheart.

In 1948, the young people of Rõuge got together for a birthday celebration. The gathering was pleasant; everybody was drinking and having a good time. When they started to sing, they sang some patriotic songs, like "Be free, Estonian seas." And of course old Õilme Teder was sneaking around there too. It seems she had a crush on Auleid, but Auleid didn't care for her. As soon as she heard that song, she threatened to go and report everyone. It would have saved the day if Auleid had agreed to bed down with Õilme, but he refused, choosing the forests over this Komsomol cow. His sweetheart wasn't lucky enough to escape — Õilme had her deported. This act became her own death sentence. Even though there were a lot of security troops staying at Õilme Teder's

place, Auleid managed to find an opportunity to carry
out his revenge.

Õilme Teder's stately gravestone stands in Rõuge Cemetery,
bearing a moving text which says that a hero has only one life to give.
But is there anyone who knows the grave of Auleid Toomsalu?

The ranks of the Forest Brothers swelled with the beginning of
the Red army's mobilization drive, which started in southern Estonia
in August and September 1944, arriving in northern Estonia some
time later. In contrast to the German mobilization, evasion of military
service this time was much harder, since the family of the evader was
targeted as well. And still, the new regime encountered terrible difficulties with the mobilization. For instance, Soviet Army Captain Purre
of Virumaa County notified the CPE Central Committee that the
Virumaa mobilization wasn't progressing satisfactorily, since the Germans had apparently succeeded in brainwashing 50 to 60 percent of
the population. In 1945, only thirty-five men of Pärnumaa County's
355 conscripts reported to the Military Commissariat; in Pärnu City,
only twenty-two of fifty-two.

In addition, desertions by the Red army's Estonian units
increased. The CPE archives contain numerous complaints about
Estonian Rifle Corps soldiers expressing "anti-Soviet views" while on
leave. In many areas, Rifle Corps men are believed to have supplied
Forest Brothers with weapons; in others, they joined up directly with
partisan units.

It is difficult to estimate how many people were in hiding from
the Soviet regime by early 1945. According to available information,
the numbers approached several tens of thousands of men, women,
and children. According to Soviet sources, these people were either
war criminals or representatives of the higher classes in independent
Estonia (intellectuals, politicians, military officers, large land owners).
In reality, not one active Forest Brother is known to have been accused
of crimes against humanity or the murder of Jews while serving in the
German army. On the contrary, many better-known Forest Brothers
participated in the resistance against the German occupation, evaded
the German mobilization, or took active part in armed combat against
German forces. One of Virumaa County's legendary Forest Brothers,
Ossip Lumiste, actually received a medal from the Soviet authorities
for destroying a German *Jagdkommando*. The man was showered with
all possible privileges. Shortly thereafter, Lumiste's brother got in the
way of a Soviet border guard patrol, who shot the suspicious man to
death during his "escape attempt." Ossip Lumiste could not endure

such injustice, and he turned to the forests, organized a group of men, and set about avenging his brother's death.

Accounts in Soviet sources about the social makeup of the Forest Brothers groups also ring false. Partisan groups included very few members of higher social classes and high-ranking military men. First of all, most people of higher social standing would have been unable to endure the hardships of life in the forest; and perhaps more importantly, most of them had already been arrested early in the Soviet occupation or had fled the country. Country people made up the vast majority of the Forest Brothers. Among them, large land owners and their descendants were a distinct minority. Many of Estonia's best-known Forest Brothers (such as Ants Kaljurand) had their origins in the poor peasant classes; a number of them were farmhands and laborers. Records from one district in Võrumaa County provide some information about the size of the farms that had belonged to Forest Brothers. According to the documents of a commission working to confiscate the household goods of Forest Brothers, the size of most Forest Brothers' farms ranked below the size of an average farm in Võrumaa County. Most of the Forest Brothers originated from middle-sized farms; the proportion of large farmers was small.

A search for some kind of social index for the formation of Forest Brothers groups is bound to fail. People joined the resistance movement not as an indication of social rank, but from a desire to stand up against the foreign power that had conquered their homeland. The young people raised in their own free country refused to accept a future without a free and independent Estonia. Most of the population reacted to the invaders instinctively with resistance. The nature of the resistance was determined not only by each individual's character (courage, aggressiveness, adventurousness), but also by circumstances. Each person targeted by the security apparatus had to decide whether to submit to slaughter willingly or to attempt resistance.

At first, the Soviet authorities apparently did not feel particularly threatened by the Forest Brothers movement, with its spontaneous origins. Reports sent to the CPE Central Committee by the counties in late 1944 mention the existence of only a few thousands of "bandits and illegals." These reports are hardly surprising. After all, during the first phase of the Forest Brothers movement (1944 through the spring of 1945), the primary goals of the Forest Brothers were concealment and avoidance of active combat. For instance, when his battalion disbanded, Major Friedrich Kurg gave his soldiers instructions to hide in the forests and farms until the spring of the following year, ready to jump into action when war broke out between the West and the

Soviet Union, ready to help in the liberation of Estonia. Most of the Forest Brothers placed their hopes solely on the outbreak of a new world war, which would mean only a brief stay in the forests. They firmly believed that the decisions and promises made by President Roosevelt and Prime Minister Churchill in the Atlantic Charter of August 1941 would be implemented after the victory over Nazi Germany.

Some of the men still regarded themselves as soldiers, remaining in uniform to symbolize the fact. A partisan unit commander from Virumaa County recalls:

> We had to raise the question of attire. Should we wear civilian clothes or army uniforms? We weighed the options: If we wear uniforms as the war continues, we'll look like fragments of German army units remaining in the enemy rear, continuing the fight instead of surrendering. But if we wear civilian clothes, we're bandits, and we'll be shot without a trial if we're caught. All things considered, we decided to remain in uniform until the end of the war. Since plenty of uniforms had been left behind with the secret arsenals, this issue was resolved.
>
> I also raised the question of discipline, because an eight-member group needs to constitute a viable unit. We are in a life-or-death situation; everyone has to fight for everyone else. In the event of attack, every man must fight as the circumstances dictate, and not run away. This is where our strength will lie. Everyone understood that there was no alternative if we wanted to be an organized force and fight as a military unit.

A number of Forest Brothers sought to flee to the West. The parents, wives, and children of many of the men had fled west, and now the men wanted to join them at any cost. The Red army knew this too, and the entire coastline was densely covered with border patrol cordons to seal off escape routes from Estonia. And still, in the autumn of 1944, escape was possible. Many men who had escaped to Sweden made daring trips back to Estonia, taking hundreds of people to freedom. Such rescues were possible only because the people held together so tenaciously. Reports by Russian border guard patrol commanders frequently include complaints about local residents refusing to help the border guards in the fight against "bandits" and "nationalists attempting to cross the border." Virumaa County security chief Matveyev submitted this report on December 7, 1944:

> When Soviet power was restored in the Ukraine
> and other Union republics, many people came to the
> People's Commissariat for Internal Affairs and security
> organs and helped to expose hostile elements. Here,
> only a few individuals will do so. Revolutionary vigi-
> lance is severely lacking. In some instances, you can ask
> a trustworthy source about the enemies of the people
> and he'll say, "There are none here," and then later you
> find out that twelve men have fled to the woods to
> evade mobilization.

One instance of a successful escape is illustrated by the adventure of Herbert Liljeberg, a man from the island of Järvsaar in the Gulf of Finland, who undertook a bold trek from Finland to Estonia to rescue his sweetheart. Herbert Liljeberg had met his future wife in Estonia in 1944 while he was there on assignment by the Finnish army. Although many of his companions had already spirited their wives out of Estonia in 1944, the object of Liljeberg's affections did not yet have any idea how much he cherished her in his heart. The lovestruck young man himself explains the situation best:

> Love had me restless. I couldn't get permission to
> visit Estonia. The postal censor confiscated my letters.
> But all's fair in love and war. Could the Gulf of Finland
> keep me away? No, because I'd sailed up and down and
> across it every which way, day and night, and I'd never
> gotten lost. I needed a proper boat, no more than five
> meters long, made of lightweight boards, so that I could
> drag it into the forest and hide it all by myself. So that's
> what I decided. I got the lumber and started planing the
> boards to get them to a thickness of ten millimeters. I fin-
> ished the boat in a week. Some people asked me why I
> was building a boat. I replied that I had to get my wife
> out of Estonia. Nobody believed this far-fetched story.
>   I did some investigating of the Russians' shoreline
> watch, trying to find out when they used their search-
> lights less frequently and so forth. What should I take
> with me? I had to have a revolver. I might run into a
> bothersome guard dog or whatever, but I could never let

myself be captured alive. I sewed a pocket under my left arm for the revolver, so I could grab it in an instant.

I planned to start my journey on August 30, 1946. I borrowed a five-horsepower outboard motor from Eino. But I didn't set out as planned, because I could see a thunderstorm raging over near the Estonian coast. The next day, the weather was beautiful. I consoled my family by saying: "If you don't hear from me within a month, then go and ask about me at the Foreign Ministry." I knew that the risk was great and that my chances of returning were slim. But my conscience forced me to go. I couldn't take it any longer.

I started out at seven that evening, dressed in pants and a woolen sweater, with a jacket and coat in reserve. I took a simple compass that I could read in the dark and an old sea chart showing the lighthouses on the Estonian coast and a straight southward course.

I had pinpointed my landing site exactly and I was to pass Prangli Island between 1:00 and 3:00 a.m., when the spotlights were turned off. In the middle of the gulf, I ran across a Russian border guard ship, which set its course directly toward me. Fortunately, a dense fog fell around us and I stopped my motor so it wouldn't betray my location. I heard the roar of the ship pass toward the east. I rode on, past Keri, Prangli, and Aksi. I rowed the rest of the way to shore, so that the roar of my motor wouldn't attract any unwanted attention. My childhood friend was extremely surprised when I rapped on his window and explained my situation. We hid the boat under some hay in his hay shed, which the enemy had searched laboriously the day before. My friend gave me some money and some identity papers that didn't have a photograph and identified me as a soldier, even though I couldn't speak a word of Russian.

The next morning I went to the train station and found out that it was 100 kilometers by train to Alice's. Asking the way, I found out what I needed to know. Alice was a teacher, and she happened to be in Tallinn and Haapsalu with her work. Finally she came. Fortunately she was alone. I couldn't let her recognize me here, being in civilian clothes and in these circumstances. I let her walk some distance from the station

before I let her know I was there, because there was a
Russian guardpost at the station and Russians all over
the place. She was astonished and surprised; and maybe
just a little happy to see me again. As she threw her
arms around me, her hand felt the pistol under my left
arm. "What do you have here?"

The way home seemed short because there was so
much to talk about. Was it fate that had brought us
together again? I'm sure she knew full well why I had
come like this, but she didn't ask. Perhaps she had some
idea. That night, I asked her straight out. It seemed that
the world stood still. Everything had come about so
unexpectedly for her. She had to make the hardest, most
serious decision of her young life.

I was in her bed and couldn't sleep. Her nearness
tempted me to take her completely, but common sense
prevented us from losing ourselves to passion. The situation was far too serious. It was hard for her to decide,
and that morning she told her mother everything.
Alice's father had been taken to Siberia. Alice herself
had made a decision from the first. Her mother said: "If
you must take such a difficult step in your life, then go
with this man. You have my blessing. But don't ever
turn back from the road you have chosen."

Alice bought some food from the market and we
went to her friend's house to eat. She had only a small
travel bag. We went toward Narva highway, where Alice
bought a chocolate bar from a kiosk. It felt just like a
school field trip. We'd gone a pretty long way when it
struck us that we should ask for help from above for the
success of our voyage, as her mother had told us. Inevitably, her mother's sermon had left its mark on me as well.
Ahead of us lay the iron curtain and Russian border
guards patrolling the shoreline with dogs. What would
stop them?

We readied the boat, putting straw on its bottom for
Alice to lie on. We were ready to go by midnight. I
pulled the string to start the motor, but we were not too
far from shore when the propeller hit a rock and the
drive pinion split in two. We were in trouble. But I had a
reserve pinion in my pocket, which I replaced in the
dark, feeling with my hands, and we finally moved

away from the shore. I was afraid of Prangli Island and
took the long way around it. The searchlights were off.
The waves rose and fell with an easterly wind, but the
wind turned southerly, being at our backs and blowing
strong.

Halfway across, the gasoline tank ran empty, and
refilling and restarting the motor took a long time. But
we were downwind and this good downwind had also
accompanied us on our trek across dry land. The night
brightened when the moon peeked out occasionally
from behind the clouds and helped us find our bearings.
The low pressure system was passing. The wind turned
northwest and blew hard. We'd never have managed
with it in the middle of the Gulf of Finland, but we were
nearing Lotan-Järvsaare. Who would have believed that
we could be so lucky? We never could have dreamed of
the adventures we'd just experienced.

When we finally reached shore at five that morning,
I took my golden treasure, the one I'd had to risk so
much for, into my arms and carried her onto the island
that would be our home. Father came to meet us on the
beach with his lantern, knowing from the roar of the
motor that his lost son was on his way home. Everyone
was overjoyed at our wonderful homecoming. And who
was this that I'd brought with me? My foolish escapade
had been in earnest, even though no one had believed in
it. We told them about the high points of our voyage,
drank the hot coffee my mother made, and felt we
needed some real rest after these nerve-wracking days. It
was time to crawl between the cool sheets next to this
warm girl, without worrying about anything anymore.
At this moment, I finally felt that life was worth living.

This was only one of several daring escapes from Estonia. One of
the most famous was the voyage of the fishing trawler *"Meretuul"* to
Sweden, which completed its voyage successfully despite being
tracked by Soviet naval vessels.

This could not go on for long. The patrols drove people away
from all coastal areas, confiscated fishing boats, and severely
restricted fishing at sea. The culture of Estonia's coastline perished.
Gradually, but firmly, the noose tightened, and soon the entire coastline was sealed off. Marine patrols increased markedly, and agents

were infiltrated into groups attempting to flee. In one instance, a speedboat transporting refugees from Estonia to Finland was seized by the Soviet fleet.

In addition, Soviet security forces launched an extensive sting operation in which their agents offered men the opportunity to flee the country, arresting them for "attempting to cross the border illegally" as they prepared to leave. An officer who fled Estonia at a later date recalls:

> One day, a close female relative of mine who knew I was hiding came to our farm with some exciting information from Tallinn. A secret organization was helping people flee to Sweden. A number of men had already made a successful crossing. When she returned to Tallinn, I weighed this proposition carefully for some time and finally decided to seize the opportunity, since it was my only chance. And so one day, with high hopes, I rode into Tallinn. I had managed to collect the necessary funds and now it was time to act.
>
> In Tallinn, I hid with my female relative. She started making the arrangements, since she was familiar with the process, having gone through it before for her husband. The days passed in nervous anticipation, and one day a man from this secret organization came to me and said I was to leave that same evening. Everything was in order and I only needed to get on my way. This good samaritan also recommended that I go ahead and write a letter about my safe arrival in Stockholm. It was twilight in early spring when I set out for the harbor to board the German ship waiting there. As expected, a Red army guard stood at the harbor gate, demanding to see my papers. With a confident gesture, I pulled out my yacht club member's license and gave it to him. He glanced at it and said one word: *"Provalivaii."* ("Move along.") I stepped onto the dock with confidence and headed for the ship docked in the distance.
>
> I hadn't taken ten steps when suddenly a three-member border guard unit emerged with their officer, who demanded to see my papers. I handed them over and he squinted at them, saying it was too dark outside to read them. Courteously, he asked me to accompany

him to his office, so that he could read my documents in a better light and inspect the stamps.

We went to his office, which was nearby. I had no choice but to follow his orders. We had barely stepped into the room and closed the door when I was shoved into a back room, stripped, and thoroughly searched. Within an hour, I found myself in a cell on Pagari Street (NKVD headquarters).

I was transferred to Central Prison, where I met a whole group of "refugees to Sweden" like myself — people who had fallen into the trap set by the NKVD "secret organization."

Rumors of these entrapments spread throughout Estonia, essentially bringing an end to organized escape attempts. Nobody panicked, however, since everyone believed that the war would end soon and that Estonia would regain its independence.

Convinced that their concealment would be brief, many groups were little concerned about making long-term plans. They did not think about building more secure hideouts or bunkers, but lived in farmhouses or sheds, often forgetting the basic rules of secrecy. Thus, the KGB was able to work with brutal efficiency, dealing many painful blows to the Forest Brothers. To trust any and all "compatriots" was to risk dire consequences. A long, gloating report preserved in the CPE archives describes the destruction of a "bandit gang" in the spring of 1945. We learn that the operation was initiated by sending the former Forest Brother "Metsnik," who had been recruited by the Soviet security apparatus, into the Forest Brothers groups active in the Vändra-Tori region.

Metsnik was accepted into the partisan unit without question, and soon the security apparatus knew the identities of not only the members of the group, but of all its helpers. On April 23, at Metsnik's direction, they surrounded the barn that served as the Forest Brothers' meeting place. The partisans caught sight of the raiders and prepared for battle. The Soviet security forces then sent two hostages, a man and a woman seized from the nearby village for being "gang collaborators," with a demand for surrender. The Forest Brothers responded with gunfire. After a fierce gun battle, the partisans were forced to give up. Six Forest Brothers and one woman surrendered; one man was seriously injured in the gunfight. The group's radio operator Herman Lillemäe refused to give himself up alive and committed suicide.

In addition to the Forest Brothers, the Soviet security forces arrested thirteen local people as "gang collaborators." The successful operation was led by Lieutenant Vaino, assisted by Comrade Hallik.

It seems that some of the Forest Brothers were slow to realize that the situation had changed thoroughly. Like the Forest Brothers during the German occupation, they tried to help with farm work at home or other places, but circumstances were no longer the same. After the front line had passed through the area in 1944, Franz and Robert Nigul hid in the farms of Mõniste Parish in Võrumaa County, where they secretly worked in the fields, frequently plowing in women's clothes. Renee Kond recalls:

> In the autumn of 1944, a destruction battalion came to our area. They commandeered me to provide transportation for them. Another horse was taken from the Horst farm, a third from someplace else. We rode to Latvia. At the Üle-Leppura farm, they seized brothers Franz and Robert Nigul, who were drunk and unarmed, and who offered no resistance. The prisoners were brought to Kuutsi and locked up in the corner room of what is now the post office. Destruction battalion member Eduard Kikas, who hadn't taken part in the raid, was placed on guard. With my horse, I had to escort Alfred Kripp, one of the raiders, to his home. It was late and I stayed the night at Saru. The next morning, Kripp rode with me back to Kuutsi. We saw that the window had been shattered and that Franz Nigul's body, arms dangling, lay sprawled over the window ledge. Robert Nigul had broken the window and jumped out, but the chair seat had broken under brother Franz's foot, his legs became tangled in the chair and he was shot to death on the window ledge.

Similar incidents took place throughout Estonia. Some men were shot as they plowed their fields.

In the autumn of 1944, a militarily organized unit of Forest Brothers was formed under the command of Estonian border guard regiment officer Mihkel Leetmaa. Together they retrieved the weaponry they had hidden in the forests of Avinurme during their retreat and built a sturdy bunker. The local farmers supplied them with food and other necessities. Mihkel Leetmaa recalls:

One March evening, our bread run was made by a sixteen-year-old boy. He was stopped by a twelve-member NKVD unit. In his sleigh they found the bag of bread and a love letter from a girl to her sweetheart who lived in our bunker. They read the letter and translated it into Russian. It was clear that the bread was meant for the "bandits."

They beat the boy and ordered him to show the way to the bunker where the bread was to go. The boy didn't know the location of the bunker, only the spot to make his delivery. The boy was beaten until he took the Russians to the logging slope and showed them the place he was to leave the bread. Not far from the bread drop-off spot, a ski trail led to our bunker. Despite the dense fir thicket, the Russians found the ski trail and started along it on foot. About 100 meters before the bunker, the trail split in two, with both trails making an arc to the door of the bunker. The right fork was longer by half a kilometer. The fork forced the Russians to split into two groups, and those that took the right-hand trail arrived a good deal later than the first group.

The guard who usually stood at the fork, 100 meters from the bunker, had just stepped inside to get warm. As he was returning to his post, the first Russians reached the bunker. The guard barely managed to shut the bunker door when its occupants heard bursts of rifle fire and the explosion of grenades. The guard was killed instantly. The men in the bunker opened fire, as planned, with four light machine guns, followed a minute later by hand grenades. The Russians screamed and swore; their raid had failed.

About half an hour later, the attack was repeated to the accompaniment of loud cries and preemptive grenade strikes. Fortunately, the Russians could not reach the windows and toss grenades inside.

Another half-hour went by and a third attack ensued, this time with fewer grenades. This assault also fell short of the Russians' expectations, because our machine guns were working well, and the grenades we threw out the window prevented the Russians from getting close.

Then they tried to blast a hole in the wall with light machine gun fire. This failed too, since the soil between the two walls kept filling up the hole.

Apparently, the attackers were running out of grenades and ammunition, because their weapons fire was subsiding. Daylight began to fade. The bunker door opened quietly and machine gun fire mixed with the blasts of hand grenades. Three partisans ran out the bunker door and vanished into the thicket, following their plan of retreat.

At first, the Russians failed to notice their escape because of the dense thicket, apparently thinking that the sudden burst was just the next round of fire, and it was already too late when they realized they were being fired upon from outside the bunker.

Three more partisans attempted to crawl after their comrades, but only one made it; the other two fell in a shower of Russian bullets.

The remaining partisans succeeded in breaking loose from the enemy in the deepening darkness without further losses. They spent the night at their next position eight kilometers away.

They visited the battle site the following day. Our three casualties had been taken away and the bunker burned to the ground. The footprints in the snow indicated that the Russians had kept close to those sides of the bunker without windows, out of our line of fire. Otherwise, all our men would have been mowed down by automatic weapons fire as they left the bunker.

All too often, surprise attacks did not end as fortunately as this one at the bunker in Sämijõe, Virumaa County. Inevitably, some sleeping partisans were torn to pieces by grenades before they could rise and resist. Edgar Ranniste describes such an incident in his recollections:

One of the village deputies told Soviet security forces operating in Vohnja Parish under the leadership of Heino Maidla that Forest Brothers were on the move in the area. The security apparatus set up a raid on the forest called Ämmassaare behind Ohepalu Village. That evening, they placed the Kolu-Pala road under surveillance, and arrested forest ranger Kirs and his family in Naelaaugu Village.

When no information was gleaned from the older family members, they took an eight-year-old boy outside to a tree and tied a noose around his neck. They said if he didn't reveal the location of the "bandits'" hideout, he'd be hanged. Deathly afraid, the little boy said he had an idea where it was and showed them the path. In the fading light, the chekists sneaked into the area and surrounded the marsh hummock they found. Our men suspected nothing. They had gone fishing at Valgejõe that day, and were now sleeping peacefully, without even a sentry on duty. In the darkness, the chekists crept up close and threw several hand grenades into the tent while firing their automatic weapons. They killed the men brutally, without warning. The men they killed were Paul Pook, Tõnu Taadermaa, Juhan Treial, Heino Juuse, and Karl Kalda. Edgar Põhjala had been killed earlier. He suffered serious injuries after being fired upon as he walked down the road. He was dragged to the township hall for identification. He died there and his body was taken back to the forest and buried in a shallow grave with his feet still exposed. His family later reburied him.

After killing the sleeping men, the murderers still weren't satisfied. They threw kindling onto the bodies and set it ablaze. Maybe they wanted to destroy the evidence, maybe they wanted to celebrate.

A few days later, when the news of the battle had spread, the families secretly went to look and found a horrifying scene — a pile of scorched human remains. Tõnu Taadermaa lay on top of the pile. Although his back was burned, he was recognizable because his hands were raised protectively to his face. His feet were tied. We had to conclude that he had tried to crawl away after being wounded, but he was captured, dragged to the fire, and tossed onto the heap. The man was burned alive.

Although the Forest Brothers suffered heavy losses in 1945, the KGB's momentum soon began to slow. Apprehending the Forest Brothers was no longer an easy task, because these partisans now had the benefit of experience. Soviet security detachments frequently ran into crushing counterattacks. In February 1945, a Forest Brothers unit led by Ossip Lumiste encountered a border patrol detachment in Loksa on the northern coast. The partisans killed one soldier and two dogs, and seriously wounded Lieutenant Trinkin. Military patrols were targets of fire in other areas as well. In the early morning hours of November 1944, a bouquet of grenades was tossed at an NKVD unit commander in Valga marketplace in southern Estonia. The officer suffered serious injuries; the assailant fled. In the spring of 1945, Kaagjärve Forest Brother Otto Lill fired at the Soviet counterintelligence chief Comrade Abahimov in the same marketplace.

Not surprisingly, the occupying army felt insecure in Estonia. A Soviet soldier who participated in the "liberation of Pribaltika" (as the Baltic States are called by the Russians) recalls:

> Estonia was one of the first territories to be "liberated" (after Vilnius) in the early autumn of 1944. My marine unit entered Tallinn harbor. All the harbor buildings and docks had been destroyed. We didn't meet a single person at the harbor. The longshoremen, like a vast majority of Tallinn's population, were boycotting the entry of Soviet forces into Estonia. The population refused to cooperate with the "liberators" because they were frightened. Later, their fears were realized. A secret letter from the Russian Communist (Bolshevik) Party Central Committee to the Communists of the marine division informed us that Estonia was the most counterrevolutionary republic, and that most of its population supported fascist Germany. The letter prohibited Soviet soldiers from meeting with local people or marrying Estonian women. We had to be vigilant. Vigilance was instilled in us every day.
>
> We were severely restricted in our treks to the city. NKVD units, made up mostly of soldiers from the northern Caucasus and Central Asia, patrolled every street corner. We were forbidden to go into the city alone. Incidents of Soviet soldiers being murdered or poisoned with tainted vodka were frequent. A marketplace stood next to the "Estonia" theater at that time. As a rule, the appearance of a Soviet soldier at that market usually cost him his life. Kadriorg (Palace

Park) was a particularly dangerous zone for us. We
could get hanged there.

It was the spring of 1945, and the war in Europe had ended.
Hopes that the Western nations and the Soviet Union would go to war
proved to be unfounded. The Western powers made more and more
concessions to their "allies." In Potsdam, the Soviet Union achieved
affirmation of the decisions made in Yalta, which gave it a free hand
in dealing with Eastern Europe. This also allowed the Soviet government to consolidate its position in its occupied territories and to begin
setting up local institutions to suit its own purposes. The promises
made by President Roosevelt and Prime Minister Churchill in the
Atlantic Charter regarding a free postwar Europe were neglected and
forgotten.

The course of events in Europe forced the Baltic resistance movements to revise their strategy. Edgar Ranniste recalls a meeting of the
Virumaa County Forest Brothers in June 1945:

There were huge forests in Vohnja Parish. A lot of
men, some locals, some strangers, lived and hid there
quietly in small groups.

One midsummer's eve, we invited them for joint
consultations. We discussed our situation, what might
happen, and how to react. Arguments ensued. Some of
the men wanted all Communists to be singled out, shot,
and destroyed. "We have good weapons," they said,
"why should we be afraid of them?" I replied that it was
not a question of fear but of consequences. "Let's say we
torch the township hall and then retreat to the forest.
What's going to happen to the local farms once the security forces come in and start raiding the area? Innocent
people will suffer, and maybe even lose their homes. We
would then lose their trust and they wouldn't dare supply us with food anymore. I think we should use our
weapons only in self-defense and in situations where we
meet up with those informers whose actions merit the
death penalty."

"Our situation is bleak, and it'll get worse toward
autumn. I think that whoever wants to continue hiding
must stay alone or in a small group. Those of you who
want to leave the forest, go ahead, but don't start informing on those of us who stay. Don't betray our positions

as the price for your freedom. I personally have decided
to remain loyal to the Republic of Estonia and not to subordinate myself to the terrorist government of Stalin,
who has occupied our homeland."

Other groups made more substantial plans. For instance, a report
sent to the CPE Central Committee tells of a "secret meeting" held at
the Laanejaagu farm near Polli, Viljandimaa County, where the partisans decided that since war was slow in breaking out, the overthrow
of Soviet power was up to them. As a first step, they planned to kill
all the people who were disrupting local life and terrorizing the
population.

The end of the war made it clear to every Forest Brother that the
occupation would inevitably persist for some time. Passive resistance
was no longer adequate if they wanted to stay alive. They had to
coordinate their planning more tightly and engage in more effective
action if they were to preserve the premises for the restoration of
independence.

A life-and-death struggle erupted in Estonia.

Chapter 5

Striking Back

In the summer of 1945, the tranquility of Estonia was shattered by automatic weapons fire and the bursting of grenades. The Forest Brothers, who had concentrated on concealing themselves up to now, launched their active resistance. All through the land, they attacked the centers of foreign authority, the Soviet Executive Committee buildings, where they carried out acts of sabotage, ambushed money shipments and transport columns, and killed the lackeys of the Soviet occupation authorities.

They directed their first strikes against the local representatives of Soviet authority. They targeted Soviet security personnel, destruction battalions made up of collaborators with the occupation authorities, and small military units, focusing on higher officers. On July 14, 1945, four Red army soldiers were killed in an attack on a Red army unit in Virumaa County's Roela Parish near Kulina Village. On July 24, a military transport carrying three naval officers was attacked at Valgejõe in Harjumaa County. All three were killed. A military transport was ambushed near Väike-Maarja in Virumaa County; Colonel Popov and Lieutenant Colonel Udayev were seriously wounded. These were only a few of the attacks carried out in the summer of 1945; such operations were conducted throughout the country. The Forest Brothers' bounty from the dead officers and soldiers came in the form of weapons and uniforms, which the partisans used during their own operations. The Forest Brothers avoided attacking larger military units. Their preferred tactic was to operate in small units, deliver their sting, and vanish.

The partisans savored lying in wait for their bitterest enemies — the high-ranking officers of the NKVD. On July 26, 1945, in Tartumaa County's Lohusuu Parish on the Narva-Tartu road, two leading workers of the Leningrad NKVD Road Construction Administration were shot to death; their driver escaped. On August 16, 1949, the Järvamaa County security chief Colonel Paul fell victim to an ambush on the

Tallinn-Paide road. A tree in the roadway blocked the colonel's car. He was taken into a nearby thicket, informed of his sentence, and summarily shot to death.

In addition to attacks on military personnel, the Forest Brothers also engaged in diversions and acts of sabotage. In his memoirs, a Forest Brother called Franz describes an all-out attack on a Soviet supply train in Virumaa County, but other written evidence of this episode is still lacking. The CPE Central Committee archives, however, do contain reports of a train crammed with Soviet military personnel that rode onto a mine on the Pärnu-Tallinn railway line near Paikuse Township on June 20, 1948. Miraculously, no one was killed. Explosions occurred on other rail lines in Estonia as well. Security reports list eighteen diversionary operations that were carried out in Estonia by partisans between 1944 and 1953.

High on the Forest Brothers' agenda were attacks on places of detention to free imprisoned comrades. Memoirs relate an attempt to attack Tartu City Prison. Accounts by German prisoners of war tell of an unsuccessful operation by the Forest Brothers to free them from a prison camp in Virumaa County. An attempt by Forest Brothers to free the prisoners in Pärnu Prison is described in detail in the CPE archives and several memoirs. Although the Forest Brothers met with little success in attacks on major detention centers, they made effective assaults against small rural prisons.

Frequently, they ambushed prisoner convoys. An excerpt from a document found in the CPE Central Committee archives describes such an attack, which was repeated in many parts of Estonia. On July 2, 1945, NKVD officer Babanin and police officer Alumets were shot to death in Saue Parish near Tallinn, and police brigadier Königsberg was wounded. According to the latter's account, the three had gone to the Arujärve farm on the night of July 2 to arrest farmer Jaan Arujärve. At a distance of about 300 to 400 meters from the farm, near the Vana-Pärnu road, they were attacked by two strangers in military uniform holding automatic weapons and waiting for them in the road ditch, and obviously aware of Arujärve's arrest. In Estonian the stalkers ordered: "Hands up!" At that moment, the arrested man Jaan Arujärve yelled: "Give it to 'em good!" The NKVD deputy Babanin drew a pistol from his holster and fired at one of the attackers, wounding him, but the bandit fired a burst from his automatic that killed Babanin. Then the bandit directed a volley at police brigadier Königsberg, wounding him in the leg, but since the wound was superficial, Königsberg threw down his rifle and escaped by running through the swamp and forest. There was little sense in pursuing

Forest Brothers in areas surrounded by forests and swamps. Even if some of them were captured, transporting the arrested men to major centers presented great difficulties to the Soviet authorities, who were forced to resort to detours and distraction maneuvers to evade local partisan units.

Freeing prisoners was often the reason for attacks on the strongly fortified centers of Soviet power — the Executive Committee buildings. Since these establishments were guarded by military or destruction battalion troops, the Forest Brothers had to plan their strategy carefully. Documents in the CPE archives describe events in Veriora Parish of southern Estonia, where the local Executive Committee chairman had been responsible for a number of acts of violence.

> On November 2, 1945, eight kilometers from the center of Veriora Parish, a group of armed bandits, comprising six persons, stopped two trucks belonging to the Võru Consumers' Cooperative and the 22nd Rifle Division.
>
> The bandits, seizing the trucks by force, drove them to the Veriora Parish Executive Committee building. Entering the building, they killed the Baltic fleet's construction unit company sergeant major and wounded company commander Lieutenant Lyadin, three People's Defense soldiers, one peasant, and a local Komsomol leader from Valgamaa County.
>
> One of the bandits wore the uniform of a police lieutenant, one of a policeman, and the rest were in civilian clothes or mixed uniforms.

The attack, launched by the group under Richard Kaldmaa and Mihkel Lutt, is described in detailed testimony recorded in Soviet security files:

> About midday on November 2, I heard a truck engine and looked out the window to see two trucks coming from the direction of Võru stopping on the street in front of the Executive Committee building. A group of men, some armed with automatics and dressed in military uniform, climbed out. Five or six headed for the Executive Committee building. Four more stayed by the trucks. Reaching the Executive Committee building,

they split into two groups. Two or three went behind the house, and three came in the front door.

Watching a group of armed men climbing off two trucks in broad daylight in front of the Executive Committee building, no one would have thought they were bandits. The police, security forces, and People's Defense units walked around with clothing and weapons just like that all the time. I was still at the inner door when a tall, heavyset, and tanned police lieutenant stepped in the front door, saying, "Hands up, everyone." We didn't obey his order immediately, so he fired several shots from his pistol into the ceiling. In the confusion, Lillo and I managed to leave the office. Lillo ran outside through the small room, but I stayed with the policeman Roostik. Someone's automatic lay on the sofa. I shoved it to Roostik, telling him to shoot when they came in. In a moment, a bandit entered our room. Roostik didn't shoot. He held the automatic by the barrel, stock on the floor.

The bandit demanded the gun. Roostik refused and asked the stranger who he was. The bandit hit Roostik on the head with the butt of his machine gun and demanded the weapon once more. Roostik still refused. The bandit hit him again and tore the weapon from his hands.

Another bandit arrived. They searched us. They took my personal documents and a pistol from Roostik's pocket. Looking at my Executive Committee Chairman's identification papers, the bandit said: "So you're the chairman. Your death will be awful." The tall gray-coated man ordered me into my office to find the key to the safe. I said that the safe was cared for by our treasurer Loreida Paal. They started looking for Paal. They found her in the propaganda corner and brought her to the safe at gunpoint.

The incursion ended quickly. Shots rang out outside and in the waiting room where the soldiers were. The gunfire ended with the burst of a grenade. When the bandits got the safe open, things quieted down as someone shouted, "Boys, come and get the money!" They came and stuffed their pockets. According to the treasurer, the safe had held 31,000 rubles. They found 5,000

more in the desk drawer. Then someone said, "Lutt's
been hit. Let's go!" In addition to the money, they took
the Executive Committee's typewriter, someone's rifle,
and an automatic from the small room.

After some of these attacks, the Forest Brothers temporarily
seized power from the Executive Committee over the entire settlement. For instance, the Hargla Forest Brothers invaded and took over
Hargla in 1945 in retaliation for the activities of NKVD battalions. Two
destruction battalion members fell in the battle; the others fled. The
largest area ever taken over by the Forest Brothers was the city of
Kilingi-Nõmme in southern Estonia.

The Forest Brothers considered it their duty to uphold the
nation's spirit of resistance while demoralizing and intimidating
Soviet authorities. In retaliation for the destruction of Estonian War
of Independence monuments, they blew up monuments to the Red
army. In Veriora Parish, a wooden obelisk honoring Red army soldiers
was tossed into a Communist's apartment through his window. On
holidays dear to the Estonian people (Independence Day on February
24, Victory Day on June 22), the outlawed blue-black-and-white
national flags were hoisted onto tall trees or buildings. Thanks to
warnings fastened to the "flagpoles" ("Mined," or "Whoever touches
this flag won't live much longer"), the flags were often able to fly for
some time.

The Forest Brothers demonstrated their strength by disrupting
a number of Soviet projects and state holidays. It is hardly surprising
that many of their major operations were launched on the anniversary of the "Great October Revolution," the widely celebrated "Stalinist Constitution Day," and other holidays. In some areas,
partisan-produced handbills urged the people not to participate in
these celebrations.

Naturally, both sides focused special attention on elections,
which the Soviet authorities hoped would legalize their conquest of
the country. Because of local instability, official elections were postponed several times. Elections for the USSR Supreme Soviet were
finally attempted in 1946. Of course, the event bore only a remote
resemblance to a true election, since every district had only one
candidate, and that individual was nominated by Moscow. Under
threat of deportation to Siberia, the people were herded into preelec-
tion meetings and later to the polls.

The Forest Brothers did their best to thwart the elections. In one
instance, they smashed a stand holding election agitation literature

near the Keeni Machinery and Tractor Station, replacing it with a poster calling on the population to disrupt the elections by casting either blank ballots or ballots with the names of anti-Bolshevik individuals. They claimed that the Bolsheviks were trying to mislead world opinion with their "elections." The poster was signed "The Forest Brothers." Similar posters were put up in other parts of Estonia. In some districts, partisans undertook more serious operations, such as stealing voter registers. They also assaulted candidates in 1946. Several of their operations in Võrumaa County's Urvaste Parish commanded widespread attention. Former Forest Brother Johannes Heeska recalls:

> A small military unit was brought into Urvaste to defend the polling station. They were a real bunch of thieves, stealing things and blaming it on the Forest Brothers, and killing one of my schoolmates. I guess the Forest Brothers decided to wipe out that gang and the whole pack involved with the elections.
>
> There was a preelection rally going on at the Urvaste schoolhouse. The township hall had been secured by the army. The Forest Brothers gathered in a small valley not far from the township hall, where we joined them later that night. They had seized a horse and wagon with a load of brushwood. They stuck their weapons under their jackets. They rode up to the door and said they were the propaganda station controllers. So the Reds let them in where they were playing cards. Lenin's portrait hung crooked on the wall. So then the "controllers" said, "Why isn't this great man's picture perfectly straight? Aren't you Party men?" They replied, "Of course we are. We are secured nice and tight, with the machine gun there and the grenades over there." One "propaganda controller" stepped out on the steps and gave the prearranged signal, and when the Forest Brothers came running in, the man drew his gun and told all the Reds they were arrested. The Reds threw their weapons on the table. One tried to run but was shot dead.
>
> Then, a couple of our men ran hollering toward the schoolhouse, shouting that the bandits had attacked and been pushed back. They yelled for the destruction battalion commander to assemble his men. The troops jumped

out with rifles in hand, but our guys whacked the guns
out of their hands outside the door. The Reds suddenly
realized what was going on. And then the Forest Brothers put them on trial. They read off the crimes, like "You
shot a farmer's daughter, you stole, you hunted our comrades, and your sentence is: the death penalty." And
they took 'em into the next room and let 'em have it.
There were seven bodies on that floor. The whole room
was all bloody, so what kind of elections are you going
to have after that?

Many Forest Brothers units deliberately inflicted damage on the
occupation authorities by attacking Soviet transport columns and
shipments of money and goods. First of all, the partisans needed these
operations to replenish their own supplies. Second, the operations
served to reaffirm their authority among the population. The confi-
dence and boldness of the Forest Brothers are illustrated once again
by an incident from a celebration in Rõuge, southern Estonia in 1946:

A Soviet army officer, Estonian by nationality, decided
to take a shortcut home while he was on leave and march
through Ööbikuorg, a popular village festival site. To his
delight, he found a festival in full swing. A band played,
some people danced, others dipped moonshine into their
mugs from a vat by the edge of the clearing.
The officer made himself comfortable among the village folk, filled his mug, and enjoyed himself
immensely. Suddenly, the words being sung to a traditional melody struck him as unfamiliar: "I want to be
home when Estonia is free, when Laidoner commands
the forces, when I hold the Estonian *kroon* in my hand."
The officer took a closer look around the festival site. In
the distance, he now noticed a neatly constructed pyra-
mid of sidearms and light machine guns with a guard
standing alongside. Suddenly, it dawned on him that he
had stumbled into a Forest Brothers' celebration. Apparently, the revelers had anticipated this moment of realization, because at that instant, a pair of armed men
stepped up to him and politely asked him to surrender
his weapons and identity papers. The officer had no
choice. After complying with the request, he was

handed another mug of moonshine and the merrymaking continued.

When the officer reported the incident to the security office the following day, he was harshly reprimanded and finally stripped of his rank, because the officials failed to understand why he hadn't arrested all those Forest Brothers.

In a more serious incident on the evening of October 4, 1946, a group of fifteen Forest Brothers stopped a bus in Võrumaa County between Leevi and Veriora. They allowed the passengers to disembark and inspected everyone's identity papers. They stole nothing and used no force against anyone. The target of the operation was a passenger on the bus, NKVD deputy Veber. He was relieved of his pistol, taken into the forest, and asked: "What have you done with our village constable?" Without waiting for an answer, the Forest Brothers shot Veber dead and drove toward Räpina Parish in a truck they had commandeered earlier.

There are tales of similar "document inspections" in recollections from many counties. An "international inspection team" made up of partisans had operated in Kuigatsi Parish of Valgamaa County, presenting itself as a joint Estonian-Latvian-Lithuanian commission gathering data on popular attitudes toward the Soviet regime.

The partisans intensified their seizures of shipments of goods and money after the regime repeatedly raised taxes collected from owners of private homes and farms in 1947. The Forest Brothers simply repossessed the money stolen from the people and returned it to its rightful owners as best they could. These twentieth-century "Robin Hoods" demonstratively refrained from touching anyone's private property. In Pärnumaa County, a tax inspector's pencil happened to be included in a forestry plant payroll stolen by the famous "Black Captain." A few days later, the pencil was returned with apologies and "compensation" to its owner with a note stating that the partisans kept their hands off private property. The partisans had a unique way of distributing some of the money stolen from Soviet establishments. The money packages were loaded into a potato basket and tossed into each yard as the men walked through the village at night.

The marauders needed detailed information on the time and place of arrival of these cash shipments to launch an effective assault. On-site informers in communications offices kept the Forest Brothers well informed. The partisans needed only to set up an ambush in the woods and relieve the escorts of their money. Typically, these operations succeeded without a single shot being fired. The cost of any resistance was paid in lives.

In order to throw Soviet security forces off the scent, the Forest Brothers did not limit themselves to operations in their home county, but made expeditions to faraway districts. For instance, the Veriora Forest Brothers of southeastern Estonia twice made off with the Sindi workers' payroll in the southwestern part of the country.

The effectiveness of the Forest Brothers' operations is confirmed by the Estonian SSR Interior Minister's letter of December 1, 1948, to the police chiefs of all counties:

> On November 30, 1948, at 6:00 p.m., a group of unidentified armed criminals forced their way into the Vao Parish Executive Committee building in Virumaa County and robbed it of 143,000 rubles at gunpoint.
>
> On December 1, 1948, two unidentified armed bandits broke into the Kooraste Parish Executive Committee building in Võrumaa County. Threatening to shoot, they forced the Executive Committee workers to open the safe. They took the Executive Committee seal and 30,000 rubles. The bandits have not been apprehended in either case.
>
> The chief of the Virumaa County Interior Affairs Office Major Pääro and the chief of the Võrumaa County Interior Affairs Office Captain Soonda have not fulfilled my directive on the strengthening of protection of socialist property. I hereby instruct:
> 1. the Virumaa and Võrumaa County chiefs to submit a written report explaining why my instructions were not followed.
> 2. the chiefs of other offices to consider this a strong warning.
> 3. the police office chief's assistant to investigate the fulfillment of my directive within 10 days and to submit a report on his findings.

Undoubtedly, the investigations were carried out. Unfortunately, the letter of instruction came too late. On that same December 1, 1948, the most sensational train heist of the postwar period took place between Sõmerpalu and Kurenurme in Võrumaa County, its echoes reaching as far as Moscow. The event can best be described by the man who directed the operation, Johannes Heeska:

We took that train with kid gloves. There were seven of us, but the operation was made to look as if there were a hundred men.

We planned it like this: when two of our men stopped the train with the emergency brake, we split up and ran toward the train. As we came down the hill, they couldn't see us unless we dropped and fired. And so we came, ten to fifteen meters apart, dropping and firing a volley, then up and to the side, dropping again and firing again. To those in the train, it would seem like it never stopped. We reached the front of the train and yelled for the engineer to come out, but he started giving his emergency signal. We were pretty close to the Sõmerpalu station. The Kurenurme station wasn't too far behind us either. There was a mail car right behind the engine; the people in there got the wrong idea and thought it was already the station and opened the door. We stuck our guns under their noses and demanded the money they'd stolen from the people. They denied having any money.

But the engineer kept on signaling. I went over to him and told him not to signal and gestured with my pistol. The passengers were in a panic.

Some people started getting off the train, so we yelled, "If you want to live, stay in the cars!" So the people drew back in. I went back to the mail car, where Ants was ordering the money escort to come out. The others were carrying packages out of the mail car. Then the guy came out with another escort, saying that he wouldn't tell us either. We lined them both up and said, "We know for sure that the money is on the train; are you really going to die for those scraps of paper?" Just then, one of our men found a burlap bag under a bench, containing another bag with writing and weighing ten and a half kilos. He yelled "Leave 'em alone, I've got the money."

We ripped the bag open with a knife and saw some ten-ruble notes. Then I ordered my men to line up ten meters apart and told the engineer to start moving when he heard the conductor's whistle. I yelled to my men to fire everything they'd got over the top of the train at my signal, to say good-bye. I whistled and gave my signal.

There was a loud rat-tat-tat and that's how we sent the train on its way.

Then, to cover our tracks, we went to the Mustajõe swamp. Switchman Saar was coming from the Kurenurme station to find out what was holding up the train. Then I told my boys to run up there along the riverbed and when Saar comes along, to chase each other around in the underbrush so he'd think we were going in that direction. That's what we did, and it really looked like several dozen men were stamping their way northward. I stopped Saar and told him to go and report that the bandits had robbed the postal train. Saar took off back to the station, and we took off in the opposite direction.

It was already twilight when we got to a familiar cottager's place. We counted our money there. There wasn't a lot; a bit more than 53,000 rubles.

We got going and when we reached the road, about half a kilometer away, we heard a couple of trucks stop. And then a couple more. We realized we were surrounded.

We had to get across the road to reach Urvaste. A ditch ran all the way up to the road. I sat in the ditch. Everything was quiet. But near us at the crossroads they were watching. We made it across the road and decided to go by the township hall. There were seven or eight trucks full of Russians there, but we managed to slip by.

Later we heard that they'd brought in several regiments of soldiers, set up a bunch of radio transmitters, and stationed a reserve unit in Sõmerpalu. They said that we bandits must be captured at any cost. For days, they combed the swamp where they thought we'd gone, but by that time we were already in Sangaste.

This incident was not an isolated one. In the late 1940s, a money shipment was attacked on the narrow-gauge railway near Lelle Parish in Pärnumaa County. On September 5, 1951, a freight train carrying a shipment of money was derailed between Kõnnu and Viluvere in Harjumaa County. After killing the escort squad, the Forest Brothers made off with a hefty sum of cash.

Increased security measures were not sufficient to guarantee the safety of transports. Lieutenant Colonel Aleksei Uibo, the former chief of the Võru police station, recalls an incident that occurred on December 2, 1948. When the agricultural tax was being collected in the parishes, canine brigade chief Titov, detention cell guard Abramov, and police squad member Virve Pau accompanied communications workers to pick up the collected tax money from the township halls. They picked up money from Lasva Township and continued to Pindi Township. In Pindi Forest, the road was blocked by a fallen tree. The car stopped and its occupants were pierced by a hail of bullets. All three were shot dead. The agricultural tax money collected from the parishes was taken by men who vanished into the darkness of the forest.

As late as 1948 and 1949, Soviet transports driving through some parts of Estonia moved only with armed escorts. Forest Brothers not only hijacked money shipments, but loads of foodstuffs or other supplies that they needed. The truckers were forced to unload their goods at a designated place and allowed to leave.

The Forest Brothers preferred to hit and run in places where they were least expected. The Veriora Parish Forest Brothers made some daredevil expeditions right into Võru City, where Communists, NKVD, police, and Russian soldiers dominated the scene. One of those daring expeditions went like this.

It was payday for the workers at the Võru electrical station when a car drove up to the office and two men got out. They entered the office holding submachine guns. In the office, they ordered everyone into a corner. One of them pointed his machine gun right at the crowd, his finger on the trigger, warning that whoever tried to resist or escape would be shot. The other man went to the cash box and emptied it while waving his gun. Then they left, saying that no one was to leave the room before ten minutes were up. Anyone seen stepping out would be shot. They got in the car and drove away. An alarm was sent to the Soviet security forces and police. They started looking for the robbers, but no one knew which direction they'd gone. The security forces drove around the roads at random, but they never caught the thieves.

The total amount of money repossessed from the occupation authorities by the Forest Brothers amounted to millions of rubles.

In addition to money shipments, the Forest Brothers raided Soviet cooperatives, collective farms, and dairies. Prized targets were the butter and cream collected from the farmers by the authorities. Often, the shopkeepers themselves invited the partisans to rob their stores, and so their assignment turned out to be rather easy. The Forest Brothers themselves treated their seizures as requisitions. They left behind neatly drawn up receipts, examples of which are preserved in the CPE archives. For instance, on November 18, 1947, four men who robbed the Riisipere store in Harjumaa County's Kernu Parish left behind the following document:

Statement No. 109
This statement is drawn up on November 18, 1947, for Kernu Consumers' Cooperative manager Comrade Johannes Bachmann, by deputy chief of the Partisans of the Republic of Estonia Major Saldre, to confirm that goods with a total value of ___ rubles stocked in the Kernu Consumers' Cooperative have been forcibly confiscated by the partisans.

This statement is drawn up in accordance with Republic of Estonia Statute No. 73-a, Section 2, for presentation to the authorities.

The statement was signed by the Forest Brothers' leader and the store manager. Typically, the notices left behind were much shorter, such as the one left by some Forest Brothers at the Piometsa store on October 17, 1948: "The men of the Green Battalion stopped at the Piometsa Cooperative on their way to Läänemaa County."
A typical store robbery is described by an eyewitness:

The Partsi store was robbed several times. The first time, someone knocked on the window in the middle of the night. The shop assistants, who were sleeping in the rooms behind the store, had no idea what was going on. So they woke us up, asking for the keys. There were seven men. We said, "We can't give you the keys because we're not the managers." They made us stand outside and said, "If you move, we'll shoot." And then they took out their knapsacks, broke the storeroom window, and dragged the stuff out. They told us not to go anywhere for two hours, and then not to say we let them in. And they told us they'd be back in a month. That first time was August 15 and they were back on September 16. This time they really got away with a haul, because their first haul with the knapsacks couldn't have been that much.

The second time they arrived at midday. The cooperative truck was delivering some stock. The bandits

emptied the entire store onto the truck and off they
went. All that stuff and the truck too, in broad daylight!

Typically, the forest men were calm, passing out candy to the
children and vodka to the men. Sometimes, however, confrontations
proved unavoidable.

The partisans had raided the Kangiste store in Võrumaa County's
Lepistu Parish several times. In 1948, the local village council chairman and People's Defense member Leo Kaljuvee became its manager,
and he turned the store into a veritable fortress. Security troops
patrolled the store frequently. The partisans saw that this situation
called for special preparations, including a masquerade. Forest
Brother Kalju Kirbits dressed up as a woman and went on ahead with
a companion to take over the store. The others followed with wagons.
Kaljuvee's son recalls the incident:

Around 5:00 p.m., the dog started barking outside. I
went to look. A stranger rode into the yard on a bicycle.
He got off the bicycle, ordered me to put up my hands,
and threatened me with his gun. That scared me. He
searched me and asked me where my older brother was,
the one going to school in the city. I knew he meant Ülo,
who happened to be in the store, but I said that he was
at school. The stranger told me to get inside and stay
there. He stayed in the kitchen, holding his pistol, watching the doors.
Suddenly my father came through the door to the
kitchen. The stranger yelled "Hands up!". Father grabbed
a pistol from his belt and slammed the door shut. I managed to run into the store with my father. The stranger
fired at him and Father fired back. I threw myself on the
floor behind the counter. A fierce gun battle broke out in
the store. When the shooting stopped, I stood up. I saw
two strangers leaning against the counter across the
room, one dressed as a man and the other as a woman.
Both were holding pistols. One of the strangers went and
yanked my dead father by the lapel, and the other bent
over another dead body. Just then, the shopgirl
Morozova started screaming outside: "Bandits! Bandits!".
The bandits ran out of the store. There were blasts of
automatic weapons fire. I saw one of the strangers from

the store riding a bicycle down the hill. The bandit in
women's clothes ran after him in long strides.

Their unexpected encounter with Kaljuvee and his security forces
could have ended badly for the Forest Brothers, but thanks to their
"masquerade," they succeeded in killing their opponents, although
not in robbing the store.

Such major offensives required detailed planning, particularly to
ensure a getaway. It is no surprise that these operations took considerable manpower. A unit of thirty Forest Brothers sacked the Maidla
Parish cooperative in Virumaa County. They stationed machine gun-
ners to guard the road leading to the cooperative, loaded the goods
onto four horse-drawn wagons, and vanished.

Often, the pursuers caught up with the partisans and brief battles
ensued, in which the Forest Brothers were usually forced to leave part of
their take behind, sometimes falling as victims themselves. In the summer of 1951, when the partisans planned to raid the Pikevere store near
Rakke Parish in Järvamaa County, local Soviet informers notified the
security forces ahead of time. Security worker O. Mäeküngas recalls:

> We were eight or nine men. We decided to follow
> the robbers at least as long as their bicycle tracks were
> still visible. The forest path was muddy and the bicycle
> tracks showed up clearly. We ran with these tracks for
> about ten kilometers. Looking at the soft surface, we con-
> cluded that the bandits were walking their bikes, and we
> hoped to catch up with them soon.
> Nightfall interrupted our tracking. The next morn-
> ing we were up early. After moving on about half a kilo-
> meter, we reached a shed in a forest meadow. We
> concluded that our quarry had to be inside. We sur-
> rounded their hideout and demanded that the bandits
> surrender. But they chose another way. They both
> grabbed their revolvers and tried to escape into the
> nearby forest while shooting. They never made it,
> because our bullets flew faster than they could run.

On some occasions, the Forest Brothers came out on top. A former
resident of Helme Parish in Valgamaa County recalls:

> After the war, there were lots of Forest Brothers
> around Helme Parish. I was a young man then, working

as a driver. One night there was a knock on the door. I
opened it to see security troops. They took me along, not
to Siberia, but to drive some security men around. The
Forest Brothers had emptied a store in Helme, and now
they needed to get on their trail quickly. Two men sat in
the driver's cab, the others climbed into the back, and
we took off. We were driving fast, when suddenly we
saw another truck heading right for us at full tilt. We
stopped, and he stopped too with his bright headlights
on. And then a man's form stepped out with weapon in
hand. My security troops suddenly stumbled out of the
truck. I found myself alone in the middle of the road.
You could hear the underbrush crackle as the security
men ran for their lives. A voice from the other truck
called: "Comrades, comrades, where are you running
to?" I went over to see who it was. It turned out to be
the Viljandi City police, out on the same assignment. It
was a while before the Helme security troops could be
retrieved from the forest; by then it was nearly morning.
We drove on in two trucks, until we found the truck
abandoned by the woodsmen. Of course, the goods
were all gone, but a note remained on the car seat:
"Thanks for the supplies. The Partisan Liberation Army
of Southern Estonia."

An inseparable part of resistance movements throughout the
world has been the elimination of the collaborators and lackeys of the
occupying powers. It was no different in Estonia.

Deliberate acts of political terror included the killing of specific
individuals after a verdict had been reached. Targeted individuals
were usually accused of collaboration with the occupation authorities. The partisans selected only those who demonstrated a desire for
active cooperation with the authorities, and not those who simply
fulfilled obligatory duties. No one was killed because of his job as
Executive Committee chairman, policeman, or People's Defense unit
member. Each execution was carried out for a well-defined reason.

A story is widely told in Võrumaa County of a young policeman
who was sent to work in a parish teeming with Forest Brothers. On
his first day on the job, the young officer, feeling slightly insecure,
tried to sound out the local situation by having a few beers with some
old men at the store. He asked them jokingly how long policemen
usually lived in their parish. The old men looked him over slowly and

replied, "That depends on you. If you're a bad guy, you won't live for more than a few days; if you're a good guy, you'll be around for decades."

How many victims did the Forest Brothers claim? The exact numbers are hard to pin down, but the official tally places the count at 891. Most of the victims were members of the People's Defense units, local Party secretaries, local Komsomol leaders, Soviet security personnel or their collaborators. Usually, the individuals representing a danger to the local population first received a letter of warning; the death penalty was carried out when the warnings proved ineffective.

Those who burdened the population with excessive duties, participated in arrests and raids, harassed or abused the local people, appropriated arrested persons' property, or went to live in buildings confiscated from their owners received these warnings from the partisans. Collaborators with the Soviet security apparatus were the most frequent recipients of more tangible warnings. A woman might have her head shaved, or fall victim to the tactic used in the Munamäe region: having a pine cone shoved up the anus. Warnings to men usually consisted of beatings.

In one incident, Heino Ploom, the new Komsomol leader in Kooraste Parish of Võrumaa County, began demanding the strict fulfillment of all tax and communal work obligations, threatening those in arrears with deportation to Siberia. Once, he called all those farmers who had failed to fulfil communal lumber transport obligations to a meeting in Kaagvere. No sooner had Ploom entered the meeting hall than he was grabbed from both sides and subjected to a serious beating. Ploom never went back to Kooraste.

If such an individual neglected to heed the warning, the partisans discussed his actions thoroughly once more, reached a verdict, and placed the condemned man's name on the appropriate list. Several groups had such lists, which they apparently traded among themselves.

Frequently, a personal vendetta resulting from the deportation or murder of a partisan's family members provided adequate grounds for execution. Recollections from Sadala Parish in Tartumaa County describe such an incident.

> The only one killed by the Forest Brothers was the
> Sadala policeman Jandak, in settlement of a personal
> account. A young man from Kadismaa Village, Vello
> Peterson, returned from Finland in the spring of 1945
> and hid in the forests. Vello had a sweetheart, Ilme

Valdmaa, on the next farm, where he sometimes spent the night. At that time, there was a military unit in Sadala that constantly scoured the villages and hunted for Forest Brothers with the help of local policeman Jandak. Vello Peterson was apprehended in his sweetheart's bed, arrested, and made to walk to the township hall under armed guard. On the way, Vello darted behind the corner of a house and escaped. The policeman Jandak and his soldiers went back to the Valdmaa farm and arrested Ilme Valdmaa and her father. On the way to Sadala through the Sadala heath, Jandak raped the girl in front of her father. Father and daughter were held for several days in the cells of the Sadala Executive Committee building, where the girl was repeatedly raped and humiliated. She was eighteen at the time. Then they were released. Ilme's mother Leida Valdmaa rode to the district police headquarters in Tartu City to file a complaint against Jandak. She was ordered to produce a witness if Jandak was to be punished. Of course, there were no witnesses to be found.

In Tuimetsa Village, Jandak dragged farmer Villem's wife into the forest and demanded that she show them where her husband was hiding. The woman did not know a place to show them, and so Jandak shot her there in the woods. He propped her body into a sitting position against a tree. That same autumn, when the first snow fell, Peterson and Villem took a cow into the forest from a farm in Sadala. The cow's hoofprints were easily visible in the fresh snow. The farmer reported the "theft" to Jandak, and Jandak followed the cow's tracks into the forest, where he was shot dead to avenge the rape of the girl and the murder of the woman.

Many recollections emphasize that the people killed by the Forest Brothers clearly deserved their fate. Indeed, random and senseless murders would have harmed the partisans' relations with the local population. The Forest Brothers would have perished quickly without popular support.

The CPE archives contain a number of formal complaints sent by Party Committees to the Soviet security apparatus, and clearly most of the grievances were submitted by the same few individuals. It is hardly surprising that some time later the archives record the notice of the "untimely demise of a loyal comrade and bandit hunter" at the hands of the Forest Brothers.

A typical example is the fate of Lasva Party Secretary Sibul. Sibul took part in arresting the population of his own parish and stealing the property of the arrested individuals. He supervised the destruction of monuments honoring the Estonian War of Independence and the eviction of Forest Brothers' family members from their homes. The final blow was the murder of six unarmed partisans in the Lasva forests at Sibul's orders. Blood had to be avenged in blood.

Two loyal Forest Brothers, Hillar Paas and Valter Liiv, were close friends of the men who had been killed in the Lasva forests. They decided to take revenge on Sibul for this cowardly murder. They soon found their chance.

As Sibul, who was then Party Secretary in Lasva, rode from the Otsa store toward Lasva, Paas and Liiv lay waiting for him in a gravel pit on the edge of the Otsa Forest. When the wagon carrying the Secretary and his driver neared the gravel pit, Liiv opened fire with his automatic. The driver was slightly wounded, but the volley tore Sibul to shreds, piercing all his internal organs. He was still alive when they took him to Võru Hospital, but it was not possible to save his life. Valter Liiv later told the other men about Sibul's murder: "Now my heart is at peace and my friends are avenged. Now we're even. That pig really screamed when I let him have it." And so the murders ordered by local Party Secretary Sibul put the final stamp on his own death warrant.

Soviet sources attribute a large number of brutal killings, particularly murder-robberies to the Forest Brothers. Later evidence often proved that these incidents were actually raids by marauding Russian "bag boys" or the handiwork of the KGB itself, which calmly passed responsibility for the crimes onto the Forest Brothers. In Virumaa County, many Forest Brothers were sentenced to death for the brutal murders of local residents and theft of their property. Only later was evidence unearthed to incriminate the local police force and security workers, when some of the stolen goods were found in their possession. Although the local People's Defense units occasionally tried to curb the violent acts by security workers, the Soviet security apparatus retained the right to operate arbitrarily.

On occasion, a series of murders that looked at first glance like senseless killings by the Forest Brothers ultimately revealed well-defined motives. A letter sent to Estonian Radio editor Leo Siimaste after the 1990 broadcast of a program about the Forest Brothers movement accused the Virumaa County Forest Brothers of killing several "completely innocent" Virumaa forest wardens. Closer investigation revealed a different picture. It seems that some of the forest wardens, following the tracks of a poacher, happened upon a Forest Brothers' bunker built of peat chunks. The wardens led security troops to the site. The bunker was surrounded, but as the soldiers drew near, it blasted skyward. The Forest Brothers had mined their dwelling before deserting it. A few days later, one of the wardens who had moved to another part of the country was wounded by a former neighbor. Two other forest wardens who had participated in the raid were shot dead.

The number of Forest Brothers engaging in political terror was small. Most Forest Brothers avoided assassinations, knowing that retaliation in the form of mass imprisonments and terrorization of the local population would inevitably follow.

One of Veriora Parish's most infamous characters was the People's Defense member Eduard Pettai, who tried his best to curry favor with the new Soviet authorities. Edward Loosaar recalls:

> Pettai mostly went around alone and harassed
> those people who he thought were anti-Commie, or
> whose family member had disappeared into the forest,
> or was away who knows where. One time, when Pettai
> came to our village again with his gun over his shoulder,
> Ulfred and Endel saw him walking along the path in the
> forest. Ulfred, who also had a gun, brought it up and
> said to Endel: "I'm going to smash him into the ground.
> How long is that pig going to keep bothering our village
> folks?" Endel stopped him, saying: "Don't shoot. Banditry isn't necessary. We've lived in the forests peacefully up to now, but after a murder like this they'll start
> interrogating the villagers and broadening their raids,
> and that'll make things hard on us."

The same line of reasoning is found in the recollections of other Forest Brothers. Unfortunately, this logic did not save many of them from destruction, because they were often killed by those they had generously spared just a short time before.

In some areas, repressions were so severe that the patience of the Forest Brothers broke completely. The outcome was widespread settling of accounts with Soviet activists, of which the most widely known is the bloodbath in Osula on March 13, 1946. Osula suffered particularly severe repressions beginning in 1944. The local destruction battalion was renowned for its enthusiastic brutality; partisans responded with counterattacks. A life-and-death struggle erupted. All too often, the victims were innocent people. The destruction battalion's attack on the Peetrimõisa warehouse in early December 1945 was the final straw. Destruction battalion commander Daniel Kängsepp had been informed that some Forest Brothers were expected to attend a celebration there. He quickly assembled a detachment of destruction battalion and security forces, who set up a machine gun in front of the warehouse before entering the festival hall. The events that followed are described by an eyewitness:

> I don't remember how many people were at
> Peetrimõisa that night, but it wasn't more than thirty.
> There was an accordion player and the people danced.
> There weren't many forest partisans at the party. Then
> the destruction battalion men came into the hall, and the
> music stopped. The accordion player tried to save the
> day by resuming playing. By that time, the destruction
> battalion men had started checking identity papers. One
> of the traitors — Rahuleid Unt, a former Forest Brother
> — pointed out the partisan leader Alfred Lehes. Two
> men grabbed Lehes by the hair and dragged him out of
> the hall. Lehes twisted one Unt brother over his arm,
> grabbed a pistol from his belt, shot the man holding him
> on one side in the chest, and the other in the head. Now
> the destruction battalion men started firing haphazardly
> into the crowd. Eighteen-year-old Hella Mäeoja was
> killed and two other girls were wounded. As a final ges-
> ture, the Reds threw a hand grenade into the hall.
> When the Forest Brothers finally escaped, they were
> mad as hornets. They scattered the destruction battalion,
> sending them running into the woods.

We can imagine how this confrontation charged the atmosphere around Osula, especially since the arrests and raids continued unabated. Forest Brothers as well as local residents, shot as they tried to escape, fell victim to KGB special commandos.

As a result, several Forest Brothers groups convoked a "tribunal," where a number of the active local Communists were sentenced to death and the pertinent list was compiled. And then came March 13, 1946, the day the Forest Brothers seized power in Osula. In the morning, partisans from many areas rode their sleighs to Osula. Some of them were in civilian clothes, some in Red army uniforms. First they seized the pharmacy. Everyone who wanted to enter was allowed to do so, but no one was allowed to leave. The local pharmacist was told to get local Party secretary Voldemar Valusk as he passed by, but Valusk refused to enter, continuing on to Võru and thereby saving his own life.

The events in Osula are also described in the official documents of the CPE archives. They describe how several dozen Forest Brothers surrounded Osula, stationed guards on the roads, and seized the Osula pharmacy, quietly placing the Red authorities they had seized down in the cellar. A witness, Ilse Iher, relates:

> When the Forest Brothers launched their operation, the authorities tried to phone Võru for help, but the lines had been cut. The Forest Brothers group included two women. They sat on the counter swinging their legs and singing "I lost my heart on the Isle of Capri. . ." and firing their automatics at the ceiling. At the same time, the partisans were hunting the destruction battalion men, who had scattered through the village. Battalion commander Kängsepp had been in the store during the assault. He even had his machine gun with him, but he didn't offer any resistance. He hid in the storeroom where no one thought to look for him.
>
> The Forest Brothers set about killing the others according to their list. Soon they realized that the list didn't include all the ones they wanted. Some of the men had gotten crazed with killing, and they started shooting women and children who were not on the list. The entire families of some authorities who had caused exceptional suffering to a few Forest Brothers were wiped out. For a while, the women succeeded in stopping the bloodshed. In one instance, they drove the partisans away from the wife of the destruction battalion commander, saying that a pregnant woman should not be killed.
>
> At the time of the assault, a soldier and a CPE Central Committee deputy were on guard in Osula. They remained untouched; the partisans told them that they'd done nothing to harm the partisans. They only took the Central Committee deputy's identity papers and money, leaving him just enough to ride to Tallinn and stop at

each major station to drink a toast to the Forest Brothers.
He was ordered to tell the authorities in Tallinn that
Soviet power no longer existed in Osula.

That was indeed the case. The partisans killed a total of thirteen people that day. These were all the Soviet activists they had captured. Security forces reached Osula late that night when the Forest Brothers, splitting into smaller units, were long gone. Some of them headed for Tartumaa County, raiding the Vastse-Kuuste village council building at Kiidjärve on March 15, destroying communications lines and wrecking telephone equipment. They destroyed all the documents and tore down the hated portraits of Stalin.

Reports of events in Osula reached Stalin himself in Moscow. As a result, special forces were sent to Võrumaa County, a wave of arrests engulfed the country, and desperate battles and confrontations ensued. There was no escaping the whirlpool of violence.

Despite its spontaneous origins, the resistance movement in Estonia began to take on a noticeably more organized character. County by county, Forest Brother units started to unite, paving the way for the rise of a nationwide Forest Brothers organization. An organization called the Armed Resistance League entered the arena of history.

Chapter 6

The Armed
Resistance League

A nationwide central command structure is crucial for the success of any resistance movement. The establishment of such an organization is indeed a formidable task. Such a command center never formed in many countries engaging in active resistance against invaders during World War II. On one hand, a centralized organization which directs all members and all activities renders a resistance movement significantly more efficient; but on the other hand, it increases the chances of detection. Moreover, participation in a resistance movement is a personal decision, demanding a greater-than-average degree of individual initiative and resourcefulness. People of this character do not submit easily to taking orders and following directives that are inevitable in the operation of a centralized organization. And yet, some kind of central command is essential for a resistance movement, if only to maintain communications with the outside world. This realization had led to the formation of the Haukka-Tümmler group, which was crushed by the NKVD in late 1944. Major L. Henriksoo had also attempted to create a blanket resistance organization in 1945, but by the end of that year, the Soviet security apparatus smashed this movement — *Eesti Päästekomitee* (The Committee to Save Estonia) — as well.

A comprehensive Forest Brothers organization was formed in spite of these early setbacks. In 1945 and 1946, Endel Redlich of Läänemaa County set up an alliance of groups in Läänemaa and Harjumaa Counties. During Estonian independence, the Redlich family had been known as ardent Defense Leaguers and good horsemen, and Endel Redlich was raised to be a patriot. In 1941, Redlich took part in battles to free Estonia from the Red army's grip. When Estonia fell into German hands, he chose to evade mobilization into the German army and went into hiding with several of his friends. It was here that these Forest Brothers began discussing the necessity of creating a nationwide resistance organization. At the end of the German occupation, Redlich took part in attempts to reestablish the Republic of Estonia, raided German transport columns for weapons, and took to the forests.

Soviet intelligence gained a truly dangerous enemy in Endel Redlich, who had an uncanny ability to predict Soviet security force operations, and to capture and punish NKVD agents. Redlich was seriously wounded in a battle that crippled one of his hands — hence his nickname, "Black Glove." In 1946, Redlich decided to create a broader Forest Brothers organization headquartered in Velise Township. Initially, the organization's network was limited, functioning only to maintain mutual communications and to seek escape routes to Sweden. Unfortunately, the group lacked ties with the Estonian National Committee in Sweden during its early days.

Since 1945, the Estonian National Committee in Sweden had been trying to contact the men who had participated in the resistance against the Germans and still remained in Estonia. A speedboat continued its shuttle route between Sweden and Saaremaa Island. Radio communications were not completely broken off, although the existence of a radio linkage was officially denied. No one knows how much the Swedish domestic investigative police knew of these activities by the Estonian émigrés. At any rate, they never acknowledged the existence of communications. To encourage political action in the West, Estonian diplomatic representatives needed communications lines with the homeland that would supply urgently needed information. The postwar period was an especially difficult time for Baltic diplomats, who suffered one defeat after another in the international political arena of a world that was turning its back on the captive nations.

Attitudes shifted as the Cold War began. Communications with the homeland were more urgently needed than ever. Within the Baltic émigré groups, men who were dissatisfied with endless talk and who thirsted for real action came to the forefront. They began forming partisan groups and acquiring supplies. Alfons Rebane, Lembit Kriisa, and others worked at recruiting resistance fighters for the Estonians. It is unclear how much of a role the Baltic States' official representatives played in subsequent events. There is firm evidence that Juozas Luozaraitis, representative of the Republic of Lithuania, had ties with the Lithuanian Forest Brothers. Luozaraitis's messages to the Lithuanian Forest Brothers contained remarkably well-focused analyses of the situation, stating how hard it was to get concrete assistance from the West, emphasizing the senselessness of bloodshed, and urging the conservation of energy for one decisive encounter. Of the Estonian diplomats, Ambassador to London August Torma was directly connected to the resistance movement. In the messages that were intercepted by Soviet security forces, he urged the Forest Brothers to continue their resistance while avoiding major operations, deeming it wiser to lie in wait for the right moment. Such were the instructions taken to Estonia by representatives of the Estonian émigrés.

Naturally, the dangerous return to Estonia was voluntary. Despite that, there were plenty of daring patriots willing to take the chance. A young woman who had caught one of the last ships out of Tallinn in September 1944 left behind her sweetheart, who could also have fled the country, but who stayed in the belief that the woman had never made it to the ship. For this reason, he gave up his spot on the ship and remained in Estonia. Now the young woman wanted to help her sweetheart leave Estonia. She describes her efforts in her own words:

> In 1944, one secret radio transmitter was still operating in Tallinn. It kept going until the winter of 1945. Late that year, our side noticed some gaps in the transmission schedule. The radiomen in Sweden got suspicious and finally broke off communications.
>
> Ants Piip, Jr. (son of Estonian Foreign Minister Ants Piip) suggested that I go to Estonia to see what was going on, and to take over some new codes to the radioman. At first I refused, since I was so involved with my studies at the time. That was the early spring of 1946. I thought it over. I knew quite well that the risk was tremendous and the hopes for success were minimal.
>
> I set out by sea around the end of 1946. Two men were with me. One was named Kadarik or Kadastik; they called him Pääsov; I think the other was named Vahtras. I had never seen them before. They were coastal folk who knew how to handle a boat.
>
> We reached Hiiumaa Island safely and went into the village, but we never made it to the mainland. My contact in the village said that getting to Tallinn was out of the question. I sent a letter and left the codes and other things in Hiiumaa. In the meantime, Kadarik had gone to Saaremaa Island but he hadn't returned. The other man and I waited for a day and then started back to Sweden.

We were solidly into neutral waters when a Soviet border patrol launch sped after us and picked us up.

Vahtras was sentenced to ten years in prison with standard regimen. He served his time someplace near Kotlas, and I think he got out of there alive. Kadarik, apparently, had agreed to collaborate with a Soviet intelligence operation, sailing back to Sweden in our confiscated boat with some Soviet security personnel posing as refugees.

I sat in a solitary cell at Pagari Prison for seven months. I got bits and pieces of information during that time. First of all, I found out that our secret radio transmitter in Tallinn had been part of a counterintelligence scheme for over half a year. That means that the station continued to operate under instruction from Soviet Russian intelligence. The radioman kept using the same old Morse code signature. But when the other side got suspicious, the scheme was scrapped.

I remember that Reichenberg was the radioman and liaison here. He got fifteen years at a distant camp near Magadan. The other one was cheerful Uno Toomla, who was sentenced to ten years.

In Moscow, I was sentenced to ten years. I was held in Lubyanka Central Prison and then sent away to a camp.

This failure and the breakoff of communications did not discourage the "Center" in Sweden. A new group was formed by the end of 1946. In early November, reconnaissance man Richard Saago and Arseeni Sagur landed on Estonia's Saaremaa Island. Saago carried a radio transmitter which was to remain in Estonia. He succeeded in visiting the cities of Tartu and Tallinn on the mainland, seeking out his old acquaintances and recruiting the best people for reconnaissance work. He gave the local agent an American-made portable radio transmitter, money, two pistols, a camera, and other equipment. They worked out transmission schedules and passwords.

After carrying out his assignment, Saago returned to Saaremaa, where a motorboat was to take him back to Sweden. On December 20, 1946, the border patrol arrested both Saago and Sagur. They seized full material evidence from Saago, including a letter to his companions who were remaining behind. Armed with this information, the Soviet security apparatus infiltrated one of its own men into Saago's network of agents in Estonia. The agent found out the numbers and members of the group and had them all arrested, but did not succeed in setting up a counterintelligence scheme with this group.

Steady communications were finally established between Estonia and Sweden, thanks to a man named Richard Saaliste, whose battle with the foreign regimes occupying Estonia had begun in 1941. Saaliste had organized a Forest Brothers unit and had fought in battles to liberate Estonia. In August 1941, Lieutenant Saaliste's right hand was pierced by three bullets in a battle near Purtse River, rendering him partially disabled.

Saaliste was then named chief of Hiiumaa Island's *Omakaitse* (Self-Defense military organization), a position he left voluntarily in May of 1944 to serve as an officer in the Border Patrol, 1st Regiment. On August 18, 1944, Saaliste was seriously wounded in the battle of Lääniste. His unit wanted to evacuate him to Germany, but he staunchly opposed the move. He was sent to Kärdla Hospital on Hiiumaa Island by way of Haapsalu on the mainland. On Hiiumaa, Saaliste helped people escape to Sweden and organized Estonian soldiers who had come to the island. As a result, Saaliste was arrested by the Germans, but he arranged his own release thanks to a personal acquaintance with the island's commanding officer. On October 2, the Russians landed in Hiiumaa, and Saaliste set out for Sweden on that same evening.

In Sweden, he soon found work as manager of a small estate farm. Saaliste's thoughts kept returning to his captive homeland, and he soon formulated a plan to return to Estonia. The Estonian Émigré Center helped him formulate his plans, since it maintained communications with the resistance groups still remaining in Estonia. Excerpts of Saaliste's letters to his friend Lieutenant Põder paint a vivid picture of his emotions:

> As my tremendous hopelessness crystallizes, I grasp for straws on which to fasten my final threads of hope.
>
> How I've longed to hear something reassuring from those I keep in contact with. But everyone seems to be moving about in a vacuum. A short time ago, a letter from America dated May 14 gave me a glimmer of faith and hope. But subsequent reports contradict this optimism.
>
> The same doubt and gray hopelessness that smother our unfortunate homeland now prevail everywhere.
>
> But I use the phrase "now prevail" intentionally, because somewhere in the depths of our subconscious

there is still one more straw, perhaps hanging in midair or as a figment of our imagination, feeding a tiny spark of hope. . . I cannot face today's reality; I want to continue believing that all is not lost.

I try to convince myself that I exist as an entity removed from time and events. That's the only way I can keep my mind resolute and principled . . . retaining my faith in all that is good and beautiful.

We and the other nations on the eastern frontier were forced to sacrifice our homes and our hearts so that those to the west could live in peace and be rid of their enemy.

And yet I fear that the Western nations will not compensate for our sacrifices with a new sacrifice of their own. If that's the case, we're done for. And yet, something may happen; an event we're not aware of may be in the making. The time has long passed for turning over a new leaf.

I just heard the radio say that Russia has declared war on Japan.

We want war, but closer to home. War would now be to our benefit. We must keep our spirit of combat alive, and stubbornly persist in demanding those rights that have been stripped from us. They can strip us of everything except our love for our homeland and the steadfastness of our character.

Saaliste retained his contacts with Hiiumaa Island, which also channeled him to the mainland, where he received information about his brother, former battalion chief of the Märjamaa *Omakaitse* Artur Saaliste, who had started a fight against the invaders. Richard Saaliste decided to join the Forest Brothers in Estonia, help them establish communications with Sweden, and coordinate the formation of a wider-reaching Forest Brothers organization. Saaliste made his first attempt to return to Estonia in the summer of 1945, but nearly sailed his boat into a Russian naval base by accident. Fortunately, it was night, and Saaliste returned his boat to the open sea unnoticed.

In October 1946, he completed preparations for a second trip. Along with three companions, weapons, and a radio transmitter, Saaliste set out for his homeland. All went well until the landing, when they unexpectedly encountered a border patrol unit. In the exchange of gunfire, two men were killed. Saaliste succeeded in breaking through, finding his brother in the forest, and getting to work establishing broader contacts. As later reports have indicated, Saaliste's escape was truly a miracle, since Soviet security forces had known of his scheduled arrival in Estonia.

Saaliste proved to be a capable organizer. He quickly succeeded in combining several partisan groups into one smoothly operating unit. These men were not "simple" Forest Brothers, but well-organized troops. Saaliste also sought to establish ties with Redlich's organization to expand the functions of the movement significantly.

Saaliste's first task was to reestablish communications with Sweden. To replace the radio transmitter lost at their disastrous landing, he quickly managed to find one of the Haukka group's radiomen still untouched by the NKVD. Vambola Orav had managed to keep his identity secret and to blend into Soviet society. The first transmission to Sweden was completed in June 1947 from the Lelle region in Pärnumaa County. After that, the transmission schedule intensified, unnerving the Soviet security apparatus. Massive raids were launched into the forests of Lelle and Järva. Buses equipped with radar equipment cruised the roads. Saaliste always managed to escape the sieges. His tactics are explained by a coconspirator, Ants Saulep:

> Soon after I bought a car from a Red army officer, my old friend Hansen came up one day and asked me if I wanted to go for a drive. I realized that something was afoot, but I agreed anyway. First we drove onto a forest road and Hansen said, "Stop here." Two men with a huge knapsack emerged from the forest and got into the car.
>
> We kept driving. Hansen said, "Just drive right through Rapla." There were lots of stories making the rounds about the Saaliste brothers, and so I had a pretty good idea who these men were. I said, "You're crazy. That town's crawling with Reds." Hansen replied, "That's why we're going through Rapla, because no one will think of looking for us there." So we drove to the forest behind Rapla. The Saaliste brothers stepped out with their bundle, stayed away for a while and then returned. Then I took them back to the other side of Rapla. When I drove back home, the area was crawling with patrols. I was stopped at least five times to have my documents checked. I helped the Saaliste brothers make several more radio transmissions after that.

By this time, the *Relvastatud Võitluse Liit* (Armed Resistance League - RVL) had expanded to areas far beyond its original home in Läänemaa County. The goal of the organization was the restoration of Estonian independence. Its program of action stated:

> The organization is preparing an armed uprising
> against the Soviet regime at such a time when England
> and the United States go to war against the Soviet
> Union, or when a political coup occurs in the Soviet
> Union itself.

Above all, in order to achieve the RVL's goals, the men had to remain hidden, and to preserve as many organized and armed combatants as possible for decisive battles in the future. Generally, engaging in combat activity was not RVL's main purpose. Its primary goal was the establishment of the structures necessary for an eventual uprising, the accumulation of weapons and ammunition, and the preservation of the population's desire and ability to resist. For this reason, RVL expended a great deal of effort on political education. Leaflets distributed through its central command as well as local organizations called on the people to continue their resistance to the invaders and instructed them in methods of passive resistance.

The structure of the Armed Resistance League was simple. It was led by a commander who answered only to the legal government of the Republic of Estonia. The central commander appointed the commanders of township organizations (or districts made up of several townships) to be responsible for RVL activities in their assigned districts. No special services or achievements were required of RVL applicants. A desire to fight for Estonia's honor and independence, and a willingness to carry out assigned duties were sufficient. Entry into the organization did have one restriction — the applicant could not be guilty of any crimes against the Estonian people. Upon his acceptance, an RVL member had to take the following oath:

> As a loyal Estonian and member of the Armed
> Resistance League organization, I pledge to dedicate all
> my physical and mental faculties to the fight for Eston-
> ian honor and freedom. While carrying out my duties, I
> pledge to act with responsibility and courage, without
> fear of giving my life for a better future for Estonia, fol-
> lowing the example of our ancient heroes. Betrayal and
> breaking of this oath will be severely punished.

II. REOCCUPATION AND RESISTANCE:

It is the spring of 1944. Now, three years after their arrival, German forces prepare to retreat and relinquish Estonia to Soviet reoccupation.

14. At a secluded camp at Männiku near Tallinn, the Germans provide military training, but not weapons, to the "Finland boys." Repatriated from service with the Finnish Army to help defend Estonia against the Soviet reinvasion, the Germans used them to cover their retreat.

15. With memories of the 1941 deportations and conscriptions still vivid, Estonians prepare for evacuation in boats of all kinds as the Soviets approach.

16. Many evacuees overloaded small boats like this for the 300-mile Baltic trip to Sweden.

17. & 18. But as the Soviets settle in during the summer, most Estonians live on the fringe between Communist puppet authority and the refuge of the forests. These Forest Brothers pose in front of their summer hideout.

19-21. Scenes of housekeeping in the forest:

19. Gathering mushrooms and berries.

20. Going fishing.

21. Making moccasins.

22-23. Disguised as women when helping with the chores at local farms.

24. On the move.

25-28. *Scenes of combat.* These four prints from a series by Axel Roosman depict the kinds of events that were never photographed:

25. An ambush . . .

26. . . . liberated deportees . . .

27. . . . a firefight . . .

28. . . . and a trial of Soviet collaborators.

29. Handwritten note distributed by Forest Brothers in 1946 on the twenty-eighth anniversary of Estonian Independence to encourage hope in national resistance.

Translation:

Today, February 24th, we celebrate the 28th anniversary of Estonia's national independence, which was redeemed by our finest sons in the Estonian War of Independence. Although the country of Estonia, as such, no longer exists among the nations of the world, we are still celebrating our independence day in the knowledge that the Bolshevik reign of terror is not lasting.

Even though the wars have ended, the fates of nations still hang in the balance. On one side are the Communist world conquerors, on the other, the free and independent nations of the world.

Estonia, you are standing at the gateway to a fateful future! The final battle for peace for all nations calls us to avenge the bloodguiltiness of the East Asiatics.

30. Jaan Roots, center, leader of the famous "Orion" group of Vastseliina parish in Võrumaa county, returns from raid on a Soviet currency shipment in 1950.

31. Roots counts the money "liberated" to pay taxes on Estonian farms . . .

32. . . . and celebrates with Elmer Käis, (left) Jaan Vigel, (behind) and Martin Parts (right).

33. Later, Roots, foreground, takes time to clown for a photograph acquired by the KGB.

The League did not seek a large membership. Rather, it emphasized placing agents in each region and each parish to maintain contact with the local Forest Brothers as well as the political resistance wing (the City Brothers). All active members of the organization were required to fill out a form. In addition to personal information, the form called for information on fluency in languages, previous combat experience, skills, and occupations. The League sent its men to work in Soviet institutions, even into the security apparatus.

The recollections of Felix Tipner illustrate how the Armed Resistance League recruited its members. Tipner fled the prison camp at Novosibirsk in the fall of 1945 and lived and worked in Estonia under an assumed name.

> At the Song Festival in the summer of 1947, I ran into my Air Force buddy Kuno Silland. He told me about the RVL. The organization was to swing into action when the time was right to defend our nation and property. Only three men were ever to meet each other: the recruit, the recruiter, and a reference. I filled out a brief form and chose a code name under which I was to exist — "Rein."

Each parish contained one appointed RVL agent whose subordinates were known only to him. The parish agents were in contact with the League's county commanders, who in turn reported to the central headquarters. The organization was operated under strict discipline, with violators subject to the death penalty. Harassing or disturbing the local population, even to obtain food, was strictly prohibited. Redlich asserted that the property of the Estonian people was sacred. There is one confirmed report of a Forest Brother who violated discipline and harassed some members of the local population; he was tried and executed.

The organization operated a printing press which published leaflets and appeals. Their leaflets proved remarkably effective. For the first time, the Forest Brothers scattered throughout Estonia learned of a command structure which was truly devoted to liberating the country. The leaflets assured them that the Western nations would not abandon Estonia. The partisans must continue to resist and preserve their strength for a decisive strike at the appropriate time. The Forest Brothers were told to refrain from harassing the regime with isolated minor operations, since these served only to incur needless losses. The League's leaflets, urging the population to continue its passive resistance to the occupiers, were also distributed in cities. The Armed Resistance League planned to coordinate training opportunities for leaders of the Forest Brothers groups, but succeeded in putting together only one training session, where Redlich taught several dozen men the use of a radio transmitter and the principles of counterintelligence.

The League's program of action was entitled "The Ideological Principles of the Forest Brothers Movement." Its first section was compiled abroad in 1945; the second in Estonia in 1948. An excerpt from one of Richard Saaliste's letters of 1945 describes the essence of the document:

> Although we lost the war and consequently our beloved homeland, our battles should give evidence to the whole world that our nation has not joined the Soviet family of nations voluntarily.
>
> We have proven that we are the members of this small nation that is known for its heroism. We have not strayed from the paths of battle marked by our forefathers.
>
> If justice one day prevails in the world, we will have our own living space and the right to exist. The day your letter came, I got another letter from a close colleague of Professor Uluots, who told me what the professor had written: "Every nation, even the smallest one, has a right to its existence and living space, even if this right falls under attack. Although the attacks have been fierce and murderously dangerous, they have faded away like storms in Nature, and the native population has continued to survive. For this reason I believe that the right which justifies the existence of a nation is greater than Man. Man must realize this right and live according to it."

While the first part of the program justifies participation in the resistance movement, the second laments the decline of discipline, the abundance of uncoordinated activities, illnesses, and other problems. It says that all groups involved in military as well as political resistance have to unite within a nationwide organization in order to work effectively toward their goal. They need to accumulate weapons and prepare for the combat that would begin at the imminent outbreak of the new World War. Apparently, Saaliste never doubted that another major war would erupt:

A new war is more likely now than it was before the war between Russia and Germany. The only things that can prevent it are famine and war-weariness. But the enemy's scales contain enough reasons to outweigh these two factors.

We can share in the joy of those who were liberated by the Western countries, but the type of freedom that Stalin brings is evident to us and to the entire world. There are only two options: Russia will be either the only victor or the only loser.

The RVL's program provides a good description of the organization's goals and plan of action. It describes the Armed Resistance League as a "voluntary, secret, armed organization of the national resistance movement to fight for the honor and independence of Estonia." The RVL sought to bring together combat-capable individuals who would take action in the event of extensive deportations or a new wave of pillaging. In the event of deportations, the RVL units were to be on alert for orders from the central leadership. They had plans to attack communications centers and railway stations, thus rendering deportations technically impossible. In preparation, the RVL men had to draw up plans of their targets, as well as discover their defenses and access. Quick action was permitted in the event of the arrest of an organization member, or in defense of his family. When war broke out, the RVL men were to act as a nucleus for the national resistance that would break out throughout the country.

The organization's other goals were to "engage in an ideological struggle," to preserve faith in the restoration of Estonian self-government, and to increase the people's will to resist by encouraging national spirit and fueling contempt for the occupation authorities and their collaborators. The organization gave high priority to the fight against traitors, as well as the economic and political disruption of the occupying regime. It was also dedicated to protecting the population from persecution and acts of terror by the occupation authorities. For the fight against "traitors on the inside and outside," the central commander appointed a Security Court, which was subordinate not to the commander but to the legal government of the Republic of Estonia. The RVL central commander could submit cases to the court and ensure that the sentence was carried out.

The directives issued to township organization commanders also gave a good characterization of the RVL program. They require a township organization commander to be well informed on events in his district, to recruit new members for his organization, and to engage in armed combat when necessary either to protect a member of the organization or to disrupt widespread deportations.

The directives repeatedly emphasized the importance of secrecy. They recommend that the organization's "legalized" members know of one another's membership in the organization. The township organization commander was instructed to collect accurate information about local Communists and traitors without passing a sentence on these individuals himself. Reconnaissance of the activities and plans of Communists was essential. The local commanders were to gather information on military units, fortifications, and arsenals in the region, and to provide supplies for the Forest Brothers. The organization was ordered to stockpile reserves for itself, either by collecting voluntary payments or by forcibly expropriating government property. The inviolability of private property was to be strictly observed. The RVL central command was to receive accurate reports of expropriation of property. The township organization commander could use armed force at his own initiative only in the defense of an RVL member or in the event of extensive deportations. In all other cases he was to wait for instructions from the RVL central commander. As their fundamental document indicated, the RVL command tried to prevent pointless actions by the Forest Brothers, strengthen their discipline, and decrease their chances of being apprehended.

Meetings were held at different places; the central staff would occasionally conduct on-site inspections of the troops. Ahto Talvi recalls:

> One time, almost all the League headquarters staff came to meet with me. Naturally, I was not forewarned. It was all done in total secrecy. One day they simply showed up. They drove around in a black Soviet Navy Pobeda. All the men wore Russian officers' uniforms. Rumyantsev spoke beautiful Russian. He could fool anybody. Those men had nerves of steel. They parked their car right in the center of town next to the Party Committee building before they came looking for me. This tactic was beautifully thought out — the presence of such a car in the town center was entirely natural, but in the outskirts it would have attracted too much attention.

There are no exact accounts of the ultimate size of the League. The major centers of the organization were located in Läänemaa,

Harjumaa, Pärnumaa, and Virumaa Counties; a total of thirty-eight parishes were under its control. Its network included Võrumaa and Viljandimaa Counties as well. The information on the numbers of League members is rather inconsistent; most figures range between 2,000 and 5,000 men. The League also united student resistance groups and underground organizations in the cities, being especially influential in Tallinn.

The combat units of the Armed Resistance League set up ambushes for Soviet transports on roads, typically selecting Soviet military or government vehicles as their targets. Railroads and communications lines were also favorite targets of Forest Brother sabotage. In 1946, communications lines were cut twenty-two times within three months in Pärnumaa County alone.

RVL units attacked Soviet shipments of goods and money, thus helping replenish the League's resources. While touching private property was strictly prohibited, the repossession of supplies taken from the people by the state was considered just. Soon, the League's activities began to weaken the authority of the Soviet regime. The RVL used its resources to help the families of people imprisoned or deported to Siberia and to help ease the tax burden of private farms.

The RVL's bitterest enemies were security personnel and their lackeys. The League avoided engaging in political terror, however, until it was left with no alternative, since the killing of any security worker was paid for dearly by the local population. Instead, the partisans had to devise methods to defang their enemy. One such incident is recalled by RVL member August Hatto:

> The owner of Võeva farm in Velise Parish had made some beer. Forest Brother Karell and his friend Ervin went to try it out. As they started to enter the farmhouse, security chief Chernov and his interpreter stepped out. Startled, the security men put their hands up. Chernov was a little slow, but Karell poked him in the ribs with his automatic, and the hands went up fast enough.
>
> The partisans took away the security men's side-arms, papers, and everything else they had with them. Then they raised their guns and asked the officials for their last wish, but the master of the farm fell to his knees and begged his friends to spare the security men's lives, saying, "Think of what will happen to me if you kill them." So the men's lives were spared.

In the bags they'd taken from the security officials,
the RVL men found complaints written by informers
and directed against some local folks. The bag also contained a notebook with instructions about how to recruit
informers. It instructed recruiters to look for poorly educated people and to promise them high-level jobs. The
recruit was to be praised in every possible way and his
importance emphasized repeatedly. He was to understand the implication that he could do anything he
wanted and be protected by the security apparatus. The
informers were to be given material aid confiscated from
deported households.

The activity of the RVL was facilitated by the fact that the resistance movement in Estonia peaked in the period from 1945 to 1947.
In those days, actual power in the countryside belonged to the Forest
Brothers. The occupiers held power in most of Estonia's villages and
towns during daylight hours, but the Forest Brothers ruled at night.
Soviet authorities lived in a state of perpetual fear. Soviet control
failed to reach some of the more remote forest villages until after the
mass deportations of 1949. In several counties, Soviet transport columns would move only when accompanied by armed escorts. Executive Committee buildings resembled strongly secured fortresses
with armed guards and even trenches. Large numbers of military
units were stationed in Estonia to ensure security for local Soviet-run
governments.

Inevitably, partisan activity in Estonia was weaker in larger cities
and densely populated counties, but greater in densely forested
peripheral areas. The Forest Brothers' operations in Võrumaa and
Virumaa Counties were the most noteworthy in all Estonia. The feats
of Pärnumaa and Läänemaa County partisans did not lag far behind.
A number of large forests and swamps lie between those two counties.
Despite its sparse forests and high concentration of Soviet troops,
Saaremaa Island was another site of extensive Forest Brothers' activity.

Estonia's most well-known Forest Brothers hail from these counties. These were daring and skilled men, whose fame extended far
beyond the borders of their areas. For the population, they were the
symbols of continuing resistance. Stories of their deeds spread
through Estonia and even into Siberia. The legendary leaders of the
Forest Brothers were the source of incessant troubles for the occupation authorities. In the aftermath, it is naturally quite difficult to
determine which exploits attributed to Forest Brothers are myths and

which are based on fact. The stories constitute a category of true folklore, a typical example of which is this story of Virumaa County's legendary hero Pargas:

> One of the most famous Forest Brothers in the Rakvere-Kiviõli district was the uncle of sports star Heino Lipp. This Forest Brothers' leader called himself "Pargas." His fame spread throughout Virumaa County. He was a tall, blond man with particularly large hands. He always kept at least one hand in his pocket. It was said that he had pistols in both pockets and he could shoot equally well with either hand. Once I was in the Uhtna cooperative store, when a large man walked in, hands in pockets, and said: "Give me two packs of 'Tallinn' cigarettes for free." The girl cashier replied impatiently, "You know I can't give you cigarettes without money and besides, I don't know who you are." The man replied: "Don't you know me? I'm Mr. Pargas." My heart stopped as I thought of the numerous tales I'd heard about the famous Pargas. The cashier took a ten-pack carton of cigarettes from the shelf and placed it on the counter in front of Pargas. The man said, "Mr. Pargas smokes only 'Tallinn' cigarettes. I don't want these."
>
> The cashier then put two packs of Tallinn cigarettes before Pargas. Pargas put the cigarettes in his pocket, gave the girl 100 rubles, and left. I felt weak-kneed for some time after that. I had seen the famous Forest Brother with my own eyes!
>
> One day, Pargas put up a sign on the Rakvere-Haljala road stating: "Pargas is accepting an unlimited number of volunteers," followed by the location of his "recruiting station." The police were afraid to take down the sign and it remained standing until the wind and rain carried it away.
>
> Another time, Pargas erected a sign near Tapa: "Hey, Stalin! Send my men some boots. We need them badly right now." The sign included the time and location for the delivery of the boots. Three truckloads of NKVD troops rode to the designated place, directly into a trap in which most of the NKVD troops were killed. Soon after, Pargas erected another sign: "Thank you, Stalin, for the boots and weapons. This is one pair we won't

be needing." A pair of bloody boots and a Russian soldier's cap lay by the sign.

Once, the Rakvere city police captured a Rakvere man and took him to the station. As soon as he was taken in, a noisy gang began breaking windows and looting stores in the outskirts of the city. When the police went to investigate, Pargas invaded the station and freed his man.

Pargas's men never lacked food supplies. One time, Pargas rode up to a store with a truck and his men started to load it with goods. All the customers were confined to the store during this operation. Upon leaving, Pargas gave each one a bottle of vodka and asked them to drink a toast to his health.

Once, Pargas robbed a car bringing money from a state bank into Kiviõli. One of his men, pretending to be deaf, stumbled onto the road and refused to budge at the beeping of the horn. The car was forced to stop; whereupon several men hiding by the road jumped into it. One took the wheel and drove the car into a forest path, where the Forest Brothers removed the money and allowed the driver and his companions to leave. Popular stories had it that Pargas's men made away with more than a million rubles.

All of Virumaa County was excited about Pargas. He was killed in 1951. A traitor led NKVD troops to Pargas's bunker, which lay near Kiviõli City. Pargas and three of his men battled thirty NKVD troops for more than an hour before they were all killed. The people mourned their hero for a long time.

Undoubtedly, most such accounts include personal embellishments. But Captain Pargas truly existed, and gained fame throughout Virumaa County with his daring escapades. Current information indicates that he was not connected to the Armed Resistance League. However, the man who was perhaps Estonia's most famous Forest Brother was a member of the RVL and the commander of one of its districts. This man was Ants Kaljurand, alias "Ants the Terrible."

He was born in 1921 to a poor farmer's family on Saaremaa Island. In the late 1930s, he left Saaremaa for the mainland to work as a farmhand, spending most of his time in Pärnumaa County. As a farmhand, Ants was in demand because of his willingness to work hard. Like most of his young Estonian contemporaries, Ants Kaljurand was fiercely patriotic, helping in the ranks of the *Kaitseliit* (Defense League). In 1940, he stood fast against the incoming Communist tide, launching a personal campaign of unrelenting opposition against it. In the summer of 1941, Kaljurand played an active role in organizing a Forest Brothers group, helped to seize the Soontagana town hall, and fought in subsequent battles against the Red army. In 1943, he was mobilized into the German army, where he fought until the autumn of 1944 as a noncommissioned officer in the Estonian Legion. Refusing to accompany the German retreat, he remained in Saaremaa, where he was captured and sent to a prison camp in Tallinn. At the end of 1944, Kaljurand escaped from the prison camp and returned to Pärnumaa County, where he quickly organized a group of Forest Brothers. Kaljurand demanded rigorous military discipline in his partisan unit. Security archives have preserved a report (originally encoded) of his group's activities, including descriptions of his discussions with his men, accounts of target practice, etc. The group's original intent, however, was to remain in hiding and avoid active combat operations. On the anniversary of Estonian independence, they hoisted the blue-black-and-white national flag in the Soontagana village center and distributed leaflets calling on the people to continue their struggle.

Many of Ants's escapades are related in numerous recollections.

Ants had a young sweetheart named Vilma from Saaremaa Island. When the NKVD learned of their relationship, they arrested Vilma and placed her in the detention cell of Soontagana town hall. When Ants heard of this, he paid a surprise nighttime visit on the town hall secretary who held the detention cell keys. He shoved the barrel of his pistol up to the secretary's mouth, and the man, in order to save his life, surrendered the keys to Ants, who then rescued Vilma. It was this incident that earned Ants Kaljurand the name "Ants the Terrible."

After that event, the NKVD succeeded in apprehending two of the men in Ants's group, who were also held in the town hall detention cell. The NKVD guards were about 300 meters away in a farmhouse with the detention cell keys. One night, Ants took a crowbar and smashed a hole in the stove used for heating the cell. His Forest Brothers escaped.

Ants the Terrible had a habit of announcing his arrival by mail. He notified the manager of the Baltika Restaurant in Pärnu that he would be having lunch there and was expecting a tasty meal. The manager took the missive to the NKVD. On the day mentioned in the letter, plainclothes NKVD men surrounded the Baltika. At the appointed time, a Pobeda with Russian army tags drove up to the door and Ants the Terrible, dressed in the uniform of a high-ranking Soviet officer, stepped out. The NKVD men did not recognize him. Ants enjoyed a fine meal at the restaurant, leaving a generous tip and a note under his plate reading: "Thank you very much for the lunch. Ants the Terrible." By the time the NKVD men realized that something was amiss, Ants and his Pobeda were long gone.

Once Ants warned the manager of a country store that he was planning to rob the place. The NKVD stationed a unit of its men around the store. The local NKVD official Allik decided he would take all the credit for Ants's capture himself and deliberately neglected to tell the city officials about the Forest Brother's plans. The unit left one soldier standing guard at the store while the others went upstairs to the store manager's office to lift their spirits with a little vodka.

A Pobeda drove up to the store and a young man stepped out, telling the guard he had to see the store manager. No sooner had the guard approached the visitor than he was relieved of his sidearm. At that instant, several more men jumped out of the car and ran upstairs, ordering the half-drunk NKVD men to put their hands up and keep still. In a flash, the rest of the Forest Brothers loaded the car with all the best goods and drove away, taking Ants with them.

Ants had long-standing ties to the local finance inspector Lilli Allmäe, who kept Ants informed of money transfers. Apparently, the NKVD got wind of their relationship and Lilli was arrested. She was pressured to reveal a great deal of information about Ants and forced to collaborate with the security apparatus, who instructed her to schedule a meeting with Ants during a dance in the village.

Ants arrived at the village at the appointed time
with a companion named Ülo. Ülo, hearing Russian spo-
ken behind some bushes, pointed his flashlight and emptied his pistol at the source, killing three NKVD soldiers.
Ants and his companion tried to flee. Ants succeeded,
but Ülo suffered a serious head wound and was captured by the NKVD. After this incident, Lilli Allmäe
hanged herself, fearing that Ants would never forgive
her betrayal.

Ants the Terrible refused to shed the blood of innocent people. This caused him to spare the life of local
Executive Committee chairman Neider, who was one of
Ants's bitterest enemies. Seeing Neider at a dance they
were both attending, one of Ants's companions aimed
his pistol at the man, but Ants stopped him from carrying out his revenge, fearing that the bullet would hit
innocent people.

Considering the fact that the archives of the Committee for State
Security contain a five-volume file on Ants the Terrible, we realize that
most of these recollections could indeed be true, even though they
may not be officially recorded.

Without a doubt, Ants Kaljurand was a cold-blooded and skilled
Forest Brother who frustrated the security apparatus. He had some
narrow escapes. One of them occurred on December 24, 1948. A Soviet
army unit had surrounded a farmhouse where Ants was staying, but
Ants and his companions managed to seek shelter in a nearby shed.
Searching through the farm buildings, the soldiers calmly opened the
door of the shed, only to come face to face with the Forest Brothers,
who peppered the entire farmyard with fire from the light machine
gun they were pointing out the door. In the ensuing confusion and
panic, Ants managed to escape. Ants the Terrible was a loyal RVL
member, operating as a district leader and commanding the Forest
Brothers of several parishes in Pärnumaa County.

The security apparatus learned of the existence of the Armed
Resistance League soon after this large-scale movement was estab-
lished. Security officials assembled their finest forces, led by Colonel
Daniel Taevere, for the fight against the RVL. At first, the men of the
RVL succeeded in slipping out of sieges by security forces, thanks in
a large part to the RVL's counterespionage chief Rumyantsev
(Rummi), who demanded strict adherence to the rules of conspiracy
from the members of the organization and succeeded in discovering

many a trap set up by security forces. Disguised either as a policeman or a security forces officer, Rumyantsev paid visits to suspicious persons who had applied for membership in the RVL, accusing them of cooperating with the Forest Brothers. If the suspicious applicant had indeed been recruited by security to infiltrate the RVL, he would sooner or later reveal his connection with the security apparatus.

The State Security Committee's next tactic was to infiltrate professional spies into the RVL's midst. The spies posed as communications men slipping in from Sweden with radio sets. Their assignment was to infiltrate RVL headquarters, seize the organization's archives, and entrap the entire organization in one fell swoop. Since actual radio contact with Sweden would have exposed the security men, however, their radio inevitably suffered a "tube that had broken on landing." Rumyantsev, however, was clever enough to keep the self-styled communications men away from the core of the organization, all the while pretending to believe their story. The game came to an end once it became obvious that a replacement tube was nowhere to be had in Estonia. Soon enough, communications with foreign countries were set up through Richard Saaliste, and the RVL could now positively identify any new communications men who came to them.

Unfortunately, the RVL's successes made the organization careless. It became less meticulous in planning operations, which began to include members who were dangerously familiar with the structure of the RVL. For a long time, the security apparatus did not succeed in capturing the most valuable RVL members alive. The men who were captured took their own lives.

In late 1947, however, the organization was shaken by a major defeat. A group of Forest Brothers with close ties to the RVL's leadership learned of a large shipment of money arriving in Järvamaa County. Although they lacked enough time to prepare the operation thoroughly, they decided to go ahead with it. It was doomed to failure from the start. The money shipment was under heavier guard than they had anticipated, and it took them much longer to seize the money than they had hoped. The coincidental presence of a police force in the vicinity added an unexpected twist to an already desperate situation. Although the Forest Brothers managed to break away, their next move proved to be a critical error. As they went to ask directions to the train station, they encountered a People's Defense member who alerted the district's entire security apparatus. Before long, the Forest Brothers found themselves surrounded in the train station. Most of them were killed in the ensuing battle, but the security forces succeeded in capturing one wounded partisan alive. They had stumbled upon a valuable prize — the driver of the RVL's central command.

This was a major setback for the Forest Brothers, leading to the arrest of one county organization leader after another, and raids on several bunkers. Although the authorities devoted a lot of manpower to this operation, they did not succeed in making a full sweep without sacrifices on their own part. Ahto Talvi recalls:

> In January 1948 I realized that someone was taking an interest in my activities. I started carrying both my pistols everywhere with me. I had my escape route planned.
>
> On December 31, 1947, I was playing carroms in the Paide fire station when the door swung open and several Soviet officers stepped in. They came over to the table wanting to play. I said to my friend, "You go ahead and play," and I quietly started to drift toward the back room where they wouldn't be able to find me easily because it was dark and full of junk. But they insisted on playing with me. I realized that this was a game for life or death. They asked me who I was, adding, "Now you're coming with us." I said, "All right. I just have to get my coat." And I slipped my hand into my pocket. Suddenly they were on top of me. But they were stupid. One jumped on my back, the others twisted my right hand behind my back, holding it above the elbow. But I was an athlete; I bent over and the guy on my back found his feet off the floor. I got my pistol into my left hand and pressed it against the chest of the guy on my right and pulled the trigger. It jammed! As soon as they saw the pistol, they started shouting and grabbed my left hand. I switched the pistol to my right, loaded the clip, and pressed it over to the right. There was a bang and one of the men fell off.
>
> The door was open now and officers ran toward us. I managed to raise my gun once more to fire. Another man fell. Then there were so many of them on top of me that I stumbled to the floor. I still held the pistol, but they tore it away. They left me sitting there in handcuffs. There I sat, looking at the two men I'd laid out on the floor, and I was completely calm. I even showed them the stretchers in the corner. And then I

asked for my pistol so I could shoot myself. But they
knew I'd be more useful to them alive.

At the same time they arrested the League command, Soviet
security forces launched large-scale operations against the bunkers of
RVL subunits. Desperate battles broke out in the forests of Estonia.
Despite the fact that they had the advantages of surprise and much
greater numbers, the security forces lost out in several areas. August
Hatto, a member of the RVL in western Estonia, recalls:

> There was a large bunker near Koluvere Township
> at Põrgupõhja. It was hidden in a dense thicket and sur-
> rounded by a meter-high earthen mound. About ten
> men lived in the bunker, and one was always on guard.
> In December 1947, after that great setback, army, NKVD,
> police, and destruction battalion troops launched a
> major raid against that bunker.
> On the day of the raid, the weather was miserable.
> Wet snow fell and visibility was near zero. That's why
> the raiding party nearly stumbled into the bunker
> guard's lap. The lookout sped back to the bunker, where
> the men were playing cards. They thought the guard
> was joking when he yelled, "The Russkies are coming!"
> When they finally grabbed their weapons and ran out-
> side, the attackers were only ten meters from the
> mound. The partisans opened fire at close range, liter-
> ally mowing down the first rows.
> A second attack was launched immediately. The For-
> est Brothers' rocket launchers wreaked havoc among the
> invaders. As the attackers' fire dwindled, the men broke
> out of the bunker and vanished, using the general chaos
> to their advantage. The Forest Brothers lost a couple of
> men, while the raiders tallied their own body count at
> near sixty.

Typically, however, the Forest Brothers did not fare so well. Taken
by surprise, many Forest Brothers were unable to resist and fell without
firing a single shot. Many were captured, particularly in Läänemaa and
Harjumaa Counties. Reports indicate that the Soviet security apparatus seized about 500 Forest Brothers. These individuals represented the
most active segment of the RVL movement. Although the central
command remained untouched, it lost most of its contacts. Mutual

mistrust spread throughout the Forest Brother units, and the relationship between Redlich and Saaliste soured. Richard Saaliste accused the RVL's leadership of excessive bravado and carelessness. He and his men broke with the organization and began conducting their operations independently, preserving only limited contacts with the RVL.

The frenzied manhunt for the Armed Resistance League leaders continued. When Saaliste attempted to return to Sweden, he learned in the nick of time that an ambush awaited him instead of a boat on the coast of Läänemaa County. It was a narrow escape for Saaliste. By this time, the Soviet security apparatus had put its finest forces into play for the destruction of the League. The Soviet security forces succeeded in capturing a few Forest Brothers only after stalking them for a long time. With brutal torture, they beat some information on the location of the League's central command bunker out of one partisan. They followed up with a large-scale raid; there was little chance of its failure. A member of the League's central command tells what happened then:

> It was the fall of 1948 when we started building a bunker in the marsh near the Kasari River. Two men went to a nearby village to gather food supplies, but they ran into a security apparatus collaborator who set a trap for them.
>
> That's how they found our bunker. They would have surprised us if Rumyantsev hadn't been sneaking around as usual. Now he came running up and saying, "A raiding party's coming. Let's camouflage with fir branches." He snapped up a machine gun. We grabbed our weapons and moved away from the bunker. A few kilometers away, they met up with us again, but we wedged our way through.
>
> They were tracking us with airplanes, and soon the way was blocked again. A few men got killed breaking through that one. They fired from the underbrush. We ran across the bog and reached the river. With Rumyantsev covering, one man swam across the river and brought a boat. We crossed the river with it. The opposite shore was higher, so we set up the machine gun there and when the Russkies reached the shore, we let 'em have it. The security forces were so furious that they burned down a farm lying in the riverbend once they got across the river.

> We were far away by then. Reedik (Redlich) said
> that there was no point in going any farther, because
> they'd be waiting for us anyway. So we made a wide
> loop and got back near the same place we'd started.

In 1948, ESSR Minister of State Security, MVD/NKVD General
Boris Kumm declared that the Armed Resistance League had been
eliminated. Although this was actually not yet true, the noose had
indeed tightened around the League. In early 1949, security forces
under the command of Colonel Daniel Taevere conducted a large-
scale operation code-named *Aknake* (Little Window). The security
apparatus had learned of Rumyantsev's weakness for music and his
frequent visits to the Pärnu Beach Casino. Security authorities
recruited a saxophone player to attract Rumyantsev's attention with
his exaggerated nationalistic behavior. This was the first time that the
security apparatus succeeded in infiltrating one of its agents into close
proximity with the RVL central command. A courier who had communicated with foreign countries for the RVL was also forced into
collaboration by the security apparatus. Neither the compromised
courier nor the security apparatus, however, succeeded in discovering the location of the RVL central command, although they gleaned
information on several farmers involved with the building of bunkers.
The security apparatus concentrated numerous forces in the suspected area and launched its raid. The bitter battle that ensued is
described in a document preserved in the CPE archives:

> On February 27, 1949, a bandits' bunker was discov-
> ered in a swamp in Halinga Parish of Pärnumaa County
> three kilometers from the town of Pärnu-Jaagupi. In the
> exchange of gunfire, nine Armed Resistance League com-
> mand members were killed. One was wounded and
> arrested; one escaped. He was followed but his identity
> remains unknown. Four soldiers of the Ministry for
> State Security were killed in the exchange, and one seri-
> ously wounded.

This document is supplemented by the doctored "official
account" given by Colonel Taevere, who led the operation. As he
describes it, two battalions raided the bunker.

> Both assault battalions burst onto the bunker
> through a dense thicket almost simultaneously. Elmar

Vertmann appeared from between the trees and sneaked toward the sentry, who succeeded in firing a shot into the air. The bandits stormed out of the bunker and rushed, firing as they ran, toward Teras's unit. There they were met with a barrage of fire. Someone fell, and the bandits stormed in the other direction, where they were met with automatic weapons fire from Gavrilov's unit. The bandits fled back to the bunker and opened heavy fire with machine guns and automatic weapons.

"Don't draw it out!" shouted Teras into the loud-speaker. "Gavrilov, block the access to the bunker opening; otherwise it'll take us forever to get them out."

The battle was beginning to subside. Johanson, gravely wounded, was screaming horribly. Eight lifeless bodies lay around the former dwelling of the bandits.

With that battle, the League's central command was annihilated. Rumyantsev and all the other leaders had fallen. Redlich had not been in the bunker at the time of the raid. The League split into smaller units that were hunted mercilessly by the Soviet security forces. It seemed that NKVD headquarters would not be satisfied until the last leaders of the underground organizations were captured. The keenest attention was now focused on the manhunt for Richard Saaliste, an operation directed personally by ESSR Minister of State Security Boris Kumm. Actual responsibility for his capture rested with one of the most notorious chekists of the day — Colonel Eduard Sisas. Although Saaliste succeeded in avoiding capture several times, the partisan forces proved to be no match for government troops. A girl who lived in the Saaliste brothers' bunker recalls:

Richard Saaliste's bunker was on the edge of Vändra Forest, seven kilometers from Eidapere. He lived in the bunker along with the following people: his brother, the chief of *Häädemeeste Omakaitse*, whose name I don't remember; his wife Ilse; his brother's wife Heili Mihkelson; and her sister. That's me.

Saaliste was in touch with the other Forest Brothers in the area, although they didn't live in the same bunker. A stranger joined those men one time; he said he was in hiding and wanted to be called "Captain" since he had been an officer in the Estonian army. Actually he was a security informer who turned people in, reported their location, and sent the security forces to raid.

On December 14, 1949, security troops raided Saaliste's bunker. Saaliste, who was outside the bunker, caught sight of the approaching troops and opened automatic weapons fire, which was supplemented by those at the windows of the bunker. Richard Saaliste fell at the bunker's door; his brother was wounded. We escaped through the bunker's rear window, taking the wounded man with us. We hadn't gone far when they saw us and directed their fire our way. When the security men found me, they beat me senseless. As they took me away, I saw that Richard had been tied up and was being dragged along the ground to the car. They threw him in. I don't know whether he was still alive or not.

I don't know where they put Richard's body in Pärnu, but people tell me that the others were thrown into a well near the bunker. When they brought the rest of the captives to trial, Evald Pärtel and Elmar Saar were sentenced to death; Pärtel's sister was tortured to death in Patarei Prison.

Despite the security apparatus's best efforts, some Armed Resistance League members remained free. When Vambola Orav, the radio operator for Saaliste's unit, was arrested in 1950, the last communications with Sweden were broken off. Of all the groups most actively connected to Saaliste, only Eerich Järlet's unit continued to operate. On September 5, 1951, Järlet's unit robbed a money shipment on the Tallinn-Pärnu narrow-gauge railway. The Forest Brothers made off with 200,000 rubles. Security forces succeeded in capturing Järlet's unit only after they had sent a false Forest Brothers group into the woods, who seized Järlet with the help of poisoned vodka.

Endel Redlich had managed to prepare a relatively secure hideout near his home town. Once when Soviet security forces were hot on his trail, Redlich killed a man tracking him and vanished. Finally, the substantial award offered for Redlich's capture seduced one person who knew of his hideout to betray it to Soviet security forces. This happened in the autumn of 1949. The only existing source is again a doctored "official report":

The roar of the engine brought the stocky redheaded man to his feet. He stormed out of the house in stocking feet and started running through the yard toward a dense pine forest.

"Redlich!" A hysterical woman's voice called from the car, "The elusive one!"

The man's head twitched, as if he were thinking of looking back at who was calling him, but he kept running. Teras ran to block his escape. Redlich realized that he was being cut off. He turned suddenly, raised his hand, and fired on the run, but Teras heard only a faint whine.

The man had apparently decided to run behind the house for a better firing position. There he encountered a soldier, fired again but missed, rounded the corner, and stormed downhill toward a nearby stream.

"Hold your fire!" called Teras, as he followed. "Take him alive!"

At that moment, shots crackled from behind the house. Redlich convulsed in a comical leap and collapsed into the stream.

"What have you done!" screamed Teras to the soldier.

He knelt over the fallen Redlich. The bandit's head lay in the stream, his still unclouded eyes arrogantly staring out from under the shock of red hair.

By any definition, the Armed Resistance Movement was wiped out by the early 1950s. The Soviet security apparatus dealt the final blow to the authority of the group by creating a phantom organization using the same name. Provocateurs (such as Artur Hamann) encouraged young people to join this "resistance organization," letting them meet and sign a few petitions, and then arresting the entire "organization."

Although the crushing of the Armed Resistance League was a true blow to the resistance movement, it did not signify the end. Most of the RVL's subunits continued to operate on their own initiative, not to mention those Forest Brother units which never belonged to the organization. There were no more attempts to form a nationwide resistance organization, although the Forest Brothers often coordinated their activities on a countywide level. Several Forest Brother groups with influence in some of the counties had their own program and plan of action, frequently reflecting the influence of the RVL. One example was the "Orion" unit operating under the command of Jaan Roots in Võrumaa County and retaining the RVL's goals in its program. "Orion" not only had ties with other Forest Brother groups, but also with underground organizations in the cities.

Most of the Forest Brothers now no longer endeavored to join larger units, preferring to operate on their own. Partisan activity subsided. Their primary interest became concealment and the obtaining of provisions for day-to-day living. The lull in active combat did not, however, make the lives of the Forest Brothers any easier.

Chapter 7

In the Forest and the City

As the resistance dragged on, concealment became more and more difficult. Life was hard in the forests and swamps. Many of the men who had fought in the battles of World War II and had taken to hiding in the forests after that claimed that a year in the forests contained as many hardships as three years on the battlefront.

In studying the life and times of the people who hid themselves in forests and swamps during the postwar years, the fact emerges that the fugitives were not always men, but entire families that were forced to go into hiding. Some took along their farm animals. Several erected sturdy dwellings and barns, which were usually built under ground and camouflaged. Some forest clearings held primitive fields for growing crops. Forest Brothers groups included a significant number of women, and sometimes children.

Naturally, a mother's heart often cried out for her child, creating a dangerous situation for both mother and child. The inherent danger of such an arrangement is illustrated by the following story. For many years, a woman called "Madonna" hid out with the Võrumaa County Forest Brothers. She and her children escaped and returned to Estonia after being deported to Siberia. Forest Brother Alfred Käärmann recalls:

> She lived like that for a couple of years, mowing
> hay for her cow in the summer and secretly doing work
> for her relatives while her children attended school. She
> slept wherever she could. The start of the deportations
> had scared people, and no one dared protect her any-
> more. And so they brought her to me, because her
> mother had sheltered me once when I was wounded.
> My only condition was this: "You don't take one step
> out of the bunker without my permission." She agreed.

The night of March 28 she got a terrible urge to visit her children in the village and to spend the night at home, if it looked safe. We argued. I couldn't convince her to forget this senseless trip. She finally played her trump card by saying: "You don't have children; you can't imagine the feelings in a mother's heart." I could say nothing except: "Go, but don't you get any chekists breathing down my neck." She left. All was quiet as I lay down to sleep, fully dressed.

About three in the morning, the roar of a motor rattled my underground bunker. I jumped outside holding my automatic. I heard a truck stop and someone shout: "The road to the village goes to the left." The rumble of a great many heavy Russian boots started toward the village, an awful rumble . . . and the village dogs didn't hear a thing. They didn't sound an alarm until the soldiers started pounding on the doors. I heard shouts: "*Atkroite*," ("Open up!"); then the squeak of a door, then "*Stoi! Stoi! Stoi!*" ("Stop! Stop! Stop!") There was the rattle of automatic weapons fire and a lot of bellowing in Russian. I went back to the bunker, took my backpack, a blanket, some food, dry socks, and all my weapons, and went to hide near the edge of the village by the road. They came back, swearing as they climbed into the car, and drove past me and the bunker without stopping. I waited another half hour until the roar of the engine was swallowed by the silence of the night. Then I went back to the bunker quietly to figure out what to do next. I lit my lamp and saw Madonna sitting on my bed in an undershirt, barefoot, with her outer clothing bunched up on her lap. I composed myself and said angrily: "I'm going to smash you to pieces. Damn you." She responded tearfully: "First, just take a look at my feet." And then I was speechless. The toes and soles of both Madonna's feet were a mass of bloody flesh. She said: "When they beat on the door, I didn't have time to dress or find my shoes. I grabbed my clothes from the chair. As the Russians broke in one door, I escaped through the other and ran across the field. They shot at me. The bullets missed me, but the bare frozen ground tore up the soles of my feet." I won't even describe the weeks it took her to heal.

That same morning at dawn, I was horrified to notice her bloody footprints on a frozen snowdrift. I quickly got an empty sack, a shovel, and my weapons, and followed the bloody footprints along the trail they had come. I shoveled the bloody snow into the sack far enough on both sides so that the blood was not visible from the road. This wouldn't have saved us from real bloodhounds. Fortunately, nobody came around the next day to sniff us out. We lived on for several weeks in a constant state of alert, watching the road to the village from a tree all day long until the snow melted and her feet healed. This time, we'd been lucky.

In October 1950, Madonna was turned in by her husband's relatives, and her daughter was taken from her desk at school. Their roads parted, with the mother going to prison, and the daughter into exile.

Some children spent their day-to-day existence in forest bunkers. The crying of a child betrayed the location of quite a few hideouts. One Forest Brother describes the life of such a child:

We felt sorriest for that little boy. He never had the chance to run around or to play with other children. Whenever we came back from somewhere, we'd bring him something good to eat, so at least we could help him that way. He didn't even have any toys. Once when we were returning to the bunker, I found a black cat in the forest. I put it in my sack and took it to the boy. That was his only toy.

Naturally, most children languished in these conditions. They either died or were sent to live with distant relatives, under whose care they had to forget their real names and their real parents.

Although most of the partisans in Estonia were Estonians, other nationalities were represented as well, not only citizens of the Republic of Estonia, but Russians and Germans who happened to be in Estonia because of the war. The ranks of the Forest Brothers swelled thanks to German prisoners of war who had escaped from prison camps.

The Estonian and Latvian Forest Brothers worked in close cooperation, exchanging information with each other and providing mutual assistance with arms and supplies. In times of danger, Latvian Forest Brothers fled into Estonia, and vice versa. Quite a few Estonian men owe their lives to the Latvians, but many laid down their lives on the neighboring country's soil. In one instance, four Latvians — three men and a woman — fled the deportations to Viitina Township in Estonia. They were given a hay shed to hide in, but the pursuers were soon on their trail. The troops surrounded the shed and demanded surrender. Automatic weapons fire burst from the shed in reply. There was no other way to get at the partisans but to burn down the shed. The troops found that the shed had contained five Latvians, since the woman had been in her final months of pregnancy.

The Forest Brothers were most comfortable hiding in homes or farms. There they had no worries about food, shelter, or boredom. Almost all the Forest Brothers lived this way for the duration of the war, for at that time the NKVD apparatus was still incomplete and its files still unfinished. Once the NKVD was armed with the information in the files, however, it started searching homes and farms, and the results were horrifying. The occupants of any home sheltering a Forest Brother were sent to Siberia. That was one reason why the fugitives began looking to the forest for shelter. It was so hard for a Forest Brother hiding in his own home to see how every bark of the dog or the roar of every car engine filled his family's eyes with fear, set his mother's or wife's hands shaking and her voice trembling. "Oh God! If they find you here, what's going to happen to us all?" As a rule, only an unmarried Forest Brother would hide in a home. Usually, it was safer for the occupants if he avoided carrying a weapon.

Some homes offered shelter in carefully camouflaged hideouts. Most partisans, however, found refuge in the forests, selecting dense thickets, swamps, and bogs for their homes. In the summer they slept under the open sky or in tents, hay sheds, and peat sheds. The arrival of fall made life extremely uncomfortable at those sites.

Under these circumstances, the Forest Brothers had to think about building bunkers. They had to select the site early and build the bunker quickly after making the necessary preparations. Speed was essential, since a single casual passer-by could render the entire effort useless. Meinhard Leetmaa recounts the requirements for a bunker site:

"— no farther than five kilometers from the village or a single-family dwelling;
— the bunker site must be surrounded by blueberry bushes or heather, so that no paths will be evident at the site or in the area of the bunker;
— drinking water must be close by;

— dried fir or pine must be available for firewood;
— at least one kilometer from the forest's main drainage ditch;
— at least two kilometers from the logging roads and slopes cut in the winter."

Frequently, the bunkers were located in hillocks, or on hummocks within marshes. Construction styles varied greatly. Forest Brother Meinhard Leetmaa describes a typical hideout in the early stages of the partisan movement:

> The bunker measured three by four meters. The walls were a double layer of wood planking, with soil in the space. The roof was covered with a layer of soil and tar paper to protect against rain. One wall had a door and window; another wall held a window. Double bunks for sleeping. A stove for heating and cooking, made of a gasoline barrel lined with bricks. A storage area was dug under the floor of the bunker to hold ammunition, hand grenades, meat, and potatoes. To prevent hand grenades from being thrown in the windows, there were winnowing machine screens that could be fastened into place from the inside. The door was covered on both sides with sheets of steel.

Although many bunkers in the late 1940s were aboveground constructions of sod or planking, the underground constructions gradually became predominant. Alfred Käärmann describes the construction of one of these bunkers:

> In October 1946, I worked awfully hard to build myself a winter bunker. I had to dig a hole two and one-half by two and one-half meters and two meters deep, cut about four cubic meters of fine planking for the walls and roof of the hole, and then carry bricks and boards from the old Tar Factory one and one-half kilometers away.
> Right after the digging was finished, the wives of some Hargla Communists went right by the hole picking berries! I recognized them by their voices. I sat near my hole all day and thought about what I should do. "What if they see it on their way back from the outing?

Should I dump them in the hole and take off? Someone
will certainly come looking for them." That night, the
women returned from their outing without having
noticed anything. The bunker was soon finished. Encir-
cling the bunker, I set up twelve 82-mm mortars with
detonators controlled by a wire. The other end of the
wire was tied around a tree six to eight meters away. The
bunker was protected on all sides.

These kinds of bunkers were carefully camouflaged and often
equipped with an emergency escape route that was disguised with
special care. Quite often, the bunker trapdoor was covered by a tree
stump or a planted fir. One bunker in Sõmerpalu Parish was built into
a ridge by a riverbank, with the entry at water level.

Emergency escape routes and secret passages allowed the men
to escape from many seemingly hopeless situations. In Helme Parish
of Valgamaa County, the story is told of a battle that raged at the
Oovest farm near the outskirts of the town, where a group of Forest
Brothers fought off NKVD units for an entire day. The Russians finally
set the farmhouse on fire. When they later pulled apart the smoldering
remains, there was no trace of the partisans, who had escaped through
a secret passageway.

Many bunkers were very well armored and equipped with well-
constructed loopholes and trenches. Near Puudli in Võrumaa County,
one bunker had on its roof a rotating turret holding a tank machine
gun. There are also reports of bunkers surrounded by minefields.

Only those bunkers with a round-the-clock guard and utmost
secrecy of location had any chance of survival. No one except the
occupants could know the location of the bunker, not even its general
area or its forest district. The bunker dwellers were guaranteed a
peaceful existence until someone happened to stumble upon them. At
least one of the residents was always on guard so that this "someone"
would not be able to leave the area undetected.

Each bunker had a coordinated plan prepared for its defense in
the event of a surprise attack. A typical defense plan is illustrated in
the recollections of Meinhard Leetmaa:

— Four designated men jump to the windows,
both of whom always have five light machine guns
standing by, two of them loaded. The man on the right
side of the window fires to the left, and the one on the
left to the right.

— One man jumps into the cellar and prepares hand grenades.

— One man loads machine gun magazines.

— The door is always bolted from the inside.

— In the event of attack, hold your position until dark, and then abandon the bunker as soon as possible.

— Before leaving the bunker, fire all weapons and throw hand grenades from the windows.

— Four men previously selected by lottery will be the first to leave the bunker, crawling or running to a distance of 50 meters in the fir thicket; the first two fire their submachine guns directly ahead; the third toward the right; and the fourth toward the left.

— After reaching a distance of fifty meters, they cover the exit of those men remaining in the bunker, of whom two fire to the right and two to the left.

— If there are enemy left behind when they reach fifty meters, all men will fire back at them.

— When the last men have reached a distance of fifty meters from the bunker, the group begins breaking off from the enemy, so that half the men will cover the retreat of the other half.

Most of the postwar bunker battles in Estonia were waged according to a similar plan. Few lasted long enough to get to the final points of the plan.

Life was hard in the bunkers, particularly in winter, when departures from the bunker had to be kept to a minimum. Every footprint was clearly visible in the snow, making outdoor activity extremely dangerous. In early spring, water from the spring thaw tended to flood the bunkers, bringing an invasion of water rats. Only strong nerves and willpower allowed the forest dwellers to endure.

How did the Forest Brothers pass their time? Daily activities, such as heating the bunker, fetching water, and cooking food all took some time. Someone was always on guard duty. At night, the men listened to the radio whenever possible. Reading was an important pastime. Research works and memoirs about the War of Independence seemed to be universal favorites. Some of the men devised other activities to escape the boredom, such as weaving nets, knitting, and doing various handicrafts. Some men did shoemakers' work for the local residents; women sewed clothing on order.

Celebrations broke the monotony of everyday life. Birthdays called for special ceremonies, and the most important events were Christmas and Independence Day (February 24). Since the Forest Brothers could not go to church, they read the Bible in their bunker, prepared traditional holiday foods, and sang hymns. Some men had to stand guard outside amid the snowy fir trees and listen only to the church bells pealing in the distance. Estonian Independence Day was also marked festively. Anyone owning a Defense League uniform wore it on that day. The national flag was placed on the table, speeches were made, and the national anthem sung. A "social hour" followed the ceremony.

Proper care of the bunker and its weapons was vitally important. Though the motley nature of the Forest Brothers' armaments made the latter operation quite difficult, they had plenty of weapons, since the Germans had left behind entire arsenals as they left Estonia in 1944. This makes Eerik Heine's account of the German "Messerschmidt" fighter plane in a forest glade entirely plausible. Of course, nobody knew what to do with it.

The CPE archives contain reports of cannons carefully dismantled and hidden by the Forest Brothers. In 1947, a farmer from Võrumaa was brought before a tribunal in Tallinn, accused of illegal possession of a firearm. A German antitank gun complete with artillery had been found in his hay shed. In response to the question of why he needed an antitank gun, the farmer muttered: "Ain't nothing a good farmer can't use."

Most Forest Brothers lacked such heavy artillery. Eerik Heine writes of mortars and other such weapons, but hard evidence of these instances is lacking. Some people recall that some groups did have mortars hidden away "just in case" they were needed for a major battle. The heaviest artillery owned by Forest Brothers was reportedly an antiaircraft gun, which the partisans fired at Red army transport planes in Pärnumaa County.

On the other hand, the Forest Brothers boasted of an extensive arsenal of lighter weapons. Of course, German weapons predominated at first, but by 1946 and 1947, it was necessary to exchange them for Russian weapons, the primary reason being problems with ammunition. The German cartridges tended to rust, and new ones were nowhere to be had. By the time their movement waned, most Forest Brothers were supplied with Russian weapons, which were captured in raids on township halls, People's Defense units, and squads of Red army soldiers. Pistols, however, were predominantly German or Belgian models. The 7.65-mm caliber "Walther PP" was especially popular. This pocket- or belt-carried pistol was widely sought after because of its modern streamlined form and self-cocking mechanism, which meant that it could be carried while loaded, since one pull on the trigger both cocked and fired the gun. Russian TT-30s (better known as "five-pointed stars") and Nagant revolvers were also in use.

Although Russian rifles and German carbines were widely used, automatic weapons were naturally the weapons of choice. Submachine guns included the German MP 38-40, as well as a few *Sturmgewehr* MP-44s, which were used during the final partisan battles in Estonia. The latter fired single shots as well as automatic rounds. An impressive weapon was the Russian submachine gun or *pepeshka*. From the start, Russian models predominated among machine guns, some of which (such as the Maxim) had been used in the Republic of Estonia. The Germans' powerful MG-42, on the other hand, demanded exhaustive care and used up cartridges far too rapidly. The Russian light machine gun *Degtyaryov* was widely used alongside heavy machine guns.

Of course, the Forest Brothers also possessed hand grenades as well as rifle grenades. Larger groups had German bazookas, and the effective "stovepipe," officially named Grenade Launcher No. 54. This 88-mm weapon of war had an electrical trigger and a maximum range of 130 meters.

There were few problems with other equipment. The Forest Brothers had no common uniform or regalia. They typically moved about in peasant dress; for operations, they wore Soviet army or security forces uniforms. Elements of the German army uniform, or on special occasions, the Estonian Defense League uniform, were widespread. Use depended on whether the Forest Brothers were interested in making their identity known or not.

The appearance of a typical Forest Brother is illustrated by a document found in the security committee archives in Kooraste Parish of Võrumaa County describing Forest Brother Voldemar Piho:

> Voldemar Piho, nickname "August," appears to be twenty-eight to twenty-nine years old, about 175 centimeters tall, stocky build, short brownish-red hair parted on the right. Round face with pimples and freckles. Dense black brows, long nose. Dress: new brown suit, black shoes, driver's black eight-cornered hat. Weapons: German automatic, two TT pistols, one parabellum, four F-1 grenades in a belt sack, four magazines of cartridges

for the automatic. Other belongings: earth-colored German poncho, one pocket watch, one wristwatch with black face. Four rings (three gold), a compass, a pair of binoculars, and one briefcase, contents unknown.

Medical care presented a major problem to the forest dwellers. No special medical facilities could be set up in the forest. The partisans took their wounded to village women with first-aid training. Only occasionally would they venture into hospitals to have doctors operate on and treat the men. Some doctors performed their services in the forest. Medical care, for the most part, was primitive.

Nevertheless, most of the wounded survived. Those who died were taken secretly to their hometown cemetery, buried in the forest near their home, or laid to rest at a cemetery near the Forest Brothers' camp. A schoolteacher from Tartu recalls:

> In the late 1940s, I was studying in Tartu, returning to my home in Vastseliina during vacation. I was a nice-looking girl with plenty of admirers. One of them was very shy and didn't dare tell me he was smitten with me. He visited me during vacation, and we often went walking in the woods together. Once we found a beautiful clearing and built a small fire.
>
> Suddenly we heard a brass band begin playing beyond the trees. I know a little bit about music, so I can tell you it was a full-fledged ensemble. We heard the rustle of footsteps. Fortunately, the fire was dying; we threw soil on it and sat as quiet as mice. The whole procession passed just a few steps from us. A man carrying a cross was in the lead, followed by the band and about two dozen people. They passed us and continued into the forest. Now we realized what it was: A few days ago, the Forest Brothers had fought a battle with the Russians, and now they were burying their dead. I have to say that I've never seen anything so magnificent or so eerie in my life. We sat there quietly for a minute and then took off.

Often, the partisans did not succeed in reclaiming their dead. In the best instance, the Soviet security forces left the dead lying where they fell. The Forest Brothers retrieved them later for burial. Entire cemeteries, complete with gardens and crosses, appeared in the forests.

Usually, however, the security forces took the bodies of fallen Forest Brothers with them. The corpses were propped up either in the marketplace or village center to be ridiculed. Some of the bodies were tied to trees, and others were taken to fox farms as feed.

The Osula destruction battalion in Võrumaa County shot a young man to death in the forest. They stripped the body almost naked and let it lie about in the town center for several days. Nobody recognized him, and so after a drunken binge, the security men ordered the youngest Komsomol in Osula to dispose of the body. The young man threw the corpse on his shoulder and took it outside Osula to the former German barracks, where he threw it into an empty well. It lay there until it rotted. The bare skull continued to shimmer at the bottom for a long time.

If the Soviet security forces buried corpses, the people marked and tended the locations of the Forest Brothers' graves. Although the security forces repeatedly leveled these gravesites, they were put in order again and remain marked to this day.

The support and sympathy of the local people were of the utmost importance to the Forest Brothers. Partisan specialist in war tactics and strategy V. Redelis once remarked that a successful partisan war requires leaders who, first, have a strong will, and second, are able to win popular support. "In other words, teamwork between the partisan leaders and the population is a fundamental requirement of any partisan movement." Only those partisan movements receiving substantial assistance from outside sources can afford to ignore popular opinion to some extent, but even then their operations ran into trouble. An excellent example is the total failure of the Soviet-sponsored partisan movement in Estonia. It would not be unreasonable to claim that popular support was the key to the Estonian Forest Brothers' long-lived fight.

Naturally, food was of primary importance to the Forest Brothers. The partisans' food was either delivered to a prearranged spot in the forest, or fetched by the men themselves. Procuring food for the winter was critical. The Forest Brothers got all their supplies, including clothes, tools, and everyday necessities, from the farms. They also relied heavily on the information they got from the local people. The partisans were well informed of the movements of the destruction battalions and even the NKVD units. Information was passed to them about Soviet transport columns and shipments of money. The Forest Brothers had friends in high places, even in KGB headquarters in Tallinn.

Who helped the Forest Brothers? According to Soviet sources, it was almost exclusively the *kulaks*, i.e., the most well-to-do peasants. This claim, however, is not confirmed in the recollections of the Forest Brothers.

Right after the war, many people helped and supported us. As the atrocities intensified, people grew
more careful, more indifferent. As Forest Brothers were
captured in increasing numbers, security forces conducted widespread reprisals against those who had
helped us. The wealthiest peasants were the ones who
tried to beat the odds by showing loyalty to the new
regime. Unbridled violence makes people want to be on
the dominant side, or at least to earn its favor in hopes
that they will be spared if they don't displease the cruel
masters. In this way, many Estonians turned their backs
on the suffering of their own people while showing a
smiling face to the oppressors, and bringing tributes to
those who held the keys of life and death. They gambled
with so many things to win the favor of the new regime
and to avoid deportation to Siberia. For instance, the
daughter of our churchwarden had to sleep with a chekist, and her mother would set a lavish table for him in
the morning as if he were the finest bridegroom. That's
how their family escaped deportation to Siberia.

In other instances, no degree of submission was sufficient. The old sayings: "Nobody can harm a righteous
man" and "He who walks behind the plow is always on
the right path" no longer applied. One story illustrates
the circumstances of a local farmer hoping to save his
family by showing loyalty to the authorities.

It was the night of December 17, dark and bitterly
cold. Two Forest Brothers, Robert Migul and I, sneaked to
the stable of the Tambelse farm. My hand had been
amputated just a few weeks ago and the open wound
oozed in the cold. The stable door was still unlocked,
which meant the farmer had not yet come out to close it,
and we did not go in. We had waited for nearly an hour
when the master of the house Julius Paas came out. Robert asked him if we could spend the night in the stable,
instructing him to leave the stable door unlocked, so that
it would look like we sneaked in without his knowledge.

The farmer locked the door and said: "Go to the Tõrvhaua meadow. No one will find you in all the hay sheds down there." Robert pleaded once more: "My companion is wounded and weak. It's twenty-five degrees below zero. We'll freeze to death there, and no one will find us until it's time to remove the hay." But the master of Tambelse remained firm.

We left into the bitterly frosty night. Julius Paas was a good person, and so he didn't betray our whereabouts. But he'd chosen to stake all his fortunes on one card — Soviet Russia. The following evening, Robert got shot and I was left alone with my wound.

All in all, Julius Paas's misplaced loyalty didn't save the Tambelse family from deportation. The farmer had gambled on the wrong card. The Tambelse farm was a wealthy one, and the parish activists, the family's "advocates," got a good haul after the family was taken away, although the Tambelse farm hadn't given one Forest Brother a single crust of bread — a number of partisans confirmed this.

I found incidents like this one to be the exception. I can only say that there were far more people who helped me and sympathized with me. Most of them were poor, not rich, and many were elementary school children.

Other accounts reflect similar views. The poorer classes really had nothing to lose to the Soviet regime since they didn't own a great deal of property or land, and thus their ranks included more highly principled fighters against the occupation authorities and their collaborators. It is hard to say how many Estonians aided the Forest Brothers directly. The population could best be split into several groups. The largest group, while not supporting the Forest Brothers actively, sympathized with them and above all did not take any action against them. For this reason, many Forest Brothers were able to hide themselves for decades without being betrayed.

The nature of each partisan group often had a bearing on the local population's relationship with the Forest Brothers. There were several different types of groups, of which Eerik Heine offers an interesting perspective. In his writings about the Forest Brothers in the collective works entitled *Eesti saatusaastad* (*Estonia's Fateful Years*), he divides the Forest Brothers into three major groups. The first comprises those individuals in hiding alone. If we include those fugitives living in the forest with family or friends, this group is enormous. These people typically lacked weapons. Any they had were used infrequently. They did not engage in active resistance; their only purpose was to remain in hiding. Their ties with the other Forest Brothers were loose and transient. All things considered, they had a good chance of staying alive, although they were treated no differently from other partisans if they were captured. Sometimes their bunkers were blown apart by grenades in surprise attacks, which struck without regard for the nature of the partisans living there.

Many "lone wolves" hid themselves successfully. They typically hid at the home of a relative or sweetheart behind false walls, in a hayloft, in an attic space, or in a cellar beneath the house. Life in a shelter known to only one other person could end in tragedy. There are numerous reports of men who perished in a sealed hiding place after the death or forced departure of their protectors.

The second group, according to Eerik Heine, consisted of the "freemen" who belonged to no particular group. They roamed through the country alone, in twos, or in threes without staying anywhere very long. Most members of this group were arrested either by chance or because of betrayal in the early 1950s, and were sent to Siberia. The percent of casualties in this group was small, since the men usually managed to avoid involvement in major battles and raids.

The third and smallest, but most energetic, group of Forest Brothers comprised the militarized, well-armed groups with designated leaders, communications networks with other units and with the outside world, and a well-defined system of bunkers and hideouts. The forests of Estonia held about 5,000 to 6,000 men of this kind at any one time, though the sizes of the active units themselves varied greatly. The groups were typically made up of two to ten men, who could unite to form units of sixty to seventy combatants if a major operation demanded. The largest bunkers found in Estonia housed about two dozen men and women.

A review of the resistance movement in Estonia would be incomplete if we did not look at the civil segment that operated primarily in the cities; those whom the Estonians called the "City Brothers."

The City Brothers, an influential wing of the resistance movement in postwar Estonia, have largely been neglected in writings about Estonian partisans. The civil resistance movement was overshadowed by the armed struggles in the forests and was gradually forgotten. And yet, it constituted an essential part of the resistance movement by being the transitional force to the next phase of the movement. Without a political wing, the ten years of resistance in the forests would not have been possible. The Forest Brothers frequently needed a temporary place to hide when danger threatened; they needed to acquire medical supplies and, most important of all, information. The City Brothers were most helpful in obtaining forged documents and in selling stolen goods in the cities. The political propaganda, leaflets, and proclamations distributed by the City Brothers represented a valuable contribution to the resistance.

In contrast to the Forest Brothers, the number of City Brothers involved in the resistance movement was smaller. Many of them had moved to the cities to conceal themselves with their forged identity papers or perhaps even to study. In his memoirs, Meinhard Leetmaa describes the process of obtaining an assumed identity:

> Estonian passports were valid up until the Soviet internal passports were distributed. In 1947, the police stations started distributing Soviet passports to replace those of the Republic of Estonia. In order to get your new passport, you had to hand in your old one, two photos, and your address and employment vouchers.
>
> In the Republic of Estonia, internal passports both with and without photos were considered valid. In order to leave the forest and get a Soviet passport, I had to obtain an Estonian passport without a photo. With the help of some good people, I managed to acquire a pictureless passport in the name of Alfred Sepp in the summer of 1947. The passport holder was dead, but the date of death had not been marked on the document because the man's father had left the passport home when he went to register his son's death. Men he knew in the township hall had simply registered the death without further ado, and so the passport remained in the father's hands.
>
> And so I became Alfred Sepp, son of Aleksander, born December 31, 1894 in Mäetaguse Township (where the real Alfred Sepp was also buried in 1942). But I had several hurdles to overcome in order to assume this identity. Early in the Soviet occupation, in October 1944, all local residents had been registered, and an entry to this effect made in each passport with the signature of the Executive Committee chairman or secretary and the Executive Committee seal. Alfred Sepp's passport had neither.

Now I absolutely had to get the passport registered at Mäetaguse Township with a date of October 1944, along with the required signature and seal. I also needed to have my departure registered, since I could not take up residence in Mäetaguse Township. After all, this was "my" place of birth and all "my" acquaintances lived here.

Because I knew the wording of the registration of entry and departure, it was no trick to write them into the passport. Signatures could also be forged, but getting the seal affixed presented the greatest problem. I found a friend who was on good terms with the Executive Committee Chairman of Mäetaguse Township. He knew that the chairman carried his precious seal in the right pocket of his jacket. My friend invited the chairman to his birthday celebration and kept the room rather hot. In addition to that, he "warmed up" his good friend the chairman with plenty of drink, until finally the man was forced to remove his jacket. My friend then took advantage of the situation and "borrowed" the seal to press into my passport.

Undoubtedly, others found simpler methods by which to obtain a passport and new identity, one being to buy them from a policeman at the market. Transactions of this nature were quite common.

The City Brothers, like the Forest Brothers, formed a diverse group. Some had extensive ties to a larger organization, while others were in hiding alone. Their "legal" status varied as well. Although a person might have forged documents, he still could operate as a "semi-illegal," i.e., lacking a permanent residence or employment. Others were fully "legalized" under their true identity, while preserving their mutual ties and those with the Forest Brothers in the countryside. Forest Brothers and City Brothers frequently exchanged status by switching residences and identities. Most of the well-known Forest Brothers had prearranged hideouts in the cities.

Some Forest Brothers managed to find themselves rather unusual cover. Former KGB-man Valter Rull explains:

It was at the end of 1948, when I went to work at the Pärnu City Security Committee. I expected some exciting reconnaissance work, but I realized right away that I'd joined a gang who went stealing and pillaging around the local farms. I spent three years writing requests to be relieved of my job before I was finally released. Fortunately, I'd been a member of the Young Eagles youth organization during the Republic. I'd been raised in a patriotic spirit, and inherited a sharp wit from my parents. It didn't take me long to decide to use my position for the benefit of my land and countrymen.

I managed to help some arrested persons a little. My greatest feat was to hide Forest Brother Ernst Anton from the security apparatus in 1949. Anton was a stockily built sixteen-year-old young man working with a unit of Forest Brothers, while keeping his job and performing as a gifted athlete with the Pärnu "Spartak" league, where I was also a member. I knew that Anton was wanted by the authorities and he knew it too. Informers followed him at his workplace, at home, and in the stadium. Anton was calm, brave, and resourceful. He knew how to get to the competitions at Pärnu stadium on time, win first place, ceremoniously accept his prize, and disappear before the security men ever got there. While Anton was in Pärnu, the Soviet security newspaper carried a story about his winning a prize in shot put at the all-Union youth championships.

As the danger to Anton's well-being increased, I let him hide in my apartment. I gave him my apartment key, but he never left the place while I was at work. His conduct betrayed no fear. Finally, Ernst Anton was forced to leave the Pärnu area. I was still working with the Soviet security apparatus a year later when I met him in a Tallinn railway station, where we drank some mineral water and talked about sports. Anton told me that things were going well. It was never clear to me what he meant by "going well."

How did the City Brothers function? On the one hand, they provided support for the activities of the Forest Brothers; on the other, they conducted their own kind of resistance movement. Besides accumulating weapons and setting up arsenals, they carried out acts of sabotage. Some of these acts are described in the memoirs of Soviet army soldiers serving in Estonia at that time. The City Brothers focused a great deal of their energies on political terrorism and the elimination of traitors and NKVD/KGB agents. One time, the City

Brothers carried out a daring attack on the Harju District Communist Party building right in the center of Tallinn. A former Party worker describes the assault:

> It happened on the last days of 1948. A parish Party Secretaries' meeting was being held in the county Party Committee house. As they listened to a lecture on the international situation, they suddenly noticed dense smoke spreading through the Party Committee building. The lecture was cut short and the nervous audience ran upstairs.
>
> Clouds of smoke billowed out from under the metal-lined door of the Party registration office. The door was locked. When they forced open the door, they saw the registration office thick with smoke. The office manager, a hefty young woman named Oleinik, was bound to a chair with ropes. A rag hung from her mouth. She had nearly fainted from fear and smoke. A trash can burned next to her and burning bits of paper floated under the ceiling. Chairs had been overturned, and the papers and documents on the desk were a mess.
>
> As Oleinik revived, she trembled as she told about the raid on the registration office. First, the bandits had threatened her with a gun and demanded the key to the safe holding the registration forms. They stuffed a rag into Oleinik's mouth, punched her, and left her groggy in the chair. Then, the bandits threw some registration forms into the trash can, added some newspaper and writing paper, and set it ablaze. When the flames grew high, they opened the door, ran out, and pulled the door locked from the outside.
>
> This happened in the middle of the day, downtown on Kreuksi Street, at the Harju County Party Committee Building.

Not even the Komsomol leaders could feel secure in Tallinn in those days. One of them, Edgar Mattiisen, recalls:

> I was shot at three times. One incident happened right here on Kreuksi Street, right in the middle of town, in front of the Komsomol house. I was coming out with Tolbat and Jaanimäe. It was night, really late. As we

stepped out the front door, we heard shots, but we didn't get hit. The police guards went looking for them and we did too, but we didn't find anyone. We heard someone running in the ruins across the street, but we didn't find them.

Eliminating some of these groups was no easy task for the NKVD. An operation to eliminate the Sorg unit is described in the collective work *Kompromiss on välistatud* (A Compromise is Excluded). Sorg had started forming his unit in November 1944, emerging with a fully organized group in January 1945. The unit kept an arsenal in some ruins on Müürivahe Street and another at Valgeristi. His group attacked stores and intimidated its enemies. Sorg also had contacts with the Forest Brothers. The Soviet security apparatus succeeded in destroying Sorg's unit after infiltrating some of its own men into it, but not without losses for the security apparatus itself. In one incident, security forces happened to stumble upon Alfred Kink, a former member of the "Erna" group, near Tondi. Kink dashed over the railroad track toward Ülemiste Lake, with the security men in hot pursuit. Shots rang out and Kink fell. The operation commander Security Captain Põder approached the fallen man. Another gunshot sounded and Põder crumpled to the ground; the "dead" Kink got to his feet and vanished. According to Soviet security files, this happened on April 17, 1948. Kink was killed several months later in a gun battle in Tartu.

Students' underground organizations comprised the most energetic segment of the City Brothers movement. Young Estonians had a strong nationalist spirit, and so it is hardly surprising to hear of "combat organizations" made up of 10- and 11-year-old boys, who gathered weapons left in the woods, supplied the Forest Brothers with information, and sent threatening letters to Communist collaborators. One such organization in Kanepi was called *Noored Kalevlased* ("Young Kalevians" — Kalev is a legendary Estonian hero). Often, the presence of an organization was not even necessary, since the spirit of the young people was patriotic enough without it. Dissident Valdur Raudvassar recalls:

> After the war, the woods were full of weapons and ammunition, everything from handguns to mines. At the first celebration of the school year, the one commemorating the October Revolution, everyone went to school carrying a rifle. They left them in the hedge by the schoolhouse to

be picked up on their way home. No one bothered to
study too much, because everyone thought that war
would break out soon for certain. Everyone thought that
either the Americans would come to our aid or that the
Germans would come back. So all the schoolboys kept
hoping for and preparing to go to war.

One time someone fired a few shots over the Loosi
School director Heino Eiche's head at a school party,
since he was suspected of being a security collaborator.
The director was sure that the Forest Brothers were to
blame, but later the whole thing came to light when a
boy told his mother all about it at home. The mother
came to school and told about the boys having guns.
After that, the security men came to the school and
investigated for a couple of weeks. They tried to find out
if the boys had any connections to the Forest Brothers.
Finally, the whole issue subsided. We were too young at
that time — fourth- and fifth-graders — to represent any
kind of organization.

The spirit of these students is also evident in the questions they
posed to the Party workers giving "political instruction" in the
schools. At a question-and-answer session held at the Kuressaare
Middle School on February 8, 1947, all 156 questions asked were
classified as "anti-Soviet." All the inquiries could be summed up in
the one question: "The war has been over for years; so why is Estonia
still occupied by the Russian army?" Naturally, the questions were
turned over to the Committee for State Security for review.

Another factor to consider is that many of the upperclassmen
were already experienced in some form of combat, had access to
weapons, and knew how to use them. All too often, these factors led
to their capture. A former teacher at the Westholm Gymnasium who
worked as the director of the Nõmme orphanage near Tallinn in the
postwar years recalls:

There I used to teach mathematics to the sixth grade
and physical education too. My students came to visit
me one time, and after they left, there must have been
some kind of incident somewhere on Falkpargi Street as
the boys were escorting their girlfriends home. It seems
that a Russian officer had bumped into one of the girls
and said something insulting, so one of the boys shot at

him. I think he'd served in the German army and he still
had his weapon. They connected me to this incident, as
if I'd been associated with this group, since they visited
me occasionally. They connected the group to me and
said they were — what did they call them — terrorists or
something.

Of course, the students did more than gather for casual meetings.
They played a large role in conducting political education campaigns
and disseminating anti-Soviet propaganda in Estonia after the war.
They disseminated true information about events in Estonia and
elsewhere in the world, listened regularly to foreign radio broadcasts,
called on the population to ignore the directives issued by occupation
authorities, and distributed "banned" literature and leaflets. They
liked to paste handbills near heavily traveled locations, such as local
Executive Committee buildings or police stations. A sample of a
handbill has been preserved in the CPE archives:

Estonians!
Do not lose your faith or hope, you suffering Estonian people! Suppress your anger and defiance in order to
preserve yourselves. We must not needlessly join the
thousands of our finest countrymen already suffering
innocently in prison.
We are still Estonians by our nature and in our
souls. Even if they strip us of everything else, we will
retain our faith and our strong will to survive.
God is watching over us!

Other handbills encouraged the people to continue their resistance. An example:

Death to the Bolsheviks and the pathetic Red army!
A Call to Action.

Estonians, all loyal Estonians, do not be too passive.
Do not let yourselves be deported or arrested by the Bolsheviks. Try to avoid this fate at all costs. All you men who
truly love our small homeland, take to the forests to form
defense units against the Bolsheviks and robbers. Forest
Brothers, maintain your ties, so that we may be able to step
out in defense of our homeland when the time is right!

Long live Estonia, soon to be free!
Publication of the Green Legion.

Similar handbills were published throughout Estonia. The city partisans were particularly interested in thwarting Soviet elections. They pasted up handbills calling on people not to vote, and tore down Soviet election agitation posters. In Järvamaa County, one group planned to insert self-igniting chemicals in the ballot boxes. During the 1946 elections for the Supreme Soviet, all election posters in Valga City were torn down repeatedly, until the NKVD set up an ambush, the outcome of which is described in a letter from the CPE archives:

On January 29, the NKVD and KBG offices posted guards in the city, and at approximately 9:00 p.m. that same day, a group of four young people was seized on Nõukogude Street, including electrician Vaine (b. 1929) and his brother. Their father had been arrested by the NKVD. The others arrested included Heino Johanson (b. 1931), the number two student at his school. Further investigation revealed that they were the leaders of an underground organization whose goal it was to disrupt preparations for the elections in every way possible.

The more impressive actions carried out by the City Brothers included the hoisting of the blue-black-and-white national flag in public places on Estonian national holidays. Nothing succeeded in annoying the new authorities more than the Estonian national banner. The flag became the symbol of the continuing resistance, similar to the letter *V* scratched on walls in France during the Nazi occupation. Discovery of a national flag in a person's home was sufficient grounds for deportation to a Siberian labor camp, so naturally hoisting the flag was a much greater crime. And still, it was hoisted in public places throughout the period of occupation (even after the end of the Forest Brothers movement). Victory Day (June 22) was one of the most beloved holidays, second only to the anniversary of Estonian independence (February 24). Once, the flag made an unexpected appearance on May Day 1946, when Juhan Udras of Valga hung a national flag on his house in the center of town. Naturally, the flag was quickly removed, and Udras gave the Soviet security interrogators a simple reason for his actions: "I did it because I detest Soviet power."

Students were the ones who tried to protect monuments commemorating the War of Independence from the Soviet demolition squads. They often held demonstrations at these sites.

When the so-called Liberators' Monument to Soviet power was blown up in Tallinn, the action sent shock waves far and wide. The explosion was carried out by a small group of female students in response to the second removal of a monument to teachers and students who had fallen in the War of Independence. Acquiring the dynamite was only half the job. A guard stood at the monument around the clock. With heart-rending screams, one of the girls began begging for help near the French Lyceum building to draw the guard away from his post. Momentarily forgetting his duty, the guard rushed to help the girl. In those few moments, the others shoved the dynamite cartridges under the monument and lit the fuse.

The number of student organizations in postwar Estonia is not accurately known, but current information indicates the existence of nearly thirty. Võrumaa County students won special fame because their organization was destroyed several times and then rebuilt with amazing defiance and tenacity. The students' underground organization had close ties with the local Forest Brothers' group, in whose bunker security forces found information about some students. Member Kalju Aarop recalls:

> At the end of 1945, a Forest Brothers' bunker was surrounded by security forces in Mersi Forest near Võru City. Twelve Forest Brothers were killed. On December 12, 1945, they started to arrest students. They targeted several organizations, and these arrests continued into January. Since the school was on holiday, some of the students managed to avoid capture. The arrested students were held in security cells for a month, then several weeks in the Võru detention center at the police station, and then taken to KGB headquarters on Pagari Street. At the end of August 1946, they held a tribunal at the Baltic Fleet. The tribunal tried thirty-nine people.
>
> Some of those on trial were not students. Thirty-five were found guilty; four were released. I think two of the released persons were from farms near that bunker. There were at least two schoolteachers. I don't know any more, except that Olev Pehka must have been one of them. He'd been in that Scouting organization since 1944 or 1945, and he'd been recruited by the

students. All the rest were sentenced to six to ten years, and nearly all of them served the whole sentence. At that time, they were all underage kids, aged fifteen to seventeen.

At first there was one organization, the Scouts. But when it got too big, they formed several smaller organizations, so that they'd have some secrecy. That's why today we don't know exactly how many organizations there were and how many members they had. But they were connected to the Forest Brothers and they helped them in some ways.

They passed around leaflets and things like that. They did some childish things like digging out an old Estonian coat of arms and taking photographs of themselves standing by it. Some of the members thought that this kind of stuff was too careless.

Their meetings were held secretly, of course, in various places. There were girls as well as boys. They tried to make these meetings look like get-togethers between sweethearts. That group had ten members. Six of them got arrested, but four managed to avoid getting caught.

In 1945 and 1946, a number of students from the Võru Gymnasium who were members of the *Eesti Rahva Võitluse Liit* (The Estonian National Resistance League) were arrested and held in Patarei Prison and in the KGB headquarters in Tallinn. In August 1946, on the final day of their trial, they were granted a final word before their sentence was pronounced. The students declared that they had a joint statement to make. Together, they rose and sang, to the astonishment and consternation of the legal tribunal, all three verses of the Estonian national anthem.

One of the leaders of the Võrumaa students' organizations, Jaan Roots, became one of southern Estonia's most famous Forest Brothers. In 1946, intimidation by the Soviet security apparatus forced him to flee to the forest. After obtaining forged identity papers, he went on to study at Viljandi Industrial School. In 1947, the security apparatus caught up with him, and Roots returned to the forest, where he became the leader of the "Orion" unit. Roots fell in battle in 1952.

A "special report" sent to CPE First Secretary Nikolai Karotamm by the local Party Committee focuses special attention on the activities of the Võrumaa County students' organizations:

Recently, our posters and slogans have been repeatedly torn down in the cities. For this reason we have stationed nighttime patrols to prevent and investigate these actions.

During the night of January 31, 1946 on Kreutzwald Street, the guards apprehended two of the vandals, identified as Maimu Sild and Aino Leies, students of the Võru Secondary School. During interrogation by the police, the girls explained that they were members of an underground organization called *Eesti Vabaduse Eest - EVE* ("For Estonian Freedom"). Upon searching their apartment at 56 Kreutzwald Street, investigators found ninety copies of anti-Soviet leaflets in a nightstand. In the room of another organization member at 55 Petseri Street, we found twenty copies of a leaflet with the following content:

"Estonians!

We call on all Estonians to rise up in united struggle against Estonia's enemies — the Communists and Russian subjugators who are trying to destroy everything we hold dear and who are forcing us to reject our national colors. Tear down the red rags that are desecrating our cities and towns.

—EVE"

Another type of leaflet contains the following text:

"Estonians!

Do not take part in the upcoming elections. Do not let your Estonian spirit be desecrated by participation in Communist elections.

—EVE"

In addition to the aforementioned, four more members of this same underground organization were apprehended later. Since it seems that this organization has been operating in Võru for nearly two weeks, we are continuing the investigation to find the driving force behind this organization.

In the early morning of January 31, 1946, a member of the electoral district commission stepped from train No. 390 to find a handbill pasted on a commemorative

plaque next to the County Executive Committee building, with a text written in red pencil. In the center is the
phrase "For the Republic of Estonia," and the upper
right-hand corner holds the words "Death to the Russian beggars." The text itself reads: "Estonians, stay
away from the ballot boxes. If you vote for the Communists, they will deport you to beautiful Siberia. The V.R.
Troop of the Võru Scouting Organization."

In 1947, a new wave of arrests engulfed the schools of Võrumaa,
but the underground organization tenaciously regenerated itself. This
time it called itself *Noored Kuperjanovlased* ("Young Kuperjanovists"
— Kuperjanov was a partisan hero in the War of Independence), and
it had particularly close ties to the local Forest Brothers. The partisans
gave military training to the students in a common bunker built in the
swamps near Võru City. In the summer of 1949, the Võru students and
Forest Brothers planned to blow up the Võru Security Committee
building. Powerful mines were placed in the building. The action was
postponed, however, since too many people, particularly children,
happened to be in the vicinity of the building on the day of the
planned attack. Some activities of the *Noored Kuperjanovlased* are
remembered by one of the movement's members:

> I belonged to the Võru students' underground orga-
> nization *Noored Kuperjanovlased*. This was an intensely
> secretive organization with ties to the Võrumaa County
> Forest Brothers. We distributed leaflets and other litera-
> ture, and relayed information.
>
> The thirty-first anniversary of Estonian indepen-
> dence was celebrated on February 24, 1949. Since we'd
> marked the day in previous years by putting up posters
> in Võru City, the security forces were watching the entire
> city carefully. In spite of that, we succeeded in hoisting a
> national flag to the top of the tallest tree in Võru's cen-
> tral park. We wrapped bunches of string and wires
> around the tree, stuffed little boxes in between the knots
> and labeled the whole mess with a sign: "Caution:
> Mined."
>
> As soon as dawn broke the next morning, the news
> of a national flag waving in the park spread through the
> city. A crowd of people gathered. The security chief
> ordered some soldiers to bring the flag down, but they

were afraid to touch the tree. They had to fetch some sappers, who didn't arrive until midday. When they started untangling the wires and found that the boxes contained no explosives, they swore something awful. The flag was brought down, but not before most of the city residents had had a chance to see it.

The people of Võru remembered this day for a long time as the last bright moment before the subsequent dark age of terror and ignorance.

The activities of the Võru students had enraged the Soviet security apparatus, and a frenzied manhunt was launched. In the autumn of 1949, security succeeded in infiltrating one of its agents into the *Noored Kuperjanovlased*. The core of the movement was apprehended, and a rash of arrests claimed a large number of students as well as teachers.

And yet, new organizations emerged to replace those that were crushed. The members of many targeted organizations took to the forests, only to emerge some time later with false identity papers to continue their studies. This kind of mobility makes the determination of the total number of participants in the resistance movement extremely difficult. According to the statistical data in Soviet archives, roughly 15,000 Forest Brothers had been either neutralized or enticed from the forests by 1947. At that time, there were at least as many still in the forests. If we add those who took to the forests later, the total number of Estonian Forest Brothers approaches 30,000 to 40,000. Most of them were armed, and nearly half belonged to organized units.

From any perspective, these freedom fighters constituted a noteworthy force that caused Soviet authorities to expend considerable resources in their drive to suppress them.

Chapter 8

Manhunt

The suppression of the resistance movement in the conquered territory quickly became a crucial issue for the Soviet authorities. Although they had hoped to nip all opposition in the bud with the terror they unleashed during the occupation, it soon became clear that crushing the fiercely independent Estonian national spirit would be no simple task. Opposition to the conquerors was too deeply rooted in the national soul. Neither the destruction of the national leadership nor the isolation of Estonia from the rest of the world proved sufficient to extinguish the flame of opposition.

The destruction battalions (given the official name *Rahvakaitse*, People's Defense Units) created in 1944 to fight the Forest Brothers, never lived up to expectations. As long as the Forest Brothers remained passive, the destruction battalions somehow managed to stay in control of the situation, but the increase in resistance activity in the spring of 1945 thwarted them. This situation upset Moscow considerably, and central Soviet authorities demanded that the CPE take decisive steps to end the resistance once and for all.

On August 7, 1945, the CPE Central Committee held a meeting to discuss battle tactics against the "bandits." The following discussion is recorded in the minutes of the meeting. Many of those attending the meeting felt that their chances of success were very poor. The partisans had succeeded in intimidating local Communist activists to the extent that no one dared to join the destruction battalions anymore. In many townships, the first men to join destruction battalions had been shot by the "bandits," and threatening letters began to appear more frequently in KGB collaborators' mailboxes. In the opinion of the security chief of Virumaa County Jaan Enger, the people of Estonia were politically retarded. He urged everyone to remember that Estonia was not Kalinin Oblast. When Enger had tried to recruit a lumberjack as his accomplice, the man had asked whether Enger himself was an Estonian. Upon hearing the affirmative answer, the lumberjack said that he did not plan to join him in terrorizing his own people.

Other participants at the meeting complained of having encountered similar attitudes. A Comrade Perov felt that the Estonian people were in need of a basic brainwashing, but since it was not possible to brainwash the entire population at once, some key individuals had to be arrested. Arnold Veimer protested, saying that arrests must be made with restraint, lest these actions put up a wall between the people and the government. Most of the others disagreed with him. Comrade Sergei Sazonov noted that a strong hand is loved by the people and feared by its enemies. They must target the core and supporters of the resistance movement in order to eliminate it. Comrade Päss reported that the resettlement of all the families of the Forest Brothers and their collaborators in several townships of his county had solved the problem. Others related similar experiences. Comrade Hanson felt that the authorities were still standing on ceremony with the families of Forest Brother collaborators, since the procurator's office insisted on following the rules and insisting on legitimate arrest warrants. Comrade Sazonov declared their handling of the situation to be impermissible, insisting that the testimony of a destruction battalion member should be sufficient grounds for arrest. The outcome of the meeting was summarized by Comrade Perov, who expressed the necessity of strengthening the destruction battalions with increases in pay and benefits, recruiting a band of informants either by enticements or intimidation, and dealing a blow to the families and supporters of the Forest Brothers. He said they should either be arrested or placed in some kind of economic vise. The actions must be well publicized. An example must be made of two or three families from each parish.

Soon after the meeting, a directive was issued ordering the strengthening of the destruction battalions and the expropriation of land and property from the supporters and families of the Forest Brothers. Similar meetings were held nearly every year to approve similar resolutions and decrees. By 1948, CPE First Secretary Nikolai Karotamm was already threatening to fire the county security forces commander and hold the local Party Secretary personally responsible if one Forest Brother was left in any county when the Fifth Congress of the Communist Party of Estonia convened in December 1948.

Even so, most of the responsibility in the battle against the Forest Brothers lay not with the destruction battalions but with the Committee for State Security, which operated under several different names in the postwar years (NKVD — Narodnyi Kommissariat

Vnutrennikh Del; then KGB — Komitet Gossudarrstvennoi Bezopastnosti), but whose purpose remained the same. During the NKVD period, the security apparatus and police forces were part of the same system. This permitted the use of police units in the fight against the resistance. The security workers were known as chekists. The creation of a Ministry of State Security within the government of the Estonian SSR affirmed the special significance of the security apparatus in postwar Estonia. The Minister of State Security was obligated to "insure domestic security"; in other words, to suppress the resistance movement. Until 1950 this position was filled by the infamous Boris Kumm, who had been at the forefront of Red terror in Estonia as early as 1940, playing a leading role in the deportation processes of June 14, 1941.

The rosters of people who worked in the state security apparatus in the postwar years clearly indicate that most of them were either ethnic Russians or Russified Estonians brought in from Russia. One such individual was the chief of State Security, Second Division, Colonel Daniel Taevere, who led the fight against the Forest Brother organizations. At that time, security workers formed a highly privileged class whose power surpassed that of the Party and Executive Committees. This gave rise to noticeable competition between these organizations; the relationship between the police and security workers was also tinged with dislike.

All too often, police and security forces proved insufficient for carrying out major operations against the resistance. In these cases, border guards, regular army combatants, or soldiers of the mobile Interior Ministry forces (subordinate to the NKVD) were brought into play. In the course of a few years, the Soviet Union transformed Estonia into a huge military base, where several accounts place 100,000 to 150,000 Soviet soldiers on Estonian soil, resulting in a ratio of one soldier for every four adult Estonians. In the antiresistance raids conducted in the autumn of 1944, regular army units were used most often, but the authorities soon abandoned this practice because the lines of soldiers became hopelessly entangled in the heavy forests, their technical backup mired in the swamps or stuck on narrow forest paths. This allowed the Forest Brothers to escape their pursuers easily. All too often, fights broke out among the raiders themselves.

August Hatto recalls a raid conducted in Läänemaa, where a small group of Forest Brothers became sandwiched between lines of soldiers approaching from two sides. The Forest Brothers stayed calm, dropped to the forest floor, let the soldiers close in, and then opened heavy fire in both directions. The soldiers responded with gunfire, hitting not the hidden Forest Brothers but their own men in the opposite line. In the confusion of the pitched battle that followed, the Forest Brothers managed to slip away. After incidents such as this, Soviet authorities quickly decided to abandon their plan to comb Estonia's forests and destroy the Forest Brothers with the help of the regular army.

Use of the air force also proved disappointing. Air surveillance occasionally succeeded in discovering groups of Forest Brothers, but curtain fire by the Forest Brothers proved to be brutally effective against the low-flying light Russian planes. The authorities were forced to find other ways to suppress the resistance.

In 1944, and even more so in 1945, Soviet authorities placed great hopes on the punitive troops of the security apparatus that were sent into rural areas. They were to discover the Forest Brothers' hiding places and destroy the men and their bunkers. Local residents refused, however, to help the security troops; even though the families and helpers of the Forest Brothers were arrested and tortured. For this reason, the operations of the punitive troops remained generally ineffective. They did manage to deal the Forest Brothers painful blows in some instances, but a decisive success remained evasive. The functions of the punitive troops were transferred to the destruction battalions, who were assigned to organize constant surveillance of the Forest Brothers and their supporters.

The destruction battalion men were ordered to stake out the Forest Brothers' homesites and identify their supporters and helpers. One Forest Brother recalls the events of those times:

> The chekists, conducting their incessant hunt for us,
> often used an ancient hunting tactic — stalking their
> prey. They watched our homes every night for months
> on end, reckoning that the "bandit" had to come home
> sooner or later. The stalkers were usually men of the
> local destruction battalion, who took up their post at the
> home of a Forest Brother or one of his relatives at twi-
> light and kept the home under surveillance until dawn.
> The surveillance was particularly thorough on family
> holidays, such as birthdays, weddings, and funerals.
> They figured that the "bandit" would return home when
> all his friends and family were together. Many men were
> shot dead in their own yard or arrested at a family cele-
> bration. The son of Mart Gustavson of Pärnumaa was
> shot in his own pasture. Old Mart told me this himself,

with tears in his eyes, in the Tiset Prison Camp No. 603
in 1955.

Even in the forests, life was for living. Young men found it hard
to remain confined in the bunkers. Most of them had wives or sweethearts, and forced inactivity in the bunker made them restless. Warm
weather permitted them to move about, and Forest Brothers dancing
at local festivals were a common sight, but the winter brought a
reversal of fortunes. Since every footprint would be obvious in the
snow, movement outside the bunker had to be strictly limited. Those
who were unable to adhere to these rules often went to their doom.
Many partisans were captured while intoxicated or with women. It is
small wonder that the last surviving Forest Brothers had the saying:
"A big throat and a big dick entail big sacrifices."

But the Forest Brothers movement lived on. Losses taught the
Forest Brothers to be more careful, and the destruction battalions
found it hard to capture these skilled and disciplined units. By 1946,
this had become eminently clear to the CPE leadership. The last straw
for the authorities was an incident in Viljandimaa County, where a
local destruction battalion managed to ruin an operation planned by
the security apparatus. Security agents had succeeded in discovering
the location of some Forest Brother bunkers, setting up an ambush
near one and sending a destruction battalion to stake out another.
Instead of lying in camouflage, the destruction battalion built a large
bonfire and started to celebrate. The noise attracted the attention of
the Forest Brothers, who were not in the bunkers at that time. They
crept up close, took out the guards, and opened fire on the drunken
destruction battalion men at close range. In the ensuing confusion, the
destruction battalion scattered and the entire operation failed.

This incident caused a scandal, and the authorities withdrew
some of their support for destruction battalions, concentrating on
strengthening the security apparatus instead. The most trustworthy
Party members were sent to work for the security apparatus; in
essence, the county Party Committees became branches of the Committee for State Security. Every report sent to the Party Committees
about an individual's anti-Soviet activities or attitude was immediately forwarded to security workers. Party workers were also directed
to help the security apparatus in recruiting local agents.

Gradually, the significance of the security apparatus in the fight
against the Forest Brothers became pivotal. The security apparatus
used its agents to discover the individuals helping the Forest Brothers, subsequently arresting them and forcing them under torture to

collaborate. The arrest of an entire family became a powerful method of coercion. By taking the family hostage, the security apparatus hoped to gain information on the Forest Brothers' routes of movement and the location of their bunkers, so that ambushes could be organized to capture them.

According to records in the CPE archives, female agents were widely used in the postwar period to entrap Forest Brothers. The results of these operations were all too often fateful for the woodland partisans. Alfred Käärmann gives an account in his recollections about the recruitment and work of female agents:

> In the summer of 1945, in August, some of the graduating female Komsomol members from Hargla School were called to a meeting, given an "antibandit" patriotic lecture, and called upon to "fulfil their honored Komsomol duty in the fight against the bandits." They were taught as follows: "Start going berry-picking alone or in groups, and don't forget to take along lots of food. In the forest, sing old Estonian songs and if you're approached by armed men, don't be afraid. They won't harm you. Be friendly to them, let them kiss you, pretend to be their sweethearts, schedule trysts in the forest. Take them food, cigarettes and vodka. Tell us everything you see and hear there. Don't ask them anything. Just look and listen." The girls were shocked, asking: "What if they start pawing at us?" "Let them, because the important thing is to earn their trust, and if things go too far, don't worry. Our doctors will take care of it." The lecturer was a woman. In reward for their services, meaning information, the girls were promised pretty clothes, silk stockings, and shoes.
>
> Two kilometers from Hargla in the Kalli railway station, some Valga girls met the Forest Brothers Evald Kont and Oskar Mölder. They hit it off right away and set up a date right there near Kalli Village in a hay shed near the forest. At the agreed time, the boys were so impatient that they couldn't bear to wait at the hay shed, but walked along the road for a distance to meet the girls. They didn't take their "girlfriends" to the designated hay shed, but to a shed half a kilometer away in the riverbend. Later, the boys told us: "We'd done everything there was to do with those girls. At daybreak, we

suddenly heard Russian chatter and the rattle of a
machine gun at the other hay shed. We had no time left
for farewell kisses. We grabbed our weapons and dived
into the river. Hidden by the riverbank willows, we ran
across the meadow into Vaskpalu, one kilometer away."

There's another funny story about these same girls.
Erich Koivupuu lived near the forest. The young ladies
with the "duty to the Komsomol" went over to his place.
They talked as if they were patriotic Estonians and
asked about the Forest Brothers. But Erich had already
been warned. He kindly asked the girls to come in, and
secretly sent his old mother to tell the appropriate
authorities that some suspicious girls who were in
cahoots with the Forest Brothers had come to his farm.
In the meantime, he engaged in some sweet talk with
the girls. Soon, the destruction battalion troops arrived
and arrested the girls. They suffered a lot on the way to
the Mõniste township hall, and they sat in prison for a
while until someone finally learned that the young
ladies were "our own Komsomol members" and not
"*banditkas.*" That was the end of their mission in Hargla.

Right after the war, the chekists used girls a lot to
achieve their ends, and they were successful quite often.
Here is one such incident that cost us dearly.

In October 1945, Forest Brother Evald Kont's
mother-in-law died in Hargla. On this occasion, a local
Hargla girl Salme Ahero showed up in Vaskpalu and
met partisans Kont and Mölder. They spent a romantic
night in a shed by the Koiva River. But misfortune was
on its way. Although winter was coming, the Forest
Brothers continued to lead a carefree life on the farms of
Gaujiena on the Estonian-Latvian border, moving
around during the day and sleeping in sheds at night.

I began to sense that something was wrong. I got
together with the boys and said: "It'll be snowing soon,
and they'll be able to see our tracks. Let's build a bunker
now so we'll have a place to stay." Mölder laughed at me,
saying "Are you crazy? The Russians won't be around
that long. We'll be free by Christmas." In the meantime,
Salme Ahero had fulfilled her Komsomol duty by informing the chekists exactly which partisans were hiding

where, what paths they used for movements, and where they spent the nights. A major raid was in the works.

Around lunchtime on October 18, I started from the Mudimetsa farm to the shed by the Koiva River to get my clothes and start building the bunker alone. West of the Tsaune forest warden's house in a clearing, several guns opened fire on me. A bursting bullet shattered my left arm above the elbow, but I managed to escape. The punitive troops continued to the Sarivariku farm. They found no one, but beat up the farm's owner August Blaum for no reason. Three kilometers from the Sarivariku farm was the Mudimetsa farm where the three Estonian Forest Brothers were staying: Evald Kont, Oskar Mölder, and Karl Täht.

Fortunately, a little girl playing outside noticed the raiders and ran indoors screaming: *"Krievi nak!"* ("Russians are coming!") The boys scrambled out the window toward the forest. They were fired at and Kont was wounded in the leg but escaped. The raid continued. That night it snowed and the troops followed our boys by their bloody tracks. Kont told the others to leave him behind and save themselves, but Mölder refused and started to hoist his friend on his shoulders. At that, Kont grabbed his pistol and shot himself in the head in the Sarivariku farmyard. Mölder tried to make his escape, but the troops were already approaching and he was shot in the legs and shoulder. The soldiers dragged him into the farmhouse and asked him if he'd been given any food at this farm. Mölder denied it and was hit in the face with a gun cleaning rod. Then they tied Mölder behind the wagon and dragged him to the next farm to ask him the same question. His denial was again followed by blows to the face. Finally, there was nothing left of Mölder but a bloody stump, and they lifted him off the wagon near Vaskpalu and shot him.

Similar accounts have been collected in many parts of the country. Edward Loosaar recalls an incident in southern Estonia, where the NKVD had long stalked two well-known local Forest Brothers, Valter Liiv and Hillar Paas. Finally, the hunters found the appropriate collaborators with whom to carry out their plans.

Forest Brothers Liiv and Paas started stopping by and visiting the potter Aljas in Lepassaare. Aljas brewed moonshine and he had two young unmarried daughters. The NKVD had recruited one of them as an informer, but both girls were very clever and never let on what they were doing. The girls started being friendly with Liiv and Paas, perhaps even lovers. This went on for some time, until the two Forest Brothers lost all caution and doubt regarding the Aljas family.

One Saturday night, Aljas heated his sauna and asked Liiv and Paas to come by, and they did. After bathing in the sauna, they drank moonshine and enjoyed themselves. One of the girls was home, and the other was supposedly visiting in the village. Actually, she had gone into Võru that morning and returned that night with some NKVD men, who surrounded the house. The partisans had no idea they were amid traitors and that they had only a few minutes left to live.

Suddenly there was a loud knock on the door. The Forest Brothers grabbed their weapons. The fog of alcohol faded suddenly, and their instincts sounded a warning. Master of the house Aljas said: "Don't worry. I'll go see who it is." They heard a woman's voice at the door and the girl came in, saying: "You're having such a wonderful time, but it's so dark and rainy out there. Look how late I am." The Forest Brothers relaxed, put away their guns and continued where they'd left off. The girls went into the back room. In a few minutes, the door to the corridor opened soundlessly and two NKVD men stood there with automatics cocked shouting: "*Ruki verkh!*" ("Hands up!")

The Forest Brothers froze in shock for a fraction of a second. Paas lunged for his gun in the corner, but was immediately punctured by a burst of automatic fire. Liiv jumped to the window, smashing it and making his way outside. The agents fired at him as he ran through the yard. They hit him about twenty paces from the house and he fell dead on the field.

And so these two young Forest Brothers, who had promised themselves never to be taken alive by the enemy, perished because of this Judas-like betrayal.

The motives that drove women to collaboration with the enemies of their people will never be clear. In some cases, it was the matter of a husband being eliminated from a "love triangle" or a woman falling in love with an NKVD or destruction battalion man.

Occasionally, the fate of a female spy sent into the woods by the NKVD took an unexpected turn. The task of exposing one of Valgamaa County's most cold-blooded Forest Brothers Karl Täht was assigned to a young girl who fell hopelessly in love with the daring partisan and confessed all to him. A series of bold attacks against local security apparatus collaborators followed. Täht was the target of several raids, but he and the girl always managed to escape. Finally, a wounded Täht and his sweetheart were secretly transported to Valga City, where they went into hiding. However, someone betrayed them. The house was surrounded and Täht was ordered to surrender. He fired at them in response, but seeing that there was no escape, shot and killed his sweetheart at her request, and then turned the gun on himself. An apartment superintendent relates Karl Täht's final words to be recorded by history: "Our love will last beyond death."

Chance played a large part in the incidents of those days. One such event happened in Vastseliina Town, where there was a small café on the corner across from the pharmacy. You could get vodka, beer, and snacks there. An NKVD detachment based in Vastseliina had been conducting raids against the Forest Brothers.

One day the NKVD received word that a Forest Brother, presumably the partisan unit's leader, was in the café drinking beer. The NKVD immediately sent its chief lieutenant to seize the man. The lieutenant told his men not to kill the partisan, but to take him alive, since he was purported to be an important Forest Brother and thus a source of valuable information. The detachment's chief lieutenant and one soldier entered the café and two men stayed by the door with weapons cocked, while the rest surrounded the building. The café was nearly empty. Two or three people stood at the counter, and one heavy man of average height, dressed in ordinary country clothes, sat at a small table.

The lieutenant marched up to the man and demanded his identity papers. The man was indeed a Forest Brother and he immediately realized the danger he was in. Rising slowly, he pretended to pull his papers from his pocket, but then in a flash shoved the table at the lieutenant and his soldier. The soldier fell to the floor. The lieutenant took several shots from the partisan's revolver and collapsed in a heap. Realizing that the doorway was blocked, the brave Forest Brother smashed a window and jumped into the street, but the rattle of automatic weapons claimed his life. Both the Forest Brothers and the NKVD troops lost their leaders that day.

For lack of sufficient armaments, the Forest Brothers often had to rely on their own cunning. Many of them gained fame by their truly fantastic escapes from the most hopeless situations.

Once, the NKVD got hold of a Forest Brother named Lumi. They tortured and beat him to make him reveal the location of his unit. Finally, Lumi agreed to reveal the bunkers where the others were hiding. A truckful of NKVD troops rode into the forest with him. The Võru city security chief Major Moskalenko rode along, hoping to take part in neutralizing a large group of bandits. When they reached the forest, Lumi was tied to one end of a long rope, with the major holding the other end. The security troops followed in single file with weapons cocked. As the men continued through the woods toward the alleged bunker site, Lumi managed to jerk himself free of the major's grasp and run. The soldiers opened fire, but in their excitement they forgot that their major was in front of them and shot him dead.

Some men were genuine escape artists. Eeri Killar of Rõuge Parish was particularly renowned for his abilities.

It's really not too hard to escape. You just have to be clever and audacious. Once when they caught me, it looked like I was in real trouble. There was a whole bunch of those destruction battalion men. Since I was a marked man, they watched me like hawks. I wanted to put them off guard, and so I made myself limp and pretended I was drunk. I kept blabbering and chattering as they carried me into the township hall. They put me in a room with one door and no windows. Several men sat guard at the door and the rest went to get a car. This was my only chance. I staggered out of the room and right up to the guards, hiccuping with laughter. They asked me, "What the hell are you laughing about? You're in deep trouble." I giggled: "Some jail guards you are, locking me up in a room and leaving the back door wide open."

"What door?" — and they all stampeded into the room to check on the open door. Of course there was no

door, but by the time they realized it, I was over the
fence and gone.

One of the most successful methods in the security apparatus's
fight against the Forest Brothers was the creation of "false" Forest
Brothers. Professional security agents and their families were sent to
live in areas known to be teeming with Forest Brother activity, and
these agents soon began "helping" the Forest Brothers. An even more
frequent tactic was the infiltration of security agents into Forest
Brothers units. These men were true professionals who were nearly
impossible to distinguish from true Forest Brothers. These "false"
Forest Brothers lived peacefully for some time within the units, taking
part in operations and all aspects of partisan life, all the while finding
out all the helpers of the Forest Brothers, their ties with other groups,
the locations of their storehouses and bunkers. When his reconnaissance work was done, the "false" Forest Brother would draw his
colleagues into a security forces' trap.

The informer's work, however, did not always bring about the
desired consequences. Farmer Leo Mandel of Kõlleste Parish, who
maintained good relations with the local Forest Brothers, passed
information on them to security forces Captain O., who was working
in Võrumaa County on special assignment. With three sleighfuls of
destruction battalion troops, Captain O. led raids on the designated
farms. The State Security Committee archives have preserved the
following report of the operation:

> On February 27, 1946, we received reports that the
> members of the Täpsi Forest Brother group might be at
> Paul Nasala's place in Kõlleste Parish of Võru County.
> Captain O., who had been posted to Valgjärve, went to
> investigate the reports along with the Valgjärve People's
> Defense Unit of nine men.
>
> They inspected Osvald Pilviste's, Paul Nasala's, and
> Oskar Viin's farms, but found no Forest Brothers. Riding
> their sleighs from the Savimäe farm toward Heisri For-
> est, the column was surprised by machine gun fire from
> the forest.
>
> Popular Defense soldier Arved Vaha was seriously
> wounded and died on the way to the parish Executive
> Committee building. Because of the darkness, no track-
> ing was attempted.

An inspection of the ambush site showed two ski
tracks leading from the Savimäe farm. The owner, Oskar
Viin, was arrested and taken to the Executive Committee
building for interrogation. After asking to use the toilet,
Viin escaped, but was fatally wounded by a convoy
about 150 meters from the building.

Forest Brothers Voldemar Piho and Kalev Arro, who had been
warned by the farmer's fourteen-year-old son, had led the ambush
against the destruction battalion troops. In retaliation, the authorities
engulfed the entire village with a wave of arrests. The Forest Brothers
soon learned the identity of the informer. The following week, they
struck at Mandel's home. Mandel's wife was killed by a stray bullet
in the gun battle, but the traitor managed to flee, and was forced to
leave Kooraste.

Over time, the security apparatus acquired sufficient experience
in dealing with the Forest Brothers, and their failures became fewer.
They succeeded in pinpointing the location of many Forest Brother
bunkers. Then they surrounded the entire area with Interior Ministry
forces and raided the bunkers with specially trained assault platoons.
The platoons were instructed to scatter the Forest Brothers from the
bunker and force them to retreat. As the Forest Brothers drew back
from the assault platoons, they were met by an ambush that cut them
down with heavy crossfire.

All too often, the Forest Brothers were unable to offer any resistance at all. Recollections gathered in Vastseliina Parish describe a
typical tragic incident of those days:

In the woods near Suuremetsa-Aesaare, four men
were evading the Russian mobilization. They lived
quietly, not bothering anyone or stealing anything. They
didn't need to, because they got food at their homes
nearby. They went home secretly at night to get supplies,
and hung around in the forest or bunker during the day.
We don't know exactly who found their bunker, but
some traitor informed local Party secretary Sibul of its
location.

Sibul immediately summoned some NKVD men
from Võru, and the security troops led by Secretary Sibul
crept to the bunker in the dark of night. No one was
standing guard, because their area was quiet and they
were fugitives who never bothered anyone. Normally,

Valdemar Valdas spent the night at home. He lived with
his mother and usually slept at home, but he stayed in
the woods that fateful night after drinking with his buddies. The NKVD could have easily arrested those sleepy,
half-drunk men, but they were so scared of the Forest
Brothers that they went along with Sibul's suggestion to
kill them in their sleep. The NKVD unit leader had suggested they be taken alive, but Secretary Sibul said that
they were dangerous bandits. And so a shameful and
monstrous murder was carried out at the local Party
secretary's instructions. They simply shot the sleeping
men to death from the threshold of the bunker.

The Soviet security forces did not always succeed in surprising
the Forest Brothers. Most Forest Brother units had a round-the-clock
guard who could signal the arrival of danger. Many of the battles that
ensued raged for hours as the Forest Brothers tried to break out of the
siege. If escape appeared to be impossible, the partisans made sure
that their lives were paid for dearly by the other side.

Forest warden Leo Lulla lived in Virumaa County with his family.
In 1944, his son had fought in battles against the Red army invading
Estonia. After the country was occupied, he was forced to go into
hiding. The Lulla residence was now subjected to repeated searches
and raids. The house was pillaged and their belongings carried away.
Finally, a good neighbor came to warn them that the entire family was
soon to be arrested. What happened after that is related by Leo Lulla's
daughter Aino:

> Father said that he hadn't raised his children to be
> sent into slavery in Siberia. We went to hide in the for-
> ests. We left my sixty-year-old aunt, who lived with us
> after evacuating from Narva during the war, at home.
> The authorities interrogated my aunt repeatedly and
> asked her where we were. They confiscated all our live-
> stock and equipment.
>
> The first night, we slept in the forest by a campfire.
> Mother and Father tended the fire so that it wouldn't go
> out. We thawed the ground with the fire so that we could
> dig a bunker. We even put a stove in the bunker, but it
> smoked badly. So we stayed outside while the stove was
> being heated. We dug a well near the swamp for water. A
> kettle stood outside to cook soup and porridge, which

made up our basic diet. We camouflaged the area around the bunker with fir trees. We gathered berries and mushrooms for those good people who helped us during our stay in the forest. We took our goods to a hiding place in the forest, where they brought us food in exchange. All the farms near the forest were under surveillance. To cover our tracks, we built a new hut near Sorumäe. It was better than the other one, because we could bake bread and cook jam there.

Ants Lepp's wife had stolen a cow from the village. Ants himself was a Forest Brother. To "redeem herself," the woman betrayed our location — a real "good deed!" In return, she wasn't arrested. But they came after us with a tank, but it got stuck in the swamp. Some of the troops stayed to drag the tank out of the swamp, and the rest came after us. We started fleeing back to Pärnassaare. There was snow on the ground and they followed our tracks.

In Pärnassaare, we had a good bunker with grenade nets and an emergency escape route into the swamp. We could shoot in every direction from our bunker. They thought there were lots of partisans in our bunker and brought in more forces. Of 200 raiders, forty-eight were killed.

Father ordered us children to flee, promising to hold off the soldiers so they wouldn't catch us. And so I ran, holding my sister by the hand, for two kilometers. When she got tired, I put her on my back. I held a revolver in my hand. Before I reached the village, I threw the gun into a ditch so I wouldn't attract attention.

Father and Mother stayed in the bunker. There was no escape for them. Father put a gun in his mouth and killed himself. The soldiers poked Mother's eyes out with a bayonet. You could hear her screams of pain all the way to the village. Night fell, and it got dark. My sister and I had escaped this time. . . but Father and Mother? Mother was forty-four years old, Father was sixty.

Occasionally, some Forest Brothers succeeded in breaking out of security force sieges. A large number of active partisans had gathered in southern Estonia along the Latvian border. They attacked Soviet military personnel and killed several Soviet security agents who had terrorized the local population. But the retaliatory strike was not long in coming. Kalju Kirbits, a resident of Rõuge and helper of the Forest Brothers, recalls:

> A couple of my friends had a bunker near Kabli by the Latvian border. One night, there was an unexpected knock on my door. I opened it and there was one of the men from the Kabli bunker, all bloody and covered with mud. After recovering, he told me this.
>
> "Several truckloads of Russian soldiers attacked our bunker yesterday around noon. They had planned to take us by surprise, but our lookout managed to sound an alarm. We withdrew into the bunker and opened fire from our machine guns through the loopholes. Then the security men started to crawl closer and tried to toss some grenades into the bunker, but we had some nets set up to bounce them off. Finally, they succeeded in destroying the net. Then Ants Looga jumped out of the bunker with his light machine gun and mowed down the first line of attackers. When he took a shell splinter in his side, we dragged him back into the bunker and kept firing. By nightfall, only two of us remained and our ammunition was running low, but the raiders were hardly faring better. As darkness fell, we heard the roar of a truck: apparently, the forces were going for reinforcements. We had no choice but to break out. We did it quietly and in different directions. I stumbled onto a guard, but I took care of him quietly with a knife and broke out of the siege that way."
>
> "The man's wounds were superficial and he was on his feet very soon. He met his end like many other Forest Brothers: a year later, he was caught in a security forces ambush and was shot to death."

Frequently, the invading forces suffered heavy casualties under partisan fire. In 1946, a battalion of soldiers attacked a small Forest Brothers unit in the Viru-Kudina district of Virumaa County. The Forest Brothers, being keenly familiar with the local terrain, went into hiding and prepared to engage in battle. The first line of attackers was mowed down straight across a field. This created confusion in the ranks of the raiders, at which time the Forest Brothers took up different positions to prepare for the next assault. The Soviet security forces lost more than fifty men. The battle ended at nightfall with the Forest Brothers breaking out of the siege. The following year, however, those same Forest Brothers fell victim to betrayal. They were brutally tortured and finally shot to death.

Similar battles took place in other areas of Estonia. One of the most famous is the attack on the bunker of the Lumi brothers near Vastseliina Parish. The bunker had been built in a hillock in the middle of a clearing next to a village. The hillock was almost entirely hollow and well supplied. The entire village knew of its existence, but no one betrayed it. Nevertheless, the Soviet security forces succeeded in capturing a Forest Brother's daughter, who was tortured so brutally that she finally agreed to reveal the bunker to the authorities. The battalion that was sent to raid the bunker made a careless approach across the open clearing. The partisans, who had seen the attack coming, let the raiders come near and then opened fire with several heavy machine guns. The battalion commander was the first to fall. In the ensuing confusion, some of the partisans succeeded in breaking through the siege on horseback. Several of the men, staying behind to cover their comrades' escape, continued firing at the invaders until their ammunition ran out. They then blew themselves up with grenades.

The fiercest battles raged in situations where the Forest Brothers realized from the start that they had no hope of escape. On April 1, 1946, the Soviet security apparatus received reports that "bandits" had been sighted near the Määritsa farm in Sõmerpalu Parish of Võrumaa County. The army and security detachments assembled quickly, and surrounded the farm with the help of ten destruction battalion men. Reinforcements arrived soon. By the end of the operation, there were two hundred men with antitank guns, heavy machine guns, and even two cannons outside the farm. The partisans trapped in the Määritsa farmhouse responded to demands for surrender with gunfire when they realized that escape was impossible. They hoisted a national flag out the window and kept firing.

To break the resistance, the attackers had no choice but to set the farmhouse on fire. Its charred remains held the bodies of about ten people, including the master and mistress of the farm. In the farmhouse stove was found a bottle containing a letter calling on the Estonian people to continue their struggle against the occupiers.

The Estonian Forest Brothers knew how to fight and how to die. The forces, however, were unevenly matched. Every fallen KGB soldier was replaced by another, while the Forest Brothers had no resources to replenish their ranks. According to the authorities, 414 armed partisan units comprising 2,386 members, along with 2,833 armed isolated Forest Brothers had been eliminated in the years 1945 and 1946. In addition, 5,868 former Forest Brothers had been "legalized" (i.e., had left the forests and resumed life and work in society). By November 1947, 8,468 Forest Brothers had been "neutralized" (i.e., killed or imprisoned) and 6,600 had been "legalized." Presumably, this same rate — about 3,000 Forest Brothers taken out of commission every year — continued until the end of the decade.

These were serious losses. By 1948, the intensification of partisan activity had subsided. The movement slowly began to dissipate.

Chapter 9

The Last Stand

The weakening of the Forest Brothers movement provided ample opportunity for the occupation authorities to take decisive steps toward "sovietizing" Estonia once and for all. As long as independent Estonian farms, farmers, and peasants still existed, a Soviet system could not take root. To destroy private farming and establish the collectivization of agriculture, nothing was as effective as mass terror, which now took the form of new deportations. In 1940 and 1941, deportations had already been conducted in the territories allocated to Soviet control by the Molotov-Ribbentrop Pact. In 1944 and 1945, several Turkic peoples accused of collaboration with the Germans were deported almost in their entirety. Deportations, carried out on a large enough scale, did indeed paralyze the people's ability to resist. First, however, the authorities needed to deal a final blow to the resistance movement.

In the spring of 1949, the time was ripe for the elimination of all "*kulaks* and bourgeois nationalist elements" from the Baltic States. The Soviet authorities had begun compiling the lists of people to be deported in 1947 and 1948, adding the finishing touches in early 1949. In 1948, Estonian Communist Party First Secretary Nikolai Karotamm and the Chairman of the ESSR Council of Ministers Arnold Veimer proposed relocating the *kulaks* to the ESSR's oil shale regions and enacting strict passport laws to keep them there. Moscow refused to support this plan and the leaders of Soviet Estonia rushed to reconsider their proposal. On January 15, 1949, Nikolai Karotamm compiled a revised report for Moscow describing the lack of progress in collectivizing the Estonian SSR. He reported that collectivization (i.e., the abolition of private property) could never succeed unless anti-Soviet elements were removed from Estonian soil. He wrote: "It is necessary to remove all *kulaks* and their families (as well as the families of German collaborators) from the Estonian SSR. In addition, we must forcibly relocate some antisocial and anti-Soviet elements. Thus, about 18,000 to 20,000 persons should be slated for removal." Karotamm recommended careful planning of the operation, proposing the formation of five-member teams in each county, consisting of the chief Party functionary, the chairman of the Executive Committee, a member of the security apparatus, a representative of the Interior Minister, and the Procurator. Furthermore, Karotamm suggested to Stalin that the deportations should be conducted simultaneously in Estonia, Latvia, and Lithuania before the start of spring planting in 1949.

In reality, the Committee for State Security was largely responsible for preparing and carrying out the operation. One week before the deportations, in March of 1949, Karotamm received the operations plan from Minister for State Security Boris Kumm, in which he notified the Secretary that 7,500 families would be removed from Estonia, representing a total of 22,326 persons, including 7,582 men, 9,935 women, and 4,809 children. In case security forces failed to seize some of those listed for deportation, they were to fulfill their quota of 7,500 families by seizing people from a reserve list of 1,906 families.

Each operations squad was assigned to round up four families. This required the formation of 1,897 operations squads, made up of Interior and Security Ministry workers, Interior Ministry soldiers, policemen, and 3,053 People's Defense members. Behind the scenes, the entire operation was backed up by the Soviet army.

The authorities decided to use Soviet sympathizers, Party activists, and "kolkhoz members under control" as general helpers, inventory takers, and drivers. The authorities requisitioned 2,772 vehicles to transport the families from collection sites to loading sites. Since the deportees were to be brought to collection sites by horse-drawn vehicles, 12,400 such vehicles had to be mobilized locally. Rail cars in the number of 1,079 were directed to twenty loading points in Estonia. The operation was to be carried out simultaneously in all parts of the country.

The operations plan gives no indication of how authorities had arrived at the lists of deportees. For the most part, they were compiled either directly by the security apparatus or according to its guidelines. A former Soviet activist and Komsomol member Marta Muruoja recalls the methods used in compiling a list of deportees in her area:

> A county representative came to our township. At a
> meeting, he said that we must identify, in the villages, all
> the elements hostile to the people. According to him,
> they were obstructing the progress of our state. The

> Party secretary or the chairman of the Executive Com-
> mittee would come over and tell us: "Now write a letter
> and say that such and such a family are *kulaks*." Some
> people in our group were eager and willing to write, but
> some of them protested and asked why they should do
> something like this. They were told in no uncertain
> terms that they had to do it. The way I saw it, the list
> had already been made up and our letters were only sup-
> posed to support its accuracy. Then the officials wrote
> up a report and everything was all legal.

Although the preparations were shrouded in secrecy, many people caught wind of the plans. Some people received warnings from
friends in the township hall; others were alerted by local Forest
Brothers. Naturally, the sudden increase of trucks and rail cars did not
go unnoticed by a people who had already suffered through one wave
of deportations in 1941. The Forest Brothers watched developments
closely, warning the local people of impending deportations, offering
thousands of them temporary shelter in the woods, or advising them
to hide with friends and relatives. Unfortunately, many refused to take
their warnings seriously.

Late at night on March 24, 1949, Soviet activists, Party members,
Executive Committee workers, and destruction battalion members
were called to meetings in city and township halls under the pretext of
discussions on "spring planting." Shortly before midnight, the doors
of these buildings were sealed and security forces surrounded the
buildings. Only then did the participants hear the decree of the Council
of Ministers which announced that the deportation of the families of
kulaks, "bandits," and nationalists from the Estonian SSR was about to
begin. The actual removal of these people was to be carried out by
hand-picked security workers, the most loyal Party members, and
military personnel. Others would be assigned to guide trucks over
local routes, inventory the property of the deportees, or serve as
temporary guards of the property. A Soviet activist who helped with
the deportations describes how some removals took place:

> Between eleven and midnight, the trucks rumbled
> up to the township hall, and soldiers stormed in and
> blocked the exits. The township's true-blue Communist,
> a woman who had been through the war, sat next to me.
> She put her arms around my neck and whispered,

"Matu, there must be a war going on. I'm heading for
the front; at least they'll feed me there."

The meeting wore on. I may be mistaken, but finally
it seemed that a man was speaking in Russian on the
radio. After that they told me that Stalin had announced
the deportations.

They started sending us out right away. They
divided us into brigades. The leader of our brigade was
a middle-aged Russian officer. There were about ten soldiers, armed with automatics, from Viljandi County. I
don't know where they sent our drivers, but we walked
to Alma Peet's. We walked in front with the armed soldiers behind us. Alma received us graciously. When we
finally told her why we were there, she and her oldest
daughter started to cry. The little ones were asleep. We
left two or three of the soldiers and one township official
with them and moved on.

When we got back to the township center, they had
already gone for Rosenberg, and we were sent to fetch
Janson's mother and father. Janson's mother swore at me
and Karl. She asked, "Have you already sent away your
own mother-in-law and father-in-law, and now you're
coming for us?" Janson's father cried so hard. I've seen
children cry like that and I've cried like that, with tears
just spurting out.

Not once did I hear the father say what we should
pack for them. Karl and I packed separate bags of men's
and women's clothing, because we were afraid that the
families might be separated at the station. Finally, their
bags were ready and the men carried them to the
sledges. I remember Janson's mother kneeling on the
sledge and his father crying bitterly.

Indeed, all of Estonia was flooded with tears. People were hunted
like animals. Those trying to flee were fired upon. The whole operation was a brutal manhunt. Many trying to escape were felled by
bullets; some were hunted with bloodhounds. On the third day of the
deportations, a bloody body mauled beyond recognition by dogs was
tossed into a rail car at Mõisaküla. No one recognized him at first, and
it wasn't until the deportees had reached Russia that someone realized
that this was the former Abja Township elder Jaan Raavel. The
wounded man lived a few days longer and finally died. He had

nothing with him but a small tattered suitcase, held tightly in his grip. The suitcase was in shreds, little more than a frame, its contents gone.

At one Võrumaa County farm, a deportation squad found the family and their friends sitting at a wake, mourning the death of the master of the farm. After the deportation squad had loaded the mourners into the truck, they stabbed the departed master with a bayonet as he lay in his coffin, just to make sure he was not playing dead.

No trace of human kindness seemed to be left on earth. Deportation squads rudely awakened sleeping women and children. No one was shown any mercy, neither women nor the elderly. Legless old men and bedridden invalids were tossed into trucks with all the rest. Some old people were betrayed into giving themselves up: they were summoned to the township hall, arrested, and loaded into rail cars. These elderly, finding themselves later in the Siberian wasteland with neither food nor warm clothing, rarely lived through the year.

Many people preferred death to a life of suffering in Siberia. Some hanged themselves in a back room; others took poison. A particularly tragic event is recorded in Põdrala Township of Valgamaa County, where the famed marksman Jaan Mihkelson lived with his parents.

> On March 25, 1949, Mihkelson rode to the Helme Parish market with his father. Several trucks passed them on the way, but he didn't learn that deportations were under way until they reached Tõrva City. Mihkelson and his father quickly turned their sleigh around and sped back home.
>
> The wave of deportations had already taken its toll at their farm. Mihkelson's mother had been taken away. The local activists were behaving imperiously in the house, registering the *kulak's* property, or rather, dividing it among themselves. Mihkelson drew out the pistol he always carried, sending the activists scurrying off to summon reinforcements. He then grabbed an automatic they'd left behind and fired a few bursts after them. In anguish, Jaan Mihkelson went into the barn, killed all the animals, and then set the barn on fire. Then he shot his father, torched all the rest of the farm buildings, waited until the fires were roaring, and then took his own life.

The inhuman brutality of the deportation squads was often fed by primitive fear. Indeed, there are some reports of drivers who had been working all day long being ordered to turn the sledges around toward their own farms to load up their own families. The brigadiers kept a close eye on the local activists, writing up the slightest evidence of human compassion in later reports. And yet, anyone could have shown some concern for what was happening to his fellow human beings. For instance, a CPE Central Committee report relates the following:

> Ennu Sau, working as secretary of the Party organi-
> zation in Leevi Township, criminally avoided taking
> part in the elimination of the *kulak* class on March 25 and
> 26, 1949. After receiving his instructions, Ennu Sau left
> the township Executive Committee building and began
> to imbibe alcohol, refusing to return to the township
> Executive Committee building despite several calls.
> Instead, he summoned the township's Young Commu-
> nist League secretary Sepman, who responded to his
> request, thereby removing himself from the operation
> and starting to imbibe alcohol with Sau and his wife.
> During the drinking party, they decried the policies of
> the Party and the Soviet government calling for the elim-
> ination of *kulaks* as a class.

Unfortunately, such incidents were the exception rather than the rule.

The exact number of people deported on March 25 and 26, 1949, remains unknown to this day. One thing is clear, however: The number of families deported exceeded the number prescribed in the plan. According to official reports, 7,785 families were forcibly relocated, including 4,507 men (most of them elderly), 10,274 women, and 5,717 children. It is obvious that the quota was exceeded mostly at the expense of women and children. The proportion of women, children, and elderly among the deportees exceeded 90 percent. These deportees were sent to live in the sparsely populated expanses of Siberia, where many of them, particularly the very old and very young, died of hunger and disease within the first few years. Some of the children had been deported to Siberia in 1941, returned to Estonia, and shipped back to Siberia in 1949.

The Forest Brothers were powerless to prevent these large-scale deportations. The situation was similar in Latvia and Lithuania. Attacks on deportation vehicles could easily harm the deportees, and the Forest Brothers were no match for the well-armed squads that accompanied the transports. And yet, the Forest Brothers took on deportation squads in many areas. For instance, in Iisaku Township in Virumaa County, a group of security operatives went to seize the Forest Brother leader Rabin, who opened fire on the approaching squad and was shot to death in the ensuing battle. On March 25, 1949, one Forest Brothers unit fired on an Interior Ministry patrol on its way to deport local families, and destroyed railway semaphores near Kadrina Township in Virumaa County. In Rannu Parish of Tartumaa County, a Forest Brother from Virumaa County stumbled upon a group of Communist activists taking inventory of a deported family's belongings. He shot them all. The man became the target of a large-scale manhunt, and finally was forced to surrender a few kilometers away in the forest.

Still, thousands of people managed to evade the security forces that came to deport them. Many were already in hiding with the Forest Brothers; others escaped directly from the hands of the deportation squads. Usually, however, such escapes did not save them from imprisonment. The sister of some men hiding in the forest, Taimi Kreitsberg, explains:

> On March 28, 1949, at 5:30 in the morning, the deportation squads showed up at our house. We were given an hour and a half to pack. They took us, my sick mother and me, with our own horse to the Varstu Village Council building near the mill. As soon as we arrived, I asked to use the toilet. When I realized that none of the soldiers were coming with me, I ran across the stream into the woods. They fired at me but missed. I went into Hargla to my relatives', but they were afraid to shelter me. I returned to my home village, wet and frozen. That night, I met up with Arno Vahesaar, who hid me under the blanket on his sleigh and took me to Richard Karisoot's. A few days later, my brother came to get me and took me to a bunker at Lihtniidu, where I became a forest dweller.
>
> We lived there the whole summer. In the fall, the situation was getting dangerous. My brother Leo was sure they'd conduct some big raids in the winter and I'd be killed. They took me to Kaika on a wagon. I lived there until my brothers were arrested. Then those people were afraid to keep me anymore. What could I do? Where could I go? I went to the Varstu Village Council building

to give myself up. They threw me in prison. They took
me to Antsla security, where I saw the informer Hillar
Roomus. They interrogated me in Antsla. Then they
took me to Võru City, where they didn't beat me, but
just left me without food or water for three days. They
said, "We won't kill you. We'll just torture you until you
expose all the bandits."

For about a month, they dragged me around the forests and the farms of the Forest Brothers' relatives, sending me into the farmhouses as a provocateur to ask for
food and shelter while the chekists waited outside. I
always told the people, "Send me away. Security made
me come in here." Finally, the security forces realized
that I was of no use, and they handed me over to some
Russian soldiers to be raped. I wasn't quite sixteen then.

In 1949, something had been shattered inside the nation's soul.
Within a few months, Estonia was collectivized and private farms
were eliminated. Naturally, this process caused an economic catastrophe, but the Soviet regime was unconcerned. It was interested only in
subjecting the captive nations to its totalitarian system. And yet, the
deportations did not immediately destroy the armed resistance movement. On the contrary, they made it grow.

The forests filled with people who no longer had anything to lose.
Their homes had been looted; their families had been murdered or
sent to Siberia. The only thing that kept many of them going was the
desire for revenge. "Better to die here than in Siberia!" became the
slogan.

A wave of brutal killings swept across Estonia. The Forest Brothers stalked and murdered collaborators. Many who had actively
assisted in the deportations were locked into their homes by the
partisans, doused with gasoline, and set afire. Up to now, the partisans
had rarely killed the families of political opponents, but now the
Forest Brothers, crazed with desperation, frequently failed to differ-
entiate among man, woman, or child. The nation's pain was at its
peak; its anguish had reached its limits.

The entire Forest Brothers movement livened. New, more skillful
and professional units formed, which planned their activities more
carefully. In the fall of 1949, they robbed banks and money shipments
in many parts of Estonia, and raided cooperative stores and dairies.
They were particularly eager to track down the security workers and
Soviet activists who had played an active part in the deportations. The

people knew all too well who they were. Documents found in the KGB archives contain repeated expressions of regret about the untimely demise of those comrades who had been most active in "eliminating the *kulak* class" in Estonia. The Forest Brothers apprehended some higher security officials as well — for instance, the security chief of Järvamaa County, who was executed in the forest after trial and sentencing. The sudden surge of Forest Brothers' activity caused deep concern among the Soviet authorities. The CPE Central Committee issued a new directive ordering the rapid elimination of the Forest Brothers movement. For a while, the directive was to remain no more than a piece of paper.

In reality, the peak of the Forest Brothers movement had already passed by this time. The indifference shown by the West toward the deportations made the Forest Brothers realize that they could hope for little help from that part of the world. Alfred Käärmann describes the feelings of that time in his memoirs:

> The most gullible of us kept hoping that the Western Allies wouldn't leave Estonia under Russian rule. According to the Atlantic Charter, all nations that were independent before the war were to regain their independence. Our people placed their hopes on America, England, the United Nations, on their "white ship" of hope, on the departure of the Russians . . . and these stupid hopes sent thousands of Forest Brothers to their deaths . . . not only in Estonia, but tens of thousands more in Latvia and Lithuania. Few of us were able to think clearly, to draw conclusions from what was happening. There really were plenty of clues. For his seventieth birthday, history's greatest butcher, Stalin received good wishes and gifts from all over the world. Moscow celebrated. And the ass-lickers in Estonia would not be outdone: They gave Stalin a huge crystal vase ("to hold all the blood being spilled") and an Estonian concert piano ("to drown out the screams of the victims"). All this, of course, to "Estonia's great friend" on behalf of all the Estonian people. On behalf of the Kazakh people, Stalin was given a huge keg of fermented horse milk. Our Forest Brothers were sure that we'd be hearing lots of farting from the Kremlin.
>
> The Western countries found out about the 1949 deportations. The radio stations broadcast the statements

of the Archbishop of Canterbury about the deportations. He said: "The methods used against the Baltic fascists by the Soviet Union were justified." I wish I could now put a wreath of barbed wire on his grave, along with Stalin's portrait and these words of his!

Why, then, did the battles and the resistance continue? Perhaps Alfred Käärmann answers the question most clearly:

> And what was this drive that forced us, the last Forest Brothers, to stay in hiding? I'll tell you: We knew that as long as we were still breathing, holding a gun, and feeling Estonia's soil beneath our feet, everything was all right. We knew that our captured comrades had it much worse. We knew that we were booked for a one-way ticket to Siberia. We knew that a bullet from our own gun would save us from enemy torture. This is the option that was chosen by Evald Kont, Karl Täht, Enn Luhtmaa, Henning, and many other partisans.

The security apparatus, having "successfully" carried out the deportations, suddenly realized the extent of its power. Its forces had rarely combed the forests before, but now the units began systematically scouring the wooded countryside. In the frequent surprise encounters that followed, both sides suffered heavy losses. Some encounters, however, passed without claiming many victims. A quick battle fought in Võrumaa is recalled by Alfred Käärmann:

> That fall, three of us lived in a temporary shack, planning to build a bunker. It was me, Kangro, and Kangro's wife. One morning they went to find something to eat and I was on lookout. Suddenly I heard something like an animal crashing through the underbrush. I clutched my automatic tighter and then he appeared — a Russian soldier looking all around him, gun hanging on his shoulder. When he saw me, he froze and paled. He said, "Hello." I said, "Hello, who are you?" He answered, "I'm a topographer." I said, "Come closer and let me see what kind of topographer you might be." And then I saw that he was slowly bringing the barrel of the gun downward. I let him have it. The man sank to the ground, and heavy gunfire broke out all

around. I threw myself down. Kangro and his wife were
already behind me, guns in hand. Kangro yelled, "Who
are you firing at? I don't see anyone." I replied, "Shoot
where you see the treetops swaying." And then we let
them have it. Suddenly it was all quiet. We heard nothing but the thunder of running feet and the clank of
guns against the trees. We had no time to lose. We had to
get out of there before they came back with reinforcements. We picked up our stove between us and took off.

Not all encounters ended so fortunately. In 1949, security forces
succeeded in apprehending the famed partisan "Ants the Terrible" in
Pärnumaa County. A tribunal sentenced him to death by shooting
along with three of his companions in 1951.

In Võrumaa County, the death of legendary Forest Brother
Haljand Koovik was a terrible loss. There was a farm near Pühajärve
Lake where Haljand Koovik had a sweetheart. Everyone knew what
was going on, but no one betrayed them. The security apparatus put
a unit on surveillance duty at the farm. Nothing happened for a few
weeks, but then Koovik showed up with a bodyguard. The guards let
Koovik and his man enter the house, but when the two emerged in
the morning, the area had been surrounded by several circles of
troops. The two men were told to raise their hands, but Koovik
grabbed his automatic and started to break through, with him and his
adjutant covering each other. The security force troops were too close
to each other and couldn't shoot if they didn't want to hit their own
men. Koovik stormed toward the forest, automatic blazing. The security men in the line on that side were unnerved by this action and let
Koovik pass through their line. It seemed that he would make it to the
forest but the bullets got him just as he reached the woods. The
adjutant succeeded in dragging Koovik to shelter in the forest. We
don't know what happened next. According to the adjutant's report,
Koovik died there of his wounds. The bodyguard left his chief's body
and fled. For such cowardice, the adjutant Forest Brother was punished with a "boycott" of several months, meaning he had to live alone
in the forest without any human contact.

Koovik's fate remains unclear, because it seems that he aroused
such fear in the security forces that no one dared follow the mortally
wounded man into the woods to see what had become of him. In their
report, the security troops crossed out Koovik's name to indicate that
he had been eliminated. According to popular recollections, Koovik
was secretly buried by local people near the place of his death. Others

claim that Koovik, after declaring himself dead, simply decided to end the game and live his last days in peace and quiet under an assumed name. We'll probably never know what really happened.

In the fall of 1949, the leaders of the partisan movement as well as the most active units were targeted for attack. Security forces had hunted the Veriora Forest Brothers with particular diligence. Although they had emptied entire villages in the Veriora area, the authorities had found no one who would betray the partisans. Finally, the security apparatus succeeded in infiltrating a provocateur into the Forest Brothers' midst. The impostor found out the forest district where their bunkers were located. The authorities then launched one of the biggest raids in the history of the Võrumaa County Forest Brothers. A former resident of Veriora Parish recalls those events:

> On November 2, a major operation was launched against the Forest Brothers. Several truckloads of soldiers armed with machine guns and mortars arrived at Veriora Station from Võru City. They had three or four tanks with them. In addition to the army, there were policemen and NKVD troops. From Veriora Station the soldiers proceeded to the forest to surround the bunkers. They didn't make it until nightfall and then the battle began. It raged all night. The noise reached out here to Orava, and the flares rose above the forest as they did on the front lines during the war. Not until the morning light did the soldiers dare to raid the bunker and take it in a fierce battle. Most of the Forest Brothers did succeed in breaking through the siege, taking advantage of the densely forested terrain. They lost four men and three women. The raiding party's casualties numbered seventeen dead and a large number of wounded. The Forest Brothers had defended their bunker bravely and repulsed the attackers several times, but because of the opponent's numerical advantage and superior armaments, the partisans were forced to retreat. The wife of Captain Randlo, a man who had been sent to Siberia, was especially helpful in the partisans' escape, holding the invaders back with well-aimed fire from her machine gun. They didn't succeed in capturing the brave woman until they lobbed some grenades her way. Two other women fought and died in the battle, but their deaths were not in vain, since they killed a large

number of attackers and kept the rest under fire, allowing many Forest Brothers to escape.

The leader of the raiding party, a captain, looked bitterly at the dead woman behind the machine gun, kicked the body derisively, and said: "Damned whore! Killed a lot of my men." They captured a woman named Roots in the bunker with an infant. Several of her brothers had been in the bunker. Some of them escaped, but one fell wounded into enemy hands and he was dragged across the tree stumps until dead. The captured Forest Brothers were taken to Veriora Station. The Forest Brothers who had escaped the siege tried to attack the Veriora railway station the next day to free the prisoners, but failed because they were far outnumbered by the soldiers in the station.

Similar battles raged throughout Estonia. Although the raiding parties suffered serious losses, they achieved their goal of destroying the bunkers. The security apparatus could subvert the dominant groups more easily once they succeeded in infiltrating one of their agents into them. Voldemar Piho's partisan unit was wiped out this way. The files of the security apparatus preserve the following report:

Our agent Metsis initiated contact with the Piho unit on September 24, 1949 through Salusaar, the owner of the Tasa farm. First he met Feliks Kilgas, then Kalev Arro, Voldemar Piho, and others. The unit was based in the Todu-Soru Forest in Kiidjärve Parish of Tartumaa County. They were planning to kill the Kiidjärve People's Defense commander Lill and the Communist Party member Hinno, and to steal the Ülenurme *sovhoz* payroll.

On September 30, the bandits sent Metsis to reconnoiter Ülenurme *sovhoz*. He contacted us and we decided to launch the operation that very night. At 8:00 p.m., we established a secret liaison center on the way to the bandits' camp with Metsis's help. We agreed that if there were no bandits at the encampment, Metsis would contact us at the secret site in a couple of hours. If the bandits were there, he would report to the secret site at 5:00 the next morning.

At 11:50 p.m., the chief of the liaison center First Lieutenant Üksik reported that fifteen minutes after Metsis's departure, three bandits had passed by the secret communications center on their way to fetch a sheep from the farm. They had been discussing their return route.

At 6:00 a.m., Metsis returned to the liaison center. He told us he'd left the encampment at 4:30 a.m. on the pretext of going to fetch some milk. He had spent a lot of time covering his trail and looking for possible surveillance. Metsis was sure that he had not been followed.

He said that there were eight bandits at the camp who were not sleeping but waiting for someone to arrive. Since daybreak was near, we could wait no longer. With Metsis's help, we surrounded the encampment. Since the bandits were awake, they noticed our movements and opened fierce automatic weapons fire on us. Our heavy machine gun overwhelmed their fire for a while. When we stopped our heavy machine gun fire and demanded surrender, they opened fire once more, threw grenades, and tried to break through the siege. Their attempt to escape failed. The battle lasted an hour. Our casualties: two seriously wounded men.

Of the bandits, the leader of the terrorist band Voldemar Piho (alias August), Feliks Kilgas (alias Einar), and five others were killed. The dead bandits include "Vello," "Leo," and "Ants." We don't know the names of the men with the aliases Jaak and Vunts.

At the battle site, the security troops confiscated six automatic weapons, one carbine, six pistols, eight grenades, 600 cartridges, three binoculars.

The facts presented in this report do not represent the whole truth however. According to the recollections of the local population, the raiding party lost nearly ten men in addition to the two wounded. Most important of all, one Forest Brother — Kalev Arro — succeeded in breaking through the siege. Since the commander of the operation did not want to spoil his report by noting a failure, he simply crossed out Arro's name, indicating that the man had been eliminated.

The Forest Brothers carried on tenaciously in spite of their heavy losses. Their numbers diminished. The remnants of several shattered groups united among themselves, forming new groups that represented a special danger to the Soviet security apparatus. By this time, the forests held only the true "professionals" whose sufferings had deadened any feelings of mercy. These men placed increasing emphasis on acts of political terror. They now hunted Soviet security workers with a special vengeance. In 1949, the Võrumaa County Forest Brothers ambushed one of the highest-ranked specialists of Estonia's Soviet security apparatus, Colonel Eduard Sisas, and killed him during a gun battle. Sisas had played an active role in the liquidation of the Armed Resistance League, receiving the title of "merited chekist"[*] for his successful fight against the Forest Brothers. Security forces responded to partisan hits with raids on the entire district, sending some of the Forest Brothers to their death and others deeper into hiding.

One of the most well-known groups at that time in Võrumaa was "Orion," led by Jaan Roots. The men in this group had fled to the forests to escape deportation. They had lost a large number of family members and friends to this tragedy in the first half of 1949. Their primary goal was revenge. "Orion" had a well-defined program of action, strong leadership and discipline, and well-planned operations. Their program foresaw the restoration of the Republic of Estonia. They set their sights on the outbreak of a new world war, which was to bring about a new popular uprising in Estonia. Until that time, they could not allow Soviet power to take root in Estonia. In order to damage Soviet authority and weaken its authority, they had to attack Soviet establishments, money shipments and cooperatives, and kill traitors and collaborators with the security apparatus.

The painful blows dealt by "Orion" caused the Soviet security apparatus to take particular interest in this group. In early July of 1950, the security apparatus received information about men living in an old peat shed in the Pille-Parkla swamp of Võrumaa County. A raiding party led by an experienced security man named Vassmann was sent to the site. The raiders unexpectedly encountered one of the Forest Brothers, Olev Kakko, whose sons were hiding at the same site. Olev Kakko let the first men go by and then fired at the officer. Vassmann fell dead. In the ensuing battle, Kakko was also killed, but his maneuver allowed the other partisans to escape. "Orion" reassembled in Kääpa Forest near Võru City, and in revenge on July 6, killed several Soviet activists collaborating with the security apparatus. "Orion" responded to each blow from the security forces with a counterattack, thus keeping the local authorities in a constant state of fear.

---

[*] "Merited" is the term commonly used to distinguish the recipient of a Soviet award or honor.

"Orion" continued to operate at the same level of activity for the next several years. The group raided stores, ambushed money shipments on the highways, and killed Soviet security force commanders, security personnel, and their collaborators. Security's attempts to infiltrate its own men into "Orion" always failed. The spies were found out and shot. "Orion" continued to suffer losses in the raids and battles, however. In 1951, the group walked into an ambush while attacking the farm of a People's Defense battalion commander. Member Rein Palosaar was killed. Despite their diminishing numbers, about ten men of the "Orion" group remained to spend the winter of 1951-1952 in a roomy bunker about half a kilometer south of the great sand cliff of Taevaskoja in Võrumaa County.

The Soviet security apparatus brought its primary forces into play to destroy "Orion." Since it was obvious that no male agents could be infiltrated into the group, they brought women into the picture. A female security collaborator who befriended the partisans informed them of a payroll that was arriving at the Veriora forestry collective. The booty was seductive. The partisans planned the operation in detail and, on June 6, the plan got under way. In Võru, the partisans hired a Pobeda taxi, but ordered the driver out in Konnametsa Forest and left him there guarded by a Forest Brother.

By this time, a special Soviet security force had placed the forestry collective under guard. No one was allowed to leave. All the workers were ordered to lie on the floor. When the Pobeda drove into the collective's courtyard, the place was quiet. Jaan Roots knocked on the door, but then spotted the security troops through a window and opened fire. The "Orion" men responded to calls for surrender with gunfire. A moment later, they were all pierced by bullets. The Soviet security forces had succeeded in destroying "Orion's" five-man core, led by Jaan Roots. Still, the Forest Brothers movement was not crushed.

By this time, the security apparatus had devised new tactics. These have been attributed to Colonel Moskalenko, who replaced Boris Kumm as the ESSR Minister of Security in 1950. Whatever the source, more and more Forest Brothers were caught by security forces in the early 1950s through poisonings. One Forest Brother who fell victim to such a poisoning recalls his experience:

> What kind of poison was it? I read a brief maga-
> zine article in which the author wrote excitedly: "Sci-
> entists have discovered a powerful agent for use in
> the capture of animals. This agent is an odorless, color-
> less, and completely flavorless but powerful liquid. It

can simply be sprayed on hay, and the animals that eat the hay will fall into such a deep sleep that they can be tied and taken wherever necessary."

How did this poison work? First it paralyzes the intellect, then it numbs the tongue, and then you lose consciousness. It seems that you lose the perception of pain along with your consciousness, because I was kicked in the chin with heavy boots, burned on the soles of my feet, and the stump of my amputated hand was bloodied. I didn't feel a thing; my memory recorded nothing. Only the injection of an antidote revived me from this death-like sleep. For several days after I'd been "brought back" from this sleep of death in Ape City, I felt like my insides had been burned. I didn't feel hunger or thirst. They didn't give me food for four days. I was overcome by extreme calm and indifference. They tried everything to get me to talk; they screamed incessant questions: "Where's the bunker? Where are the others?" The only result was that I lost consciousness in the hands of my torturers. My thought process was extremely sluggish, and my reactions have remained slow ever since that time. I'll never be able to drive a car again.

The Võrumaa County Forest Brother Alfred Käärmann relates the events that ended his freedom:

The autumn of 1952 was a rainy one. Aleksander Kangro, his wife Heini Kangro, and I had just finished building a winter bunker near the Liivaku-Mudimetsa road in a corner of Latvia, where the Estonian-Latvian border turns south toward Tambelse Village. One day in early November I visited the master of Mudimetsa farm, Ruudi Cirulis.

Why should I be suspicious of this man and his family, whom I'd known and trusted for seven years? I never bothered them much; I never even went into their house. I never asked them for anything. A couple of times each summer as I passed by I'd watch there in the forest until I saw somebody and then I'd ask them what was going on in the neighborhood. This time, it was the same story. As I was leaving, Ruudi asked: "So when are you going to stop by again?" Without suspicion, I said

I'd be by after the holidays if it didn't snow. I had no idea that this statement would be my doom.

The snow came down soon after that and stayed on the ground about a week. By the evening of November 11, the sun had melted the snow. I told my bunker companion Heini: "While you're finishing the soup, I'll go visit Ruudi and come right back." I set off; I had to go a couple of kilometers.

It was a beautifully clear and crisp fall evening. I sneaked close to the Mudimetsa farmhouse from the southwestern side. An empty grain drying hurdle stood in the yard on the northern side of the farmhouse. A slaughtered sheep was tied to the uppermost rung by its feet, and old Ruudi was skinning it there alone. No one else was in sight. I picked up a dried branch and knocked it against the trunk of a pine tree; that was our signal. Ruudi heard it, dropped his bloody knife, came over to me, and asked me to come in. I refused, saying that we could talk right there.

Ruudi told me to wait a minute while he went inside. He went. I waited and Ruudi returned in a few minutes, carrying a bottle of the Latvian vodka "Kristalldzidrais" and a common tea glass. "What's the occasion?" I asked, surprised. "My daughter Margarita just had her birthday and there was some booze left over," Ruudi replied. We sat at the edge of the forest behind some dense bushes. Ruudi poured the vodka into the glass. "Half is enough for me," I said. "I don't really care for vodka." I drank that 100 grams and now I remember how it made my head buzz. Ruudi poured the same glass full to the brim from the same bottle and drank it. We talked. Ruudi poured me about fifty grams more, because that's all I wanted, and drank the rest himself.

We'd only been together for about twenty minutes when Ruudi's oldest daughter Austra emerged from the house carrying a basket of food and a three-liter earthen mug with a brownish liquid. Austra looked at both of us and said: "Are you insane, drinking like this!" I told Austra that it wasn't much, just one bottle for the two of us. I remember that my tongue didn't want to cooperate, it was numb. I also remember I didn't eat or drink anything

else. I took my German canteen, poured some of the
brown liquid into it and screwed it shut. My hand wasn't
shaking. Then I remember how Ruudi looked at me, his
eyes overflowing with tears. After that I remember nothing, except for the western sky. The blood-red setting sun
was shining behind the treetops; the sun of my freedom
was setting then too.

I came to in the Ape security cell, where they woke
me up by kicking me.

Poison facilitated the capture of most of the remaining Forest
Brothers who worked alone or in small groups. This method was less
effective with larger groups. Near Veriora Parish, Soviet security
personnel tried to capture one group with tainted beer, but the Forest
Brothers simply accepted the goods and left for an unknown destina-
tion, leaving the generous "donors" behind. In the raid that followed,
security forces managed to seize only one Forest Brother who had
fallen asleep on a village lane; the rest apparently "slept it off" in their
bunker or got wise to what kind of drink they were dealing with. In
revenge for its failure, the security apparatus dragged nearly all of the
village's adult population into the Security Committee offices for
interrogation. The population of the village was taken away.

Slowly, the Forest Brothers movement began to subside. As the
numbers of partisans decreased steadily the Soviet security forces
could zero in on them more easily. One of Võrumaa County's last major
battles is recalled by Valdur Raudvassar, who was then a schoolboy:

In the spring of 1953, a huge battle between the Forest Brothers and the security forces took place in Puudli,
not far from the road I took to school. I was walking to
school with the boys one morning when we saw some
unfamiliar horsemen on the road. Later that morning the
noises of battle started. At first there were only isolated
gunshots, then the encirclement tightened and we heard
the rattle of automatic weapons and machine gun fire, as
well as the bursting of grenades. Suddenly, everything
went quiet, and we assumed that the Forest Brothers'
bunker had been destroyed.

A few days later, the boys and I went to look at the
battleground. The soldiers had taken away all the bodies
and the weapons, but there were cartridges all over the
place. The battle had been fierce. The partisans' bunker

had been built into a small hillock, with a well in the valley nearby. We also found a tree with sticks pounded
into it to make climbing easier. That had been the Forest
Brothers' lookout tower.

There had been six or seven Forest Brothers in the
bunker, including several women. They had lived
quietly without bothering anyone. But then, someone
had betrayed them. The partisans resisted fiercely, but
finally they were pressed into their bunker, where they
realized that all hope was lost and they blew themselves
up with grenades. The military raiding party lost more
than twenty men, with even more wounded.

We were mortified by the shattered bunker in the
hillock. We took off our hats and one of the boys said the
Lord's Prayer. We knew of nothing else we could do.

Other bunkers were destroyed about that same time. Now, there
remained only three- or four-member units of Forest Brothers without a permanent encampment. According to the Security
Committee's own files, the last battles with Forest Brothers were
fought in 1955 and 1956.

These years can be considered the final moments of widespread
armed resistance. The Soviet Union's suppression of the Hungarian
uprising and the total inactivity of the West brought an end to all
hopes for Western assistance to the captive nations. Resistance had
become meaningless. When the Soviet regime declared amnesty again
in 1956 and 1957, masses of men and women emerged from the forests.
A local resident describes how one man gave himself up in the Vändra
district of Pärnumaa County:

There was a man in our area who had lived in the
forest for a long time. They hunted him and chased him
but never caught him. When that last amnesty was
announced, he decided to give himself up. He marched
out in full regalia, with a light machine gun on his back
and an automatic in his hand, pistol at his side and grenades on his belt, into the local police station. He kicked
the door open with his foot. The police guard turned
pale, thinking the man had come to kill. But the Forest
Brother unloaded his weapons right there on the table
and said: "My war is over now."

Indeed it was. Some of the "legalized" Forest Brothers were arrested, but some were allowed to go free as an enticement for those who still refused to come out of the forests.

In 1956, Soviet tanks ended Hungary's quest for freedom. The world reacted to the tragedy with indifference, offering no more than feeble protests in response. Watching events in Hungary, the captive nations finally realized that they could expect no concrete assistance from the "Free World." However, the nascent political thaw in the Soviet Union allowed the Estonians to begin influencing political trends in their country by achieving positions in the offices of the occupation government. The thaw also opened doors for political resistance. In the late 1950s and early 1960s, secret student organizations formed the vanguard of this new trend in Estonia. From the late 1960s onward, political dissidents led the movement. Despite these new trends, there were men who stood fast by their refusal to surrender.

With the end of armed conflict, some of the Forest Brothers emerged from the forests to live legally under assumed names, but most of them were exposed before long. In one instance, Ants Aunvere, a man who was working as a road inspector in Kose in Harjumaa County, was arrested for his past partisan activity. Other former Forest Brothers were hunted and captured in Latvia.

Some men, however, continued to hide, refusing even an ostensible compromise with the occupation authorities. Although these men were fully aware of Estonia's current status in world affairs, they still refused to abandon resistance. Perhaps we will never know exactly how many of these men there were. They were destined to die nameless on a forgotten front. Not until recently has the veil of secrecy begun to rise from the events of those days. The best approach is a chronological review of the events about which we have information.

It is the year 1964. Early that year, newspapers carry the story of two brothers, Aksel and Arnold Ojaste, who hid themselves for nineteen years in the Jõgeva district. They have been fully amnestied by the authorities after their voluntary departure from the forests. In May that same year, several newspapers print an article about Jüri Keskküla, who hid himself in a secret room on a farm in the Paide district of Saaremaa Island for twenty years.

On February 26, 1965, the official Estonian news agency ETA reports on the imprisonment of Forest Brother Raimond Mölder. At the initiative of the Ranna *kolkhoz* policeman Simson, a frenzied manhunt was launched in early 1965 near the Mustvee district for the "dangerous criminals and collaborators with Germany hiding themselves on the *kolkhoz* territory." Mölder was apprehended in this manhunt. Mölder did not give up without a tough fight, seriously injuring two members of the manhunt squad.

Not all such incidents were publicized. Many, such as the following story, were kept secret. In the summer of 1967, two middle-aged men in typical country clothes emerged from the southern Estonian forests near Kraavi. One of them had a suspicious bulge in his breast pocket. At the edge of the forest, they were ambushed from several sides by men in police uniform. The Forest Brothers staggered under the onslaught before they were forced to the ground. In the scuffle, one lost an automatic weapon that fell from his pocket with a clatter; the other was relieved of a nine-round Nagant revolver. The man told its new owner not to fiddle with it if he didn't want it to go off. The chief of Võrumaa County security had reason to rejoice: his squad had seized Võrumaa County's legendary Forest Brothers Hugo and Aksel Mõttus.

The events preceding this incident are described by one of the brothers:

> Väntra, our father's farm, lies right on the border of
> Võrumaa and Valgamaa Counties, in Antsla Township. It
> was a thriving farm that had been in the family for gener-
> ations. Centuries of hard work had fertilized the land
> and built grand barns, stables, and granaries. Our father
> had been the Antsla Parish elder for a number of years.
>
> There were lots of children in our family, four broth-
> ers and two sisters. Our family was harmonious and
> happy, although our mother and some of the children
> fell victim to a dreaded disease — tuberculosis. In 1944,
> when the war raged in Estonia after the retreat of the
> Germans, Aksel fought on the front at Narva and was
> seriously wounded. Then he fled from the invading Red
> army, finally reaching home after a dangerous and diffi-
> cult trip. At home, the new system of government had
> already taken root. Aksel was forced to go into hiding,
> as was his older brother Hugo, who had worked as mas-
> ter of the farm.
>
> Among our brothers and sisters, Ülo and Maimu
> were marked with tuberculosis. Even though both of
> them were on file at the tuberculosis dispensary, they
> were still forced to do exhausting manual labor for the
> *kolkhoz*.

The new authorities levied heavy taxes on the farm of our father, the former parish elder. If we hadn't secretly helped him with the farm work, Father never would have managed to pay the taxes with the help of the two children still living with him. The new authorities demanded the fulfillment of ever-increasing obligations.

Ülo was forced to climb into a flax retting pool already icing over in late autumn to throw out the flax remaining in its bottom. After that, his health took a sudden turn for the worse. The *kolkhoz* refused to grant him permission to go for treatment. More and more often, they threatened him with imprisonment. Ülo no longer dared show himself in the farmyard, and he hid himself in our bunker at the slightest hint of an impending raid. Not even the endless threats and constant danger could force our farm into cooperation with the senseless destructiveness of the new regime.

There were more and more raids and ambushes on Väntra farm. Since we no longer felt safe in the bunker in our home forest, we dug a new hideout near the southern tip of Ahijärv Lake, 150 to 200 meters east of the Antsla-Saru road. In the dark of night, we chopped down a load of logs ten to twenty centimeters thick, dug a deep cave in the sand, and lined it with the logs. The roof was level with the ground. The bunker contained five bunk beds, since we didn't know when the whole family might have to seek shelter there. It was painstakingly camouflaged, so that neither it nor its entryway was visible. We also camouflaged the hearth.

On September 15, 1952 a huge raiding party headed toward Väntra. The family grabbed a few belongings and vanished into the woods. Now none of us would ever return to our home farm, not even little Maimu. We'd never be taken alive!

We had stored potatoes at our new bunker. Bread was a problem. The 1,500 rubles that Maimu had brought along were quickly spent on bread and foodstuffs in distant towns. We risked our lives to haul them back to the bunker. We learned to cover our tracks and to listen to the forest birds, particularly the oriole, because he signals the movements of any animal or person in the forest.

Life in the forest wasn't easy. Around Christmas, some wild boars came over the Latvian border and ravaged our potato stash, and the rest of our potatoes froze. We were in danger of starving. The dampness and cold of the bunker as well as hunger took their toll. On top of that, the forced inactivity in our stuffy bunker made us even weaker. Whenever we were off somewhere getting food, we were always in danger of capture, and so the others had to sit quietly in the bunker. This went on for years.

Father was the first to go. He got weak, refused to eat, and died right before Christmas in 1953. We set out through the snow and darkness of December on our difficult and dangerous journey to carry Father's body to our home forest. While we dug the grave and placed Father in the coffin, Maimu stood guard in the roadside thicket with an automatic. Because we had no ropes, we lowered the coffin into the grave with young birch trees that we had tied together at the top. These were also the only flowers to adorn Father's grave. Then we replaced the sod on the grave in its original position, so that there would be no trace of it in the spring when the snow melted.

Now we lived in the bunker in our home forest once more. It had been a long time since anyone had thought of looking for us there. But we were right in the path of some logging operations. One day, we were on one of our usual searches for food. Maimu and Ülo were in the bunker alone when the loggers reached that area. The workers removed the underbrush covering the bunker and immediately realized what they'd found. One of them saw the entry trapdoor, opened it, and realized that there were people inside. But he quietly closed the trapdoor and followed the others without a word. We returned soon after that. Our brother and sister met us outside with this awful news. What could we do? Holding our weapons tightly, we followed the loggers, who had settled down to rest by a campfire. We stepped up to them. Our message was brief: "You know who we are. If any of you breathes one word of what you've seen. . ." Fortunately, the men were not strangers. One was even a fellow student from the gymnasium. They were Estonians; they were human beings. We were left in peace.

Even so, we had to start the back-breaking work of building a new bunker, because none of us really knew whether someone would expose us or not. This time, we made a mistake by selecting a site with unbearably cold and damp clay soil. The water came in with the autumn rains. Ülo was already very sick. We also made a serious mistake by melting snow for drinking water all winter, and in the spring we could barely stand up because of mineral deficiency. Later, we dug holes in low-lying areas and drank the water that seeped in there. This water, filtered through the soil, gave us new strength.

Now we transferred our bunker into the forest near the formerly large farm of Mähkli, into a triangular thicket formed by the intersection of three roads. We had learned to prefer the proximity of roads, where no one thought to look for us, and where it was much easier to slip in and out without leaving tracks.

It was more and more dangerous to buy bread locally. We stole some bicycles and rode far into areas where no one knew of the Mõttus family. Locally, the hunt for us continued in full force. The local people saw us in the forests repeatedly. They knew quite well who was stealing from their potato bins and milk buckets — but no one said a word.

What did we do on these long winter nights in our crowded bunker? All the light we had came from a miserable little petroleum lamp that never burned properly in the stuffy air. Nevertheless, we managed to fill these long hours by reading. We took books set aside for destruction in school and public libraries. If we needed more, we'd steal them from the local library on moonlit nights. We couldn't keep our books in the bunker because of the dampness. Storing them in barrels proved to be wiser. Near each bunker, there was a hidden barrel full of books, a total of about 600 to 700. These books represented our life experiences and the education that had been cut short for all of us.

Our move into the more comfortable bunker came too late for Ülo. In the summer of 1954, he closed his eyes forever.

After our brother died, we never left our little sister in the bunker alone. Whenever we went out, she'd hide in the woods and wait, and we'd go back to the bunker together. This kind of activity, as well as living in the forest under the open sky in summer, helped Maimu regain her strength. She put up with four more years of living in the woods, but then one summer her strength gave out. She begged us to take her to our homestead. We carried our dying sister through our home forest to let her die in the farmhouse she loved. But even this small wish was to remain unfulfilled. When we got to our home forest that morning, the *kolkhoz* reapers were there harvesting the grain from the fields that used to be Väntra's, and we couldn't risk being seen. By evening, Maimu had died without ever feeling the walls of home around her again. Her final resting place is in our home forest next to our father and brother.

Times changed. We dared to come out in the open more often in distant areas. We did some work for the farmers without staying in any one spot for long. With our bikes, we rode to Viljandi and other cities to buy things. I'm sure the farmers knew they were dealing with Forest Brothers, but they never denied us work and they paid us well. We did all kinds of farm work and nobody betrayed us. We rarely associated with any other Forest Brothers. But then came the fateful summer of 1964, when we decided to go visit our old bunkers.

The Mõttus brothers were arrested and taken to Võru City, where the local investigator found their crime to merit only two to three years imprisonment, for unlawful possession of weapons and concealment from the authorities. Ten days later, the Soviet security apparatus ordered their transfer to Tallinn, where it could carry out its revenge. The Mõttus brothers were sentenced to ten years in a forced labor camp, and their once-thriving homestead was razed as they served their term.

Aksel and Hugo Mõttus survived their imprisonment and returned to Estonia, but there was no employer who would give a job to two men without a single entry in their work records. They finally found work as orderlies at Pelgulinna Hospital in Tallinn. It was only in 1988, during the advent of the new era, that the brothers were relieved of their status as second-class citizens.

In the summer of 1974, Soviet authorities in Poka Village of Võrumaa County stumbled upon a man who they thought was hiding from the authorities. The capture of this famed Forest Brother, Kalev Arro, is recalled by former political prisoner Enn Tarto:

> As soon as the authorities heard that a stranger had been sighted at the Kirjase farm, all hell broke loose. The village council said that the man had to be flushed out of the forest and captured. They got the local people all excited about it.
>
> On June 2, 1974, two drunken tractor drivers stopped at a roadside thicket to relieve themselves. To their surprise, they saw a stranger in the woods watching them. The men decided that it must be the same vagrant they'd been hearing about, and ordered the stranger to come closer. At that, a shot rang out and one of the men fell dead. Even though Arro could easily have killed the other one too, since the man was scared stiff, he let him go. That tractor driver, sobered by shock, mounted the tractor and sped into the village center. He notified the police immediately. A massive raid was launched.

The Põlva district police chief Hans Salm, who led the operation, recalls:

> We weren't sure what was going on. We had no idea exactly who the fugitive was and how well he was armed. Some people were saying it was a lunatic who had escaped from the asylum.
>
> When we reached the scene of the crime, we divided the men into squads and started combing the swampy thicket in that area. One man happened to rush ahead of the others. Suddenly, the bushes started to rustle, and a ragged man emerged from the underbrush, firing the high-caliber Walther pistols he held in both hands. The man at the head of the line sustained serious facial wounds, but succeeded in returning fire. After firing a few shots, both the stranger's pistols jammed. He threw them aside, drew a knife from his boot, and kept coming toward us. By this time, he had several bullets in his body. Finally, about five or six paces from the head of

our line, he staggered as we fired on him, and then he
collapsed, punctured by bullets.

The man was dead. The police had an idea who he was, but no
one wanted to tell the security men investigating the incident. The
investigators found some documents in the archives of the State
Security Committee that put them on the right track. Most likely, the
man was the famous Forest Brother Kalev Arro. To confirm the theory,
they summoned Kalev Arro's brother and sister, who claimed they
did not recognize the body. Their claim was ridiculed in the Soviet
press. However, anyone who knew what usually happened to the
relatives of captured Forest Brothers needed no explanation of their
"inability to recognize" the body.

Now the Soviet security apparatus hunted down the former
Forest Brothers of the Valgjärve district. They found one and took him
to Tartu City to identify the body. The man gazed calmly at the corpse,
denying ever having known the man. There was nothing else they
could do but to put him back into the truck and take him home. At
home, as they let the man out of the truck, they saw that he had gotten
drunk on the way home, and now he sat numbly in the back seat, his
face wet with tears. Only then did the Soviet security men realize that
he was mourning his fallen friend. . .

Who was Kalev Arro? His name appears frequently in the
accounts of the Valgjärve and Kooraste Forest Brothers. He was born
into a relatively poor family of Valgjärve Parish. The fir forest near his
family's Vasara farm was the village festival site, where young people
gathered to dance. Kalev's sister Manda was a brilliant actress, and
her brothers' talents were nearly as good. Since a strong nationalist
spirit reigned in the family, it is not at all surprising that Kalev Arro
began fighting the agents of the foreign government as early as 1941.
Arro's brother and sister also took part in the resistance. The Arro
family suffered severe repression with the second Soviet occupation.
After their mother died under suspicious circumstances, Kalev Arro
had no more mercy for his enemies. He became a Forest Brother
known by the nicknames "Värdi," "Jüri," and "Butcher."

Kalev Arro continued his partisan activity until the crushing of
the Piho group in the fall of 1949. He was the only man to break
through the massive siege that wiped out his comrades. The raiding
troops, not wanting to ruin their report by admitting that a man had
escaped, recorded Arro's name on the list of eliminated Forest Brothers. As a result, no one hunted him for decades, until the tragic events
of 1974.

From any perspective, it seemed that this chapter of history was finally closed. Many of those who took part in the raiding operations received medals and awards for their role in discovering and neutralizing the "dangerous criminals." The courts sentenced the helpers of the "dangerous criminals" to long prison terms. And still, one man who had never surrendered lived in the forests of Võrumaa. His name was August Sabe.

According to Hans Salm, the police chief of the Põlva district in those days, August Sabe was the son of a miller. From childhood, he loved to venture into the local forests, learning his way through every thicket and polishing his skills as a swimmer. As a citizen of the Republic of Estonia, Sabe supported neither the German nor the Russian occupation. He took to the forests to escape the Soviet mobilization in 1941 and helped in the founding of the "Vastseliina Republic," a parish in Võrumaa County liberated by Forest Brothers before the German occupation forces arrived in 1941. When the German army mobilization was announced, Sabe vanished into the forests again. No one pursued him, and so he lived in peace until 1944. As the Germans departed, the incoming Russians once again sought Estonian men to use as cannon fodder. Sabe knew he must live the life of a Forest Brother once more. Having faith in the amnesty declared after the end of the war, Sabe emerged from the forest and returned to his job at the mill.

The mill was a place where the villagers exchanged news of local events, which interested the Soviet security apparatus as well as the Forest Brothers. One evening, two somber-looking men came to see August Sabe at the mill and notified him that, beginning the next day, he was to work as a Soviet security agent, informing the security apparatus of everything going on in the region. Several months passed, and the KGB received no reports from Sabe. Such "insolence" could not go unpunished. A large gang of comrades set out to "teach Sabe a lesson."

As soon as Sabe saw them coming, he knew what was going to happen. The security men began firing at Sabe from a distance. He ran to the millpond and dived into the waterfall. The troops lined the riverbank. Some ran downstream and fired into the water; others lobbed grenades. But all was quiet. They found neither Sabe nor his body. The security men ransacked the mill thoroughly, waited for a while, and then left. Only then did August Sabe climb out of the water. Good swimmer that he was, he did not swim downstream, but upstream against the current to the still water behind the falls, where he raised his head out of the water and waited until the raid was over.

When he saw that his home had been destroyed, he knew there was only one place to go. Sabe took to the forest and joined the "Orion" group headed by Jaan Roots.

In 1952, the central figures of "Orion" fell into a trap and perished. Because Sabe was assigned to secure the rear, he managed to escape. Realizing the precariousness of his situation, he went to live alone. He spread the story that he had died of tuberculosis in the forests. Sabe had an abundance of friends who fed and sheltered him.

The years went by. The old people passed away, and the young ones flocked to the cities. Forest villages stood empty. One by one, those who aided Sabe died. He was forced to emerge from hiding more frequently, significantly increasing his risk of capture. Põlva police chief Hans Salm relates the following:

> In the mid-1970's, a series of mysterious thefts plagued the Võhandu district. In one incident, someone had poured several cases of vodka into a bucket right at the store; in another, some old stage curtains had been stolen from the community house. Cream and milk disappeared from the dairy.
>
> One time, something strange happened. The watchman, who was usually drunk, came to work without his booze and sat at his post sober. Sitting sadly in the dairy, he saw a man come around with a three-liter jug and fill it with cream.
>
> The watchman was so surprised that he didn't react right away. Only when the stranger had already gone out the door did he recover, storm after the man, and shout: "Hey! Where are you going with that cream?" The stranger ignored him and kept walking. Yelling and protesting, the night watchman followed him. The stranger turned around and said, "If you keep on making a racket, I'll shoot you." The watchman wouldn't stop, so the stranger drew a pistol from his pocket and fired a shot into the air. Panicked, the watchman scurried away. The stranger went on his way. No one at the police station believed the watchman's story. They thought the man was delirious.
>
> Another incident took place in the summer of 1978. Local authorities launched a raid against poachers on the banks of the Võhandu River. During the raid, a deputy stumbled upon a hidden hunting rifle. Surprised at

III. THE ANTAGONISTS:

Very few photographs of Forest Brothers are known to exist; their Soviet antagonists were publicized as heroes. The following selection is illustrative.

Some who served Moscow:

34. Boris Kumm, Minister of State Security, 1944-50.

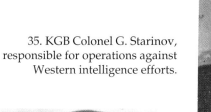

35. KGB Colonel G. Starinov, responsible for operations against Western intelligence efforts.

36. Uno Kask, KGB counterintellgience officer.

37. Eduard Sisas, KGB Major shot by partisans.

38. P. Paul, KGB Commander in Järvamaa County, shot by partisans.

39. O. Põder, KGB Captain and provocateur, shot by partisans.

40. Maps, money, and radio equipment seized from alleged CIA agent Kalju Kukk.

41. Similar equipment seized from alleged CIA agent Hans Toomla.

42. Karl Talpak, in Estonian Army captain's uniform, mid-1950s.

43. Ants Kaljurand, alias "Ants the Terrible," a legendary Forest Brother in Estonian Army uniform, mid 1940s.

44. Alfred Käärman; on the back of the photo is the inscription, "In my uniform jacket in my last year of freedom, 1952."

45. Toomas Hellat, member of the Erna Unit, organizer of the National Council, and leading member of the Haukka-Tümmler reconnaissance group.

46-48. The Mõttus family of
Antsla, Võrumaa County.
Aksel (above) was captured
with his brother Hugo (left)
in 1964, but both survived their
prison sentences; after surviving
in the forest for over a decade,
another brother, Ülo, died in 1954,
and their sister, Maimu (below)
died in 1958.

45-49. *The last free man.*

49. August Sabe in a 1950 photograph. Sabe lived and operated in the forests of Võrumaa county until September 28, 1978 when he went to fish on the Võhandu River. There he met two men who claimed to be fishing but who were in fact security officers on his trail. Sabe was caught, but broke free, dived into the river, and drowned. This series of photographs, taken by the KGB officers before and after his death, document the last moments of his freedom and his life.

50. The setting.

51. On the verge of a catch, Sabe is trapped by the KGB officer behind him.

52. The remains retrieved.

53. Sabe's effects are catalogued and the case is closed.

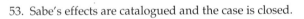

his find, he remained in the area to see if anyone came to retrieve the gun. It wasn't long before a stranger crashed through the underbrush and headed straight for the hideout. Drawing his gun, the deputy charged out of his hiding place and ordered the stranger to raise his hands. The man turned around and put his hands up. When he saw his captor, he dropped his hands, turned around, and calmly began retracing his steps. The deputy shouted, "Stop, or I'll shoot!" The man muttered, "No you won't," and vanished into the forest. The man had nerves of steel. The deputy did not fire.

It didn't end with that. The deputy turned the rifle over to the authorities, and after some drinking with his buddies to celebrate the raid, he went home that night in a good mood. As he reached the top of his steep and narrow staircase, someone grabbed his arm in the darkness and growled, "What the hell did you do with my gun?" This startled the deputy half to death, and he fell down the stairs and broke his arm. Sabe never did get that gun back.

The Põlva security apparatus saw the connection between these incidents, and the new chief of security concluded that a Forest Brother was hiding in the woods of his district. Eager for a promotion and some medals, he combed the forests and swept the Leevi and Võhandu districts with raids. He found nothing suspicious.

On September 28, 1978, several raiding parties were combing the forest near Paidra. The security chief and his assistant got into a rubber boat and floated down the Võhandu River. It wasn't long before they discovered a strange man fishing on the bank. The men went ashore and walked up to the stranger. They introduced themselves as fishermen from Võru and started to ask about the identity of the strange old man.

They even took some photographs with the fisherman, first one security man, then the other. Finally they asked the stranger where they could mail the pictures. And then August Sabe — because that's who it was — made his only mistake by growling that he didn't need the pictures and implying that their conversation was over. At the security men's insistence, he gave them the first name that came to his mind, but by then the security men knew what was going on.

They shouted at the old man: "Don't lie. Your name is August Sabe. We're from State Security and you're under arrest." Things happened quickly after that. The only thing that saved the security men was that Sabe was sitting on the riverbank by his rods and did not have enough time to turn around after rising and grabbing the Walther from his pocket. At that instant, one of the security men, a karate specialist, threw the old man into the water. The other captor dived in after him and they fought fiercely in the water. Finally, the old man could no longer oppose the two young men who were threatening to drown him, and he surrendered. As the men shoved Sabe to shore, Sabe felt some solid ground under his feet, tossed the security men back into the water, and dived back into the Võhandu River. He never appeared on the surface again. Whether he drowned while trying to escape or had drowned himself intentionally is something we'll never know. When the security forces finally retrieved Sabe's body, caught on a branch over the river, they did not succeed in reviving him.

The last Estonian Forest Brother had perished. The authorities planned a television program to dramatize the capture of "the dangerous criminal who had concealed himself for decades," but the Committee for State Security banned its airing at the last minute. It felt that neither Estonia nor the rest of the world must know what had happened, but in 1979, the underground publication "Supplements to the Free Circulation of News and Ideas in Estonia" published an article about the death of the last Estonian Forest Brother. Although the resistance movement in Estonia had undergone a metamorphosis, it had never died.

Chapter 10

Caught in the KGB Net

A review of the postwar period in Estonia would be incomplete without a description of the encounters among the intelligence services of several countries during the latter half of the 1950s in the Baltics, when the resistance movement was in retreat. Taking advantage of the weakening of the Forest Brothers, the Soviet security apparatus succeeded in infiltrating the remaining Forest Brothers units and using them in a counterespionage game against Western intelligence services. In all three Baltic states, a "false Forest Brothers movement" began to flourish, and the KGB succeeded in deceiving Western intelligence services in almost all their operations. Indeed, the blame lies partly with the Western intelligence services themselves, since they waited too long to involve themselves with events in the Baltics. This reflects a certain naïveté and inexperience on their part. It is interesting to note that although Western experts initially underestimated the strength of the resistance movements, they later fell victim to their overestimation of the strength of the resistance movements. The Baltic resistance movements began crumbling by the early 1950s because of the lack of effective support from abroad. And now, suddenly, the West was interested, although it was more interested in using them rather than in helping them directly.

The prelude to the major encounter in the Baltics of several national intelligence services dates back to the mid-1940s, when the British intelligence service SIS established contacts with Baltic national resistance movements while the Baltics were still under German occupation. The liaison officer between the Baltic independence movements and British intelligence in Stockholm was Alexander "Sandy" McKibbin, who had been SIS representative in Estonia until 1939. Agents supplied with radio transmitters were sent into Lithuania, Latvia, and Estonia to establish communications. Some of the agents were apprehended by the Germans, and the others suspended their operations in 1944 and 1945 and left the area when the

Red army forced its way in. At any rate, communications with resistance groups in the Baltic States had broken off by the end of 1944. In Estonia, Alexander McKibbin had been the contact with National Committee figures, specifically with Toomas Hellat. With the destruction of the Haukka-Tümmler group, communications with Estonia were lost.

In the spring of 1945, when Estonia, Latvia, and Lithuania had already been reoccupied by the Soviet Union, the SIS succeeded in restoring communications with the Lithuanian partisan movement. During the latter part of that same year, they started training the men to be sent into Estonia and Latvia to establish contacts with the local resistance movements in these countries. Unfortunately, a strong wind blew the boat carrying these Estonians from Sweden to England off course, and the men were apprehended by British police. Naturally, the men could not tell the police of their true reasons for entering England, and they were placed in an internment camp.

The Latvians recruited by the British fared better, and in October 1945, the SIS sent four well-equipped agents from Sweden to the shores of Kurland in Latvia. Unfortunately, the ship capsized as it approached the shore. The border guard patrol discovered the wreckage and a manhunt began. Soon, all the agents were seized by the KGB, who claimed the radio transmitter with all its ciphers as a special prize. Major Janis Lukasevics planned to start a counterespionage game with the SIS, but the imprisoned Latvian agents proved to be stoical men who preferred death to betrayal. All four gave up their lives in the torture chambers of the Latvian KGB house in Riga. Major Lukasevics persisted. Soon, he found one man, a Latvian resistance movement member who had communicated with Sweden during the war, who was willing to cooperate with the KGB. The traitor's name was Augusts Bergmanis. Together they established communications with Sweden. Initially, the SIS did not trust the new agent, and the KGB had no choice but to wait. The KGB also tried to establish a "partisan headquarters" in Lithuania, but the Lithuanians caught wind of the fake and escaped large-scale entrapment.

In 1946, two SIS agents landed at Zvejniekciems harbor in Latvia's Skulte Parish to establish communications with Latvian partisans. Agents Rihards Zande and Eriks Tomsons were assigned to investigate the fate of the preceding group and to start helping Soviet-held nationalist figures escape from Latvia. A new boat was to arrive in four months.

At first, all went well. Zande established contacts with several partisan groups. Radio communications were set up with Sweden, but soon problems developed with the transmitter: Zande could receive messages from Sweden, but his own transmissions did not get through. In a fateful step, the SIS ordered Zande to contact Bergmanis, who impressed Zande as a trustworthy man. The trap was set. Within a few weeks, the KGB had a complete list of Zande's and Tomsons's contacts. The KGB did not arrest them immediately, since they hoped to make a bigger haul by including the next boatload coming from Sweden.

By December 1946, the SIS, with the help of the United States, had outfitted a powerful speedboat for the trip to Latvia. On December 19, 1946, the vessel went to sea, setting its course to the previously agreed spot on the Latvian coast, where the KGB lay in wait. To the KGB's astonishment, the boat's captain sensed the danger. Following an inexplicable premonition, he turned his vessel around and returned to Sweden. The boat and its equipment were seized by Swedish authorities. The SIS took its time in finding a new boat, and thus foiled the KGB's plans for a major attack. Zande and Tomsons continued to operate until the KGB was forced to halt their operations when the intelligence information they sent to Sweden began touching upon sensitive areas. The Soviet collaborator Bergmanis transmitted a panicked report to Sweden of the group's "exposure" and suspended operations. The trap remained set for other victims.

The SIS, stung by its failure, did not hasten to send new agents to Latvia. But now the KGB decided to speed up developments by "allowing a Latvian partisan communications man to escape" to Sweden. In reality, this man was KGB provocateur V. Sveics. In October of 1948, Sveics was in Sweden as a new SIS group was preparing for its trip to Latvia. Naturally, the group was placed under the leadership of the "Latvian specialist" V. Sveics. The group, consisting of two Estonians, two Latvians, and two Lithuanians, underwent thorough training. In late April 1949, the six men boarded what was supposed to be the fastest vessel — an S-208 speedboat — and headed for the Lithuanian shore near Palanga. They planned to land on May 1, when the border patrol's vigilance was expected to be lax because of the "workers' holiday." Their assumption proved correct, and the Soviet border patrol failed to notice the white speedboat or the men coming ashore on rubber rafts.

At the first opportunity, Sveics separated from his companions and alerted the border guards. In the ensuing battle, both Estonians (whose names will forever remain unknown) and one Latvian were killed. The other men escaped and scattered. Sveics was taken to Riga, where, as instructed by the KGB, he sent a radiogram to Sweden describing his "miraculous" escape and reporting that the agents in Latvia were ready for action. Through Sveics, the KGB obtained the names of other agents sent to Latvia by the SIS through other channels, and by 1949, the entire network of agents in Latvia was under KGB surveillance. The stage was all set for a grand espionage game, and the SIS fell into the trap.

By the early 1950s, Western policy toward the Baltic States had shaken off its lethargy. The escalation of the Cold War stimulated the intensification of Baltic operations by the American and British intelligence services. With the outbreak of the Korean War, Western governments needed information on possible mobilizations being carried out in the Soviet Union's westernmost regions. By the end of the 1940s, contacts intensified between the CIA and the SIS, who up to now had almost singlehandedly controlled Baltic operations. The SIS was convinced of its agents' loyalty and the Americans believed their claim. In reality, the KGB controlled not only the SIS agents in the Baltics but, through Kim Philby, also the training of SIS agents in London and Germany.

In the late 1940s, SIS had established a special center in London for the training of agents to be sent to the Baltics. The center operated in cooperation with the Baltic embassies in London. Its leaders included Colonel Alfons Rebane, Stasys Zymantas, and Rudolph Silaraijs as the Estonian, Latvian, and Lithuanian experts, respectively. The operation carried the code name "Jungle." The SIS procured a house in Chelsea for the center's use. This is where the agents-in-training lived, and where they learned radio transmission techniques, codes and ciphers, and other theoretical skills. Field training (shooting, swimming, camouflaged movement, hand-to-hand combat) was conducted in the countryside. The training concluded with a trip to the hills of Scotland, where the trainees were to demonstrate their skills to the instructors. The purpose of these exercises was to train professional SIS radio operators, and not partisans.

In late October 1949, a speedboat transported the first of these agents to the shores of Latvia. Here they were met by a unit of "Forest Brothers" consisting of KGB agents with the collective name of "Maxis." The "partisans" of Kurzeme forest were led by KGB Major Alberts Bundulis. By the autumn of 1950, cooperation between the SIS agents and the KGB impostors was going so smoothly that one SIS man started giving the "partisans" courses in radio operations, planning to send several of the most talented of them to be trained in London. Once, the SIS men chanced to meet a group of genuine Forest Brothers, which was eliminated several days later by the KGB.

London was thrilled with the achievements. The CIA, whose interest in the Baltic States was growing, felt that things seemed to be going a little too smoothly. In a conversation with Henry Carr, his colleague Harry Rositzke expressed doubts as to whether the British intelligence operation wasn't "infected" with KGB agents. Carr categorically denied this, but failed to convince his colleague. American intelligence began dealing with the Baltic States on its own, sending agents into the Baltics without coordinating its operations with the SIS.

The SIS continued its operations at full speed. They thought they had established close communications with the Latvian Forest Brothers; now they turned their sights toward Estonia. In the spring of 1951, the S-208 speedboat brought four new agents to the Venta River delta near Ventspils, including one "partisan" sent to London by the KGB. The group included three Latvians and one Estonian with the code name "Gustav," whose identity remains a mystery. Gustav was assigned to go to Estonia with a Latvian agent without contacting the Maxis group, and to contact the Estonian Forest Brothers. Unfortunately, the Latvian disobeyed his instructions and marched right into a trap. Both agents were placed under KGB surveillance, and since the Estonian KGB was not ready to work with its "guest," it decided to arrest Gustav instead. On April 24, 1951, the Estonian left the Latvian "partisans" and headed for Estonia. A few hours later, his body was recovered from the Ujava River. Walking into the ambush that had been prepared for him, and realizing his situation was hopeless, Gustav managed to swallow an ampule of sodium cyanide. His suicide set the KGB's Estonian operation back by six months.

By the autumn of 1951, Alfons Rebane (code name Robert) had recruited and trained new volunteers to operate in Estonia. According to Rebane's instructions, the men were to be liaison officers between the Estonian Forest Brothers and the British. Rebane foresaw the creation of an underground organization in Estonia modeled after the Defense League, with a membership of at least twenty thousand men. They were to spring into action at the outbreak of a new World War, which seemed more than likely in 1951.

In 1951, the Estonian agents and one Latvian were taken from England to Hamburg, Germany. This team heading for Estonia included Leo Audova (code name Ants) and Märt Pedak (code name Otto). Both men had fought on the eastern front against the Red army. Audova had earned the Iron Cross, Second Class and the Eastern Medal. Though Pedak's motives for undertaking this life-threatening mission were unclear, Audova was a principled freedom fighter who was also a deeply religious man. The group that left Hamburg in late

September on the S-208 speedboat was equipped with four radios, code books, forged documents, three automatics, six pistols, 2,000 cartridges, and 150,000 rubles.

On the night of September 29, the S-208 with its motors muffled slipped into a small bay six kilometers from the Ujava lighthouse. The location represented a "blind spot" for Soviet radar, and everything progressed as it had in training. The S-208 launched a rubber raft named "Lady Jane Russell," which took the men ashore. Here they were met by the Maxis Forest Brothers, one of whom was to return to London with a real SIS agent for training. The incoming agents were taken to the Maxis group's camp, where they were met by a "liaison officer" from Estonia. The Estonian KGB was now plugged into the network.

In Estonia, preparations for the entry of the SIS agents were thorough, just as they had been in Latvia. A number of "Forest Brothers'" bunkers were built in the woods and equipped with all the necessities. The operations of the "Forest Brothers" were led by experienced KGB specialists Jaan Mägi, Uno Kask, and Voldemar Rosin. Their preparations may well have included a notebook found in Põltsamaa in the 1960s containing the "Estonian woodland partisans' league" program, bunker equipment list, drawings of uniforms, and military school graduation emblems. Reports say that the language in the notebook was teeming with Russian terms, leaving no doubt as to the nationality of its compilers. The goal of the Estonian KGB was to give the SIS the impression that a powerful partisan organization was operating in Estonia, and the notebook was supposed to be part of the charade.

First of all, the SIS agents had to be transported from Latvia to Estonia. To establish their credibility with the real Estonian partisans, the KGB "Forest Brothers" introduced themselves as members of the group led by Arnold Sirel, a war buddy of Rebane, who had at one time operated in Läänemaa County. As "proof of their authenticity," they produced a watch given as a gift by Alfons Rebane. The KGB had already enticed Sirel's actual group into a trap. The carefully planned operation nearly failed on the bridge over the Pärnu River when traffic inspectors tried to stop the truck carrying the SIS agents. The incident passed quietly, giving a green light to the KGB's operation, which sought to place Ants and Otto under full control of the "Forest Brothers'" leader "Karl."

Soon, communications were established with Sweden. Colonel Rebane's vigilance was dulled by the fact that the "Forest Brothers'" leader had turned out to be an old friend whom he had no reason to doubt. After an exchange of reciprocal code phrases, the formalities were over and "Robert" sent a radiogram to Estonia greeting the Forest Brothers organization and promising to continue sending assistance.

In Estonia, the SIS agents were not given any part in other operations. They were fed third-rate information, which they transmitted to London. Ants soon began to feel uneasy about his forced inactivity. He left the bunker with his weapons and radio transmitter and radioed messages to London, keeping their contents secret from the rest of the group. These actions alarmed the KGB and Ants was arrested. Now the KGB exposed its charade to Otto, who was forced to work for the Soviet security apparatus.

On April 20, 1952, new SIS agents came ashore in Latvia, including Eerik Hurma (code name Georg), with forged documents in the name of Georg Kuuse. Georg brought along 60,000 rubles, a wealth of supplies, and blank Soviet passports. The KGB was seriously troubled by the quality of these passports, the products of a very capable CIA factory for the preparation of forged documents. Georg was sent to live in Ants's bunker and placed under strict surveillance. In 1953, Heino Karkman (code name Albert) reached Estonia by way of Latvia, bringing along new sums of money. Albert's assignment was to obtain photos of military and industrial targets and mail them to a designated address in England.

In 1954, SIS decided to conduct an inspection of its Latvian and Lithuanian agents, and called the "partisans'" representatives to England for this purpose. After extensive preparations, the operation was undertaken in the autumn of 1954. On November 1, 1954, a motorboat picked up "Forest Brother" Juhan Luks on the coast of Saaremaa Island and transported him to a speedboat waiting on the open sea. The same speedboat brought new SIS agent Raimund Jantra (code name Harry) to Estonia. Luks was questioned for several days in London by SIS officers, who were unable to unearth anything suspicious. Luks underwent thorough training and was sent back to Estonia. On April 20, 1955, Juhan Luks landed in Estonia. The same speedboat carried SIS agent Albert and KGB Lieutenant Olaf Jürisson back to England. By November, the KGB lieutenant, now code-named "Harald," was back in Estonia, bringing supplies and instructions to "intensify operations." At the same time, another "partisan" sent to England by the KGB was being trained at the London center. This Soviet spy, called Olev, had fought in Rebane's unit during the war, but was subsequently pressed into collaboration with the security apparatus for reasons unknown. Soviet security got Olev to Bornholm Island, where he gave himself up to Swedish authorities. Rebane soon contacted Olev, who told Rebane that he had been brought to the West at Karl's orders.

It was now agreed that the landing site of the agents sent into Estonia would be the area near Loksa and Hara Bay on Estonia's northern coast. The agents were put off the cutters in special small speedboats, which had enough room for one man, his supplies, and gasoline tanks. The boats were expertly camouflaged and rode low in the water. The pilots had undergone special training in concealment from border guard ships and searchlights.

The KGB's grand operation entered its crucial phase. Apparently, its final goal was not even clear to its local leaders, who seemed to be more interested in enticing some well-known Estonian public figure to Estonia and arresting him — Operation "Trust." The KGB's goals, however, were more ambitious: with the unwitting help of Baltic exiles, to infiltrate Western intelligence centers, thus gaining the ability to eliminate Western intelligence personnel in the Soviet Empire. But its heady success had rendered the KGB careless. In addition to the others it had recruited, the KGB tried to recruit Heino Karkman for its own interests, but succeeded only in arousing his suspicions. Karkman had no proof to back up his suspicions, but he began taking notice of events while continuing to "play dumb." He succeeded in dulling the KGB's vigilance and returned to London where he expressed his doubts to Rebane, who had also become suspicious because the operation was going too smoothly.

They decided to get to work on the KGB officer in London. Because Rebane despised physical force, he decided to use psychological pressure, particularly since the man was a soldier from his own wartime unit. Rebane displayed full trust in the man from Estonia, giving him gifts, taking him to the best restaurants, and assuring him that only because of the recommendation of his infinitely trusted friend, was he prepared to travel to Estonia to inspect the Forest Brothers units. The "false Forest Brothers" had already sent such an invitation to Rebane by way of Juhan Luks. The KGB agent endured for a whole week, but then broke down and confessed to Rebane that he had been sent to England by the KGB to entice Rebane into a trap in Estonia. Because of Rebane's trust and generosity, the KGB agent could not go through with such a dirty plan, and he told Rebane not to go to Estonia because the invitation was a KGB setup. All was now clear to Rebane. In a gentlemen's agreement, Rebane did not immediately inform the British of what he had learned, and allowed the KGB man to return to Estonia. The game continued, but Rebane was now the hunter, stalking "Karl," the leader of the "Forest Brothers."

In August 1956, Rebane accompanied Karkman to Helsinki, as if accepting the invitation brought by Luks to take a speedboat from Finland to Estonia or to meet somewhere at sea. Several months passed and winter arrived. Finally, Rebane informed them that he would not go to Estonia, but ordered Karl to come to Finland. "Ice solid on Finnish coast. Unmanned floating lighthouse. Automatic lighthouse operates constantly. Contact man named Bolton." Karl, however, did not dare to undertake such risky business. A radiogram arrived in Finland: "Operation has become impossible. Wind piled ice on shore near Loksa." Things were now more than clear to Rebane.

The espionage game went on. Rebane continued to speak of his imminent return to Estonia, all the while making every effort to bring his own men out. The KGB, however, became suspicious. "Georg," who had tried to distance himself from the "Forest Brothers" group, was arrested. Jantra was pressed into collaboration with the KGB, but the man succeeded in outwitting them. Jantra managed to convince the KGB that he would be much more effective in London, and thus managed, at the request of Rebane, to be sent back to England, where he was to infiltrate deep into the British intelligence services. The KGB had made a fatal mistake: Jantra remained loyal to Rebane and explained the entire game in detail to the SIS. Jantra finally changed his name, worked for years in British intelligence, and is currently in retirement in Great Britain.

The game, however, still had not come to an end. Through Rebane, the SIS had sent other agents into Estonia, but nearly all had unwittingly come under KGB control. Rebane did manage to warn one of these agents, and the man left the bunker built for him, leaving the KGB emptyhanded. After a series of adventures, this man also succeeded in escaping to the West, and is now retired in Great Britain.

By the end of 1956, the extent of the SIS's deception was clear. By this time, they had concrete evidence that the KGB had infiltrated the Latvian Forest Brothers as well. In December 1956, Alfons Rebane sent his final radiogram into Estonia, saying in no uncertain terms that the Estonian Forest Brothers had been infiltrated by the Bolsheviks. Operation "Jungle" had failed. Colonel Rebane went to live in West Germany. Heino Karkman, the man who had played such a key role in foiling the KGB's plans, became a sailor. The KGB, however, was not inclined to forgive and forget, and on April 14, 1958, Heino Karkman fell off a ship under suspicious circumstances in the Swedish harbor of Köping and drowned.

Of course, the KGB's ire was understandable. Disguised as "freedom fighters," a substantial number of Soviet spies had been shunted to the West from the occupied Eastern European countries in the late 1950s. After the failure of the operation, they all came under suspicion and were exposed. Of the Estonian spies, Artur Hamann-Tuldava, a man who had come across Soviet Karelia and through Finland into Sweden, deserves special mention, since he had the talent to become a top Soviet spy. Now his career came to an abrupt end. Western special services quickly recognized the nature of Hamann's activities and quietly placed him under intense surveillance. Artur Hamann-Tuldava realized his back was to the wall and fled back to the Soviet Union in 1963.

The British intelligence service was not alone in its interest in Estonia during the postwar years. Swedish, and through them, the American intelligence services started gathering information as early as the mid-1940s. Swedish intelligence knew of Robert Saaliste's group that had returned to Estonia in 1946. No one knows how many of Saaliste's radiograms from Estonia were handed over to Swedish intelligence by the émigré groups. At any rate, it would be hard to believe that the Swedes had no knowledge of the émigrés' activities.

For whatever reason, a new stage began in the operations of Swedish intelligence in 1947 and 1948. The Swedes exhibited a marked increase in interest about information coming out of the Baltics; the influence of the CIA was apparent behind this. Arkadi Valdin became a central figure in Sweden; his liaison with Swedish intelligence was K. Andreasson. In a house at Gimmerstavägen 24 in Älvsjö near Stockholm, recruited agents were given thorough training. The men sent to Estonia were to maintain communications with the Swedes. The secret organization *Elu Tee* (Path of Life) in Finland also worked for Swedish intelligence, transporting agents across Finland back into Sweden. To establish contact with this network, one had to telephone the Helsinki number 484 487, ask for Mr. Kindbärg, and say the password *Helsingfron Kullenberg*. According to Briton T. Duvall, who helped transport Estonians from Finland to Sweden, the Finns pretended that they knew nothing of the operation. There were occasions, however, on which the Finns warned Duvall of impending danger.

Traffic between Estonia and Sweden was quite heavy during those years. According to a Swedish Foreign Ministry source, most of the men sent to Estonia made it back to Sweden with better information than the authorities could have hoped for.

Swedish intelligence was not alone in working with Arkadi Valdin. The British and the Americans also turned to him by way of Colonel Alfons Rebane. Contact with the Americans took place through the former chief of long-distance reconnaissance for the

German general staff, General Gehlen, who worked at recruiting and training men from refugee camps on behalf of the CIA. Thirty agents, all of whom had been trained in Pullach near Munich, were sent into the Baltics as a result of General Gehlen's efforts. Gehlen had at his disposal one mine-laying boat and two speedboats, which made quick visits to deposit men on the smaller islands around Hiiumaa Island or on the mainland coast south of Pärnu City.

The first man sent to Estonia in this "cooperative endeavor" was Ernst (other sources say Endel) Mumm, who landed in Estonia in 1947 or 1948. Mumm (code name Nixi) landed safely and got right to work. In October 1948, a large group of men followed him: Harri Vimm (alias Villu), Johan Maltis (Joonas), and a reconnaissance man with the code name "Susi." Their first attempt to reach shore on Hiiumaa Island near the Osmussaare lighthouse with a speedboat directed by Captain Albert Lilleberg was unsuccessful. The speedboat encountered a fleet of Russian border patrol vessels and was forced to return to its home base on Ture Island. They managed to reach shore on the third try, when they headed for Lohusalu Point. The men went ashore with rubber rafts, crossed the border zone by jumping on large rubber balls, and headed inland. The group was assigned to contact the Forest Brothers led by Richard Saaliste in Estonia. All too soon, however, the Soviet security apparatus detected the appearance of unfamiliar radio waves on the air.

A manhunt began. Villu was supposed to contact the border patrol regiment commander Major Paul Lilleleht, who had hidden in Estonia for a long time, but encountered a document checkpoint and killed himself by biting an ampule of poison. The security apparatus had more luck with Joonas, who became discouraged by a series of failures in his operations and gave himself up to security forces. Along with Joonas, Soviet security forces seized not only the radio transmitter but also information on the third agent Susi. Susi was placed under surveillance by security, surrounded by security agents posing as "resistance movement members," and turned into an unwitting mouthpiece for the Soviet security apparatus.

Meanwhile, Valdin thought that everything was going according to plan. Only Nixi sensed danger. Realizing that the men sent to contact him had been compromised, he acted to save himself. At Valdin's request, another team was sent to Estonia: a Lithuanian, and Estonians Evald Hallisk (alias Habe) and "Ermo." The team landed on the Lithuanian coast and was immediately placed under security surveillance. Actually, Soviet security had planned to wipe out the entire team right away, but in the battle with border patrol troops, the

Lithuanian was killed and the Estonians escaped. Unfortunately, this escape didn't save the Estonians, who were graciously met by KGB "Forest Brothers" who took them to their "base camp" in Estonia. The men were allowed to operate freely for a time, to prevent Valdin from becoming suspicious.

The Soviet security apparatus had devised a plan to deal an effective blow to "Western intrigues" in Estonia by imprisoning "the enemy's spy cadre and its entire team" in one swoop. Security forces made colossal preparations, including "field training" and other such operations. It seemed that nothing could prevent the operation from succeeding.

September 2, 1951 came along. The boatload of new agents was scheduled to land at 11:30 p.m. The morning was beautiful, but by nightfall, a storm was brewing. The situation was complicated by a forest fire that had erupted the night before. The men on the speedboat could not see the flashlight signals from shore against the light of the fire, and turned one and one-half kilometers to the south, directly toward the border patrol cordon guarding Matsalu Bay. Here, an alarm sounded when the roar of the motor was heard. At 11:00 p.m., a group of people was heard splashing through the water; everything on shore was ready. At 11:40 p.m., machine gun fire clattered toward the "illegal border crossers." They responded with automatic fire, trying to break through the siege in the darkness. Some of the men got quite far, but they were unevenly matched against the border patrols. Cordon commander Kozlov fell in the fighting, and many border patrol soldiers were wounded. All four of the Estonian agents — Lembit Ustel, Aksel Ports, Kreums, and Friedrich Põld, who had escaped from Estonia in 1947 on the fishing schooner Meretuul — perished.

For all practical purposes, this brought Valdin's operations in Estonia to an end. No more teams were sent to Estonia. The entire operation shifted more and more into the Americans' hands. In the mid-1950s, the CIA's interest in the Baltics increased markedly. Fearing KGB infiltration of the British intelligence network, the Americans began preparing agents who were exclusively their own, with little coordination with intelligence agencies of other countries. Despite these precautions, the KGB succeeded in impeding CIA operations by infiltrating one of its own men into a group of agents. The collaborator turned in his companions after they had parachuted into Latvia. The KGB also began a radio counterespionage game with the Americans, but the compromised radio operator succeeded in notifying the Americans that he was being controlled, and the operation was scrapped.

One of the best-known incidents in Estonia is the capture of CIA agents Kalju Kukk and Hans Toomla in 1954. Kalju Kukk was recruited by the American intelligence service in 1953 in Casablanca and was sent to Munich for training. After exhaustive drills, Kukk (code name Karl) was whisked across the ocean to the U.S.A. on August 7, 1954, where he received thorough training from American instructors at Fort Bragg in North Carolina. Two other men — "Ants" and "Artur" (Hans Toomla) — underwent training with him. Some time later, the men were returned to Germany for supplemental training in radio communications. These actions indicate that the Americans had learned from the Britons' experience. They did not assign Kukk and Toomla to establish communications with the resistance movement, but rather instructed them to work as genuine spies, tracking the movements and possible concentrations of Soviet forces, collecting information about current events in the Soviet Union, obtaining documents, and other such activities. Kukk and Toomla were given the locations of some of Valdin's men. Their main liaison was to be the Swedish agent Nixi who had been sent into Estonia in the 1940s. Nixi (Ernst Mumm) was working in an automobile repair shop and running a successful espionage operation, according to American intelligence assessments. He had recruited his own network of agents. As proof of their authenticity, Toomla and Kukk were given several items and half a photograph, of which Nixi held the other half.

On May 7, 1954, an unmarked transport plane took off from the Frankfurt-am-Main airport. Kukk and Toomla parachuted into southern Estonia near Auksaar Village, moving into Kergu Village near Vändra, where Toomla's mother Liis Toomla lived with his sister Helgi Noormaa. Kukk and Toomla were assigned to familiarize themselves with the situation in Estonia, recruit agents, and prepare to receive a larger group of operatives into Estonia. Toomla's old friend Robert Hamburg was recruited as resident in Estonia, with the code name "Ats." Kukk and Toomla moved through Estonia and gathered information. On June 30, 1954, they made their first broadcast. They felt confident and secure. Their only tense moment had been an encounter with identification checkers on the Pärnu-Tallinn train, which ended without incident. The men had no hint that the KGB had launched an extensive search for them under the direction of Colonel Gavriil Starinov, and was already on their trail.

In June, Liis Toomla's farm was placed under KGB surveillance. Early in the morning of July 11, the watchers reported two bicyclists riding toward the farm; shortly afterward, a radio broadcast was detected in the area. The encirclement tightened. Kukk and Toomla were unsuspecting, and so the KGB was able to ambush the two men as they returned to the farm on their bicycles. Kukk was taken prisoner. Toomla, reacting with lightning speed, managed to grab his pistol and mortally wound KGB operative Lukyanov, after which Toomla himself collapsed, fatally wounded. The KGB tried to set up a radio counterespionage game to mislead the Americans with the help of the imprisoned Kukk, but Kukk refused to cooperate, protecting the identity of his network of agents in every way he could. Despite his efforts, the KGB tracked and arrested the resident Ats. During the military tribunal held in February 1955, Kukk was sentenced to death and his agents to varying terms of imprisonment.

Nixi continued to vex Soviet intelligence. Contacting him had been Hans Toomla's assignment, and therefore Kukk knew nothing of him. And so, Mumm continued to operate until December 1956, when Soviet security trackers located his radio transmitter and arrested him. Further information about Mumm is lacking. Apparently, he was executed.

Stories of the activities of American intelligence in Estonia also remain hearsay. From accounts by individuals who dealt with the recruitment and training of Estonians during that time, we know that the Americans sent into Estonia other agents who escaped the fate of Toomla and Kukk and returned successfully to the West. This may indeed be true, but evidence has been nearly impossible to obtain.

The failure of the Western intelligence service operations serves only to prove that a resistance movement cannot be led or organized from the outside. Its strength depends above all on the resoluteness and spiritual power of the nation itself. Although the West provided precious little help to the captive nations, their resistance movements persisted with amazing tenacity. A new generation rose to replace the killed or imprisoned Forest Brothers, and continued to resist the conquering authorities with changing methods in changing circumstances.

Epilogue

The Resistance Lived On

The end of armed combat in the late 1950s still did not represent national submission to foreign rule. The dream of freeing Estonia with weapons had proved to be illusory; new circumstances demanded new methods for continuing the resistance.

The death of Stalin brought a respite from Soviet terror. The heirs of the great dictator realized that his policies of coercion and violence would take them nowhere. The first to realize this was the notorious KGB chief Lavrenti Beria, who began liberalizing Soviet foreign policy and making plans to transform the Baltic States into "people's democracies." Moscow began withdrawing ethnic Russian Party functionaries from the Baltic States. Soviet border guard units prepared to depart. Several government figures of the Republic of Estonia, recently released from jail, were approached by Soviet authorities asking them to assist in the establishment of a "people's democracy" government in the Baltic States, following Bulgaria's example. These changes were cut short by the coup in Moscow and the execution of Beria. Before long, however, the plotters who had accused Beria of "overthrowing Soviet power and favoring bourgeois nationalists" were forced to follow his lead and begin reforming the system. In 1956, at the initiative of Nikita Sergeyevich Khrushchev, the Twentieth Congress of the Communist Party of the Soviet Union finally condemned Stalin's "cult of personality." A "thaw" spread across the Soviet Empire.

The thaw brought changes to Estonia. Many Estonians who had survived the harsh conditions in Siberia were allowed to return home. The economic system was liberalized, Moscow loosened its reins, and the right of native Estonians to chart their country's course increased markedly. As a result, agriculture began to recover from the shock of collectivization, industries came under Estonian control, and national culture reawakened. Many people now hoped to build a career in the Soviet Estonian power structures, rise to high-level positions, and use the system to do some good for their own land and people. They decided to join the Communist Party, crowd out the Russians and the "Yestonians," and start taking care of things themselves. The proportion of Estonians in the Communist Party of Estonia slowly began to rise.

Estonians, however, soon realized the futility of trying to accomplish anything useful within the ranks of the Communist Party. The Soviet regime had only switched masks; its basic character remained unchanged. Russification continued unabated. The large number of surviving Estonians returning to their homeland from Siberia was outweighed by the number of Russian colonists entering Estonia. According to the 1959 census, the proportion of ethnic Estonians in Estonia had fallen to 74 percent, down from 90 percent during the independence era; by 1970, Estonians made up only 68 percent of Estonia's population. Cities populated solely by non- Estonians (such as Paldiski and Sillamäe) appeared throughout the land. For this very reason, it was only after Estonia's reassertion of independence in 1991 that the Estonian people learned that an atomic reactor had been operating for decades at the Soviet military base at Paldiski. The Soviet intent to ruin Estonia was eminently clear.

The brief renaissance came to an end when Estonian factories were once more placed under direct control of Moscow and industrialization ran rampant. As Estonia's economy slid downhill, the rape of all her natural resources reached unprecedented proportions; an ecological catastrophe seemed inevitable. Thousands of hectares of land were rendered unusable. Northeastern Estonia became one of the Soviet Union's most polluted areas. The Estonians who had sought to help their country by making their way into the corridors of power quickly forgot their ideals and became obedient Soviet bureaucrats, driven by a thirst for power and the desire to retain the privileges of the *nomenklatura*. Supreme power within the Estonian Communist Party was retained by the older generation. The proportion of Estonians in this organization did not exceed 50 percent until the mid-1960s. Actually, the "Estonianization" of the local Communist Party structure would have changed nothing. The Latvians had succeeded in becoming a national majority within their Communist Party by the late 1950s, but harsh intervention by Moscow worsened the situation once again.

As pressure persisted, however, so did the resistance. One form of resistance was the stubborn preservation and advancement of national culture. The guiding principle for this drive was a statement by Jakob Hurt, a man who had sown the seeds for Estonia's national awakening in the nineteenth century: "If we should not become great by our strength or our numbers, then we must become great by our spirit, our culture. A nation that is culturally strong and wealthy cannot be stripped of its national identity." This principle sustained the Estonians during the most difficult decades of Soviet rule. Art and literature played special roles in an environment where free expression was strictly limited. Between the lines, readers could comprehend the bittersweet yearning for truth and justice, the insatiable thirst for freedom. Estonian writers and poets called on the people to remain true to their principles and to cherish and preserve their native language. By maintaining its cultural heritage, Estonia could retain its historical ties with Europe, a fact which was especially important in the existing circumstances.

In addition to the work of professional cultural figures, the people nurtured their national culture. The strongest statements of national identity were the nationwide Song Festivals held every four years, drawing hundreds of thousands of people from all over Estonia. By singing their old beloved national songs interspersed with the officially prescribed Soviet works, the people reaffirmed their existence and their inner faith, giving them strength to endure the hard times. The survival of the church against all odds also played a crucial role.

Naturally, this was only one aspect of the resistance. Without a political struggle that could manifest itself in public campaigns, passive resistance would have faded quickly. The people needed reassurance that the struggle was continuing, tangible proof that the spirit of resistance lived on. And so, each year, on February 24, the anniversary of Estonian independence, leaflets appeared on bulletin boards and fences, and "forbidden literature" was passed from hand to hand. On national holidays, blue-black-and-white flags were hoisted onto trees and posts. On Christmas Eve, candles were lit on the graves of freedom fighters, according to the old custom. Bouquets of flowers kept appearing with undaunted regularity at the sites of national monuments obliterated by the occupiers. All these actions served to remind the Estonians to preserve their national spirit.

The City Brothers units represented the connecting link between the battles of the woodland partisans and the political resistance movements. Though the armed struggle in the woods came to an end by the mid-1950s, the underground organizations in the cities continued to work vigorously. A typical example of such a group was the underground organization of students from Tartu, called *Sini-must-valge* ("The Blue-black-and-white"), which included the later renowned dissident Enn Tarto. In accordance with the spirit of the times, the organization had a constitution, an oath, secret weapons, and hand-printed leaflets. Distribution of these leaflets led to the group's downfall in 1956, when the members of the organization were apprehended and sent to Siberian prison camps. In 1955, another well-known dissident, Erik Udam, had been sentenced to prison for belonging to a similar organization. After their release, neither Tarto nor Udam remained free for long. In 1962, both were sentenced to five and a half years of internment in a hard labor colony for their work in the organization called the *Eesti Rahvuslaste Liit* (Estonian Nationalist Union).

In contrast to the widespread support enjoyed by the rural Forest Brothers in the preceding decades, the urban organizations had a very narrow base of support to draw from. The public had become fearful; their finest leaders were discouraged and disillusioned. Indeed, in the early 1960s, during the peak of the thaw, the organized resistance movement seemed to be in its final stage.

Young people opposed to Soviet rule, however, felt it logical to prefer the use of legitimate Soviet-imposed structures, particularly the Komsomol, to their own advantage in furthering the opposition. This trend became particularly strong in the late 1960s at the University of Tartu. University Komsomol leaders focused on building "socialism with a human face" and kept a keen eye on the changes occurring in Czechoslovakia. The university student demonstrations of that time tended to boil over into condemnations of the Soviet system.

The hopes to further the opposition movement by using Soviet establishments crumbled when Soviet tanks crushed the Prague Spring movement in 1968 and sparked the subsequent crackdown within the Soviet Empire. The opposition movements that had arisen within Soviet-imposed establishments were closed down. Intellectual groups were subjected to a thorough purge. Some of the opposition activists accepted these events as inevitable and continued climbing the career ladder within the Soviet system. Some withdrew into silence and avoided public activism. A smaller number joined the dissident movement that had taken root in Estonia. The era of the dissidents had begun.

The first of these groups arose as cooperative endeavors between Russians and Estonians in 1968 and 1969. In 1969, three officers of the Baltic fleet in Tallinn and four Estonians from Tartu were arrested and accused of illegal possession of firearms, among other charges. The first real dissident organizations — the *Eesti Demokraatlik Liit* (Estonian Democratic Union) and the *Eesti Rahvuslik*

Rinne (Estonian Nationalist Front) — formed in Estonia in the early 1970s. In 1972, they sent a joint appeal to United Nations Secretary General Kurt Waldheim demanding the restoration of Estonian independence. Furthermore, the new Estonian dissidents managed to reestablish contacts with Estonian émigrés in the West. The renewed vigor of the dissident movement encouraged Estonian émigré political leaders to assert their demands more strongly in the world political arena. The West gradually began turning its attention to the Baltic issue.

Naturally, the Soviet security apparatus was not content to sit by and watch. In 1975, a number of members of the Estonian Democratic Union were arrested and sentenced to varying terms of imprisonment. Dissidents responded with a new campaign of protests and open letters; the authorities retaliated with a new rash of arrests and imprisonments. Cooperation with dissident movements in the other Baltic States intensified. On August 23, 1979, forty-five Estonians, Latvians, and Lithuanians sent a letter to the governments of the Soviet Union, the German Democratic Republic, and the Federal Republic of Germany asking for the repeal of the consequences of the Molotov–Ribbentrop Pact. Many more joint appeals followed in 1980.

Naturally, in their early years the dissident campaigns failed to influence significant changes. The activities of dissidents were no more than the whine of an annoying mosquito to the great Russian bear. The Soviet Union refused to depart from its plans. The Estonian economy continued to decline. The Soviet policy of centralization and its quest to build gigantic enterprises were transforming most of Estonia into a backward, overindustrialized borderland. The fact that Tallinn had become a quaint kind of Soviet port of call for Western tourists gave the Estonians little satisfaction.

In the late 1970s, the land was swept by a new wave of Russification. All manner of privileges encouraged colonists to settle in Estonia. Russian colonists were allocated new apartments, leaving Estonians to live in older buildings. More than 70 percent of all foreign nationals in Estonia lived in fully-equipped apartments, while the proportion of native Estonians living in such dwellings was barely 50 percent. The proportion of Estonians in Estonia fell to 61 percent. The tentacles of Russification stretched even farther. In 1978, the Central Committee of the Communist Party of Estonia issued an ultrasecret directive at Moscow's orders calling for even more extensive Russification of Estonia. It called for an increase in the use of the Russian language in everyday business, throughout the educational system, and even in kindergartens. It seemed that nothing could save Estonia now.

And yet, in this very era of hopelessness, the roots of change took hold. A new generation emerged on the scene. These individuals were not tied to the independent Republic of Estonia by personal experiences, but only by the recollections of their parents and grandparents. The experiences related by the older generation seemed like fairy tales amidst the miserable reality of Soviet life. But the nation, by preserving its memory, had actually preserved its identity. The legacy of their forefathers who had fought and died for Estonian freedom aroused the spirit of the younger generation. Since they had grown up within the Soviet system, this generation should have been unquestioningly submissive to it, but it took the opposite track. The young people had no illusions about the Soviet system; they were indeed blessed with a certain immunity against the all-pervasive ideology. The impending destruction of their nation called them to action. There was nothing to lose, since the future held nothing but national annihilation. The youth of Estonia chose the way of their forefathers. Resistance became their only option.

The Estonian resistance movement underwent a rapid reanimation in the 1980s. Opposition groups sprang up in many parts of the country. All forms of public protest actions against the Soviet system, such as the dissemination of leaflets and the hoisting of the national flag, increased in frequency. Underground publications flourished throughout the land. The most influential of these was the "Supplements to the Free Circulation of News and Ideas in Estonia," a collection of documents issued by several dissident movements. The young people's demonstration in Tallinn in the autumn of 1980 confirmed the widespread grass-roots nature of the new opposition. Young people calling for an end to Russification and the restoration of Estonian independence were scattered by special police units, who beat some of the demonstrators and arrested a great many of them. These acts of violence jolted the Estonian intellectual community into a public declaration of their opposition to the current system. In the appeal known as the "Letter of 40," forty well-known Estonian cultural figures openly protested against the policies of Russification in Estonia.

The authorities responded to the snowballing resistance with repressions. In October 1980, Estonia was besieged by a wave of searches and arrests, followed by a series of trials. In 1981, ornithologist Mart Niklus and chemist Jüri Kukk were sentenced to lengthy jail terms. Protesting against the unfair verdict, the renowned Estonian scientist Jüri Kukk embarked on a hunger strike which took his life on March 27, 1981. In 1983, the persons involved with the publication of "Supplements" were arrested and sentenced to various terms of imprisonment. The resistance movement seemed to retreat into stunned stillness.

The silence, however, was deceptive. The embers of resistance continued to glow under the ashes, often manifesting themselves through violence. Many young people saw no other way to stop the onrush of colonization but to resort to terrorism. Large-scale gang fights, some involving the use of firearms, became more frequent between Estonian and Russian youths.

It is hard to predict where it all would have ended if the Soviet central leadership had not finally acknowledged the impending implosion of the Soviet empire. Mikhail Gorbachev, the man who had become First Secretary of the Soviet Union's Communist Party, set about advocating his programs of *glasnost* and *perestroika*. He decided that repairing the facade of the empire would continue to guarantee the receipt of foreign loans that would invigorate the Soviet economy. The goal of *perestroika* was to put on a show of liberalizing the Soviet system while preserving its basic character. Unfortunately, the Soviet leadership failed to realize that democracy is like toothpaste: once you squeeze it out, you can never get it back in the tube. Estonia's resistance movement, now deep underground, used the opportunities presented by *glasnost* and *perestroika* to the utmost.

The autumn of 1986 saw the founding of the Estonian Heritage Society, which set about advocating the necessity of protecting Estonia's cultural treasures and returning the nation's history to its people, thus also advocating the concept of a "new era of national awakening." Although Soviet authorities attempted to limit its activities, the Heritage Society movement flourished. In the spring of 1987, it was joined by the Greens movement, which received its initial thrust from the popular protest against the gigantic phosphorite mining projects planned for Estonia by Moscow. For the first time in decades, the people brought their demands to the streets. The authorities, stunned by the organized protest movement, put a stop to the intended projects.

The resistance movement reached a new high on August 23, 1987, when Tallinn became the site of a political demonstration organized by former political prisoners who urged the people to demand the repeal of the Molotov-Ribbentrop Pact and the elimination of its consequences. Although Tiit Madisson, the organizer of the demonstration, was expelled from the country, the movement had already gained momentum. The Estonian people, realizing their power, could no longer be easily stopped. Subsequent demonstrations organized primarily by young people and aging freedom fighters took place in many parts of Estonia, often accompanied by encounters with the police and security forces. The Joint Plenum of the Leaders of the Cultural Unions of the Estonian Soviet Socialist Republic in April 1988 bluntly attacked Russification policies and demanded more rights for Estonians to decide their own fate. At the Heritage Festival held in Tartu a few weeks later, the most impressive mass demonstration since 1940 brought the symbol of the Estonian nation — the blue-black-and-white flag — out in the open once more. Over the next several months, the flag of national independence and new patriotic songs swept the land, encouraging the people to cast aside decades of fear and humiliation. In the first days of June 1988, 100,000 singing and dancing young people gathered at the Song Festival Amphitheater in Tallinn, as scores of national flags flew above them. The chairman of the CPE Karl Vaino ordered tanks sent in to quell the demonstration, but times had changed. Moscow backed off, Vaino was relieved of his post, and restructuring began to take place in Estonia.

The Estonian Popular Front, created in April 1988, played a leading role in subsequent events. The Estonian National Independence Party, an organization demanding Estonian independence since the day of its creation in 1988, also stood at the forefront. After three years of tenacious struggle, Estonia and the other Baltic nations succeeded in exercising their will, and in August 1991, the three independent Baltic States appeared once again on the world political map.

One question has been asked frequently: Where did the Estonian people, a nation downtrodden for decades, get the strength to rise up and fight for their rights? This question is obviously a difficult one to answer. One essential factor in the tenacity of the resistance, however, was the Estonians' recognition of and refusal to relinquish their fundamental rights. The basis of this position is found in their retention of close ties between the past and the present by the preservation of collective memory. The people's refusal to bury their historical memory preserved the attitudes and values of their forebears in the nation's innermost soul. It is said that only a nation which has fought for its freedom deserves to have it. Estonia fought for its freedom, paying perhaps a greater price than many other nations. It is because of this tenacious struggle that the Estonian people prevailed.

The battles fought by the Estonian Forest Brothers in the postwar years ended in defeat. They failed to free their homeland from the grip of the invaders; they failed to save their families, much less themselves. And yet, their spirit of relentless resistance ignited a deep patriotism and steadfastness of character in the smoldering soul of later generations, who used these treasures to lay the foundation for the "Singing Revolution" that finally began in 1988. The desperate but uncompromising resistance shown by the Forest Brothers, and by all the men and women who followed in their footsteps, saved the Estonian soul. It is to these men and women who gave their lives in the forests and swamps that we owe our deepest respect and gratitude.

Appendix A

Description of a Forest Brothers Bunker

- Selection of the Site
- Construction of the Four-Man Bunker
- Placement of the Bunker
- Layout of the Bunker
- The Interior of the Bunker
- Camouflaging the Surroundings
- Food Supplies
- A Final Note

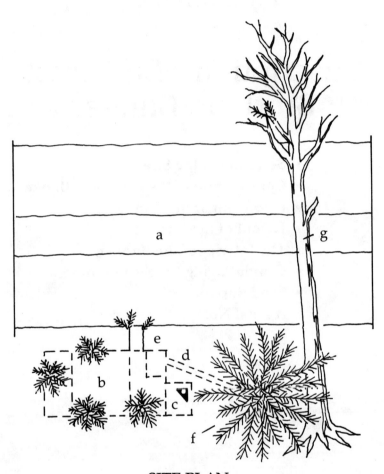

SITE PLAN
SCALE 3/32" - 1'

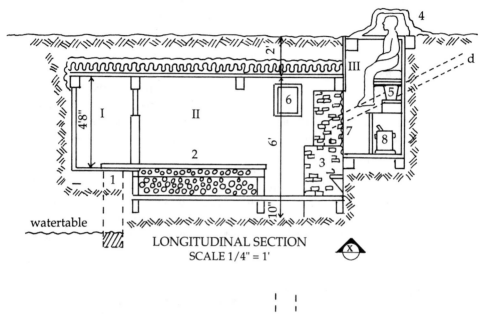

LONGITUDINAL SECTION
SCALE 1/4" = 1'

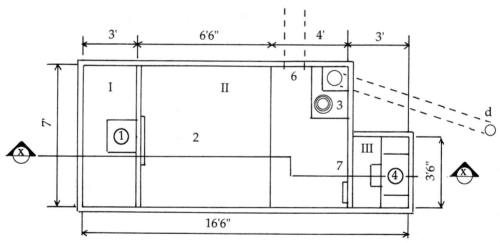

FLOOR PLAN
SCALE 1/4" = 1'

Description of a Forest Brothers Bunker
Selection of the Site

In the autumn of 1945, in a forest with a large swampy area, we selected a spot where the ground water level was relatively deep. The site was an earthen mound created by the digging of a drainage canal. The mound already had large trees growing on it. The mixed vegetation in this forest area, which consisted of clumps of young pine and fir trees underneath taller deciduous trees, was advantageous for concealment as well as strategic for fighting defensive battles and escaping potential raids.

Another essential consideration in selecting a site was the proximity of a heavily used forest area with a logging road and footpath. Footprints on such a path would not betray the presence of the Forest Brothers, and the path could be used at night to bring food from farms and food pickup points, as well as to transport construction materials for the bunker.

Before construction was begun, a friendly forest warden helped us find out whether logging operations were planned for this section of the forest in the winter of 1945–46. There were no such plans.

We built one four-man and one three-man bunker. The bunkers were built about fifty paces from each other to give us the advantage of surprise if we needed to open fire in self-defense to cover ourselves in the event of a raid, exchange of gunfire, or attempts to escape.

Construction of the Four-Man Bunker

At this carefully selected site, a hole 17' x 7'6" in length and width and nearly 9' deep was dug into the earthen mound of the drainage canal. In the fall, before the leaves fell, we loaded the soil into boxes and carried it to the edge of the swampy area some distance away. There, we cut the mossy sod into strips and rolled it up. The soil was spread evenly onto the stripped area. When the moss was carefully unrolled onto the fresh soil, the transported earth was completely concealed.

We pulled up the floorboards at an old deserted farmhouse some distance from the bunker. We also sawed props and girders at the farmhouse into the lengths we needed for the bunker and then transported them into the forest. The farmhouse also provided us with bricks, an iron stove plate, and a metal pipe for the bunker chimney. We built our forest bunker with hardly a single telltale blow of a hammer or whine of a saw.

Between the floor-girders of the bunker, we placed some drainage pipes which would direct the overflow into the bottom of the canal if the ground water should rise. On top of the girders, we placed floorboards; we used these boards also to line the walls. We then put up joists and ceiling boards, topping them with roofing tin. A layer of straw was scattered over the tin for insulation. Fir branches went on top of that, and a final layer of twelve to sixteen inches of soil. This kept the snow from melting on the bunker's roof and prevented loss of heat from the bunker itself.

Placement of the Bunker

(See site plan.)

In a mixed forest, beneath an earthen mound along a drainage canal (a) 18′ wide.

(b) 16′6" x 7′0" underground bunker. With the arrival of cold weather, young fir and pine trees were "planted" on the "roof" of the bunker.

(c) 3′0" x 3′6" bunker lookout station, latrine, and entrance.

(d) Underground chimney whose vertical pipe directed the smoke into the upper branches of a tall fir tree (f).

(e) Daylight shaft in the bank of the canal, hidden by young fir trees.

(f) An old fir tree, about 40′ tall. The base of the tree was covered with needles, which did not show footprints. The base of the tree remained free of snow, even in wintertime.

(g) A pine tree with a straight and smooth trunk, uprooted with ropes by the Forest Brothers. The wind blew the snow off the smooth trunk, which served as a "bridge" allowing the Forest Brothers to walk to the opposite side of the drainage canal without leaving footprints.

(h) A refuse hole with a tight-fitting lid was located on the treetop end of the pine in the earthen mound along the canal. A small fir was "planted" on the lid.

Layout of the Bunker

(See floor plan and longitudinal section.)

The bunker contained three rooms. The cold storage room (I), 3′ x 7′, was used for keeping food supplies and a milk jug. It also contained a well (1) about 12" in diameter and 4′ deep with lid. The living room (II), 10′6" x 7′0", contained bunks (2) for four men. The bunk boards were placed loosely on an 18-inch-high frame, with firewood reserves stored underneath. The living room also contained a stove/oven (3) built of bricks. After dark we used very little wood to prepare our meals, because the firewood consisted of small and well-dried hewn logs sawed from telephone poles, which burned almost smokelessly. The foyer (III), 3' x 3'6", contained the latrine and a bench for the guard/lookout, who sat high on a seatboard and cushion with his head in a hollow tree stump (4). Under the seatboard was the refuse bucket (5) with lid.

An old, hollowed-out tree stump was mounted onto a hinged trapdoor which could be opened to exit the bunker. The stump had natural as well as man-made narrow slits which allowed the Forest Brother acting as daytime lookout to observe the surroundings from the height of the earthen mound, about three feet above the level of the surrounding forest floor. The only obstruction to the line of sight was the trunk of a large fir (f) about three paces away, as well as some smaller trees.

The large fir standing by the entrance to the bunker fulfilled an essential function. When darkness fell and the fire was lit in the stove, the vertical chimney pipe (d) was extended from the bunker up along the trunk to direct the smoke up into the upper branches of the fir and thus to prevent the smell of smoke from lingering in the vicinity of the bunker. The well-dried wood burned with little smoke or odor.

The pine tree (g), uprooted and pulled down with ropes by the men, had a smooth trunk and few branches. It too fulfilled an important function. Since snow did not adhere to the smooth pine bark, we used the trunk as a "bridge" to the opposite side of the canal. On the opposite side, at the treetop end, there was a hole lined with boards and sealed with an airtight lid, where we dumped our dried waste. A small fir was "planted" and attached to the lid, which could be opened by grasping the trunk of the fir, and the waste bucket (5) was emptied into the refuse hole (h) at night.

The Interior of the Bunker

The cold storage area contained supplies of potatoes and root vegetables, a tub of butter, and a barrel of salted meat. Smoked meat and sausages hung on hooks fastened to the ceiling.

Shelves in the living room held sacks of dried bread, flour and barley, salt and sugar, candles, and a small petroleum lantern and matches. Cooking pots and dishes hung on the walls. The walls also held weapons: automatic pistols, Russian sidearms, one precision gun, holstered revolvers, and waist belts. Some shelves held ammunition chests and hand grenades.

The bunker's only window (6), about 12" x 14" in size, was located beside the stove/oven. A "tunnel" (e) angled upward at about 30° and lined with boards led up from the window and became horizontal before exiting the earthen mound of the canal. Several small fir trees grew around the opening, helping to conceal it but also restricting the entry of light.

A heavy blanket covered the opening (7) leading to the vestibule, with its raised lookout post and latrine. The petroleum can and tools, such as axes, saw, wedges, and rope were kept in a storage area (8) under the latrine bucket.

Camouflaging the Surroundings

We had to take special care to camouflage the area and cover our tracks. The forest floor had to look natural and undisturbed. We brought abandoned anthills to the vicinity of the bunker in sacks. We spread dried pine and fir needles over areas that inevitably bore traces of the work and movements in the bunker's vicinity. The bed of evergreen needles rarely betrayed any footprints, and the needles could be smoothed with a broom.

With the first frosts, we "planted" young fir trees on the roof of the finished bunker. They would stay fresh until spring. Upon exiting the bunker, we would step out under the large fir tree and onto the trunk of the "fallen" pine. After reaching the opposite side of the canal by walking across the pine trunk, we continued toward our destinations, choosing a new zigzagging trail with each excursion from the bunker. When a thick layer of ice had formed on the surface of the water in the canal, we could leave the bunker in either direction by walking on the ice wearing soft felt boots or peasant moccasins. Of course, this was only possible if no snow had fallen.

Food Supplies

We brought food to the bunker on dark nights from food pickup points — farmhouses or other previously agreed-upon outbuildings. Because these farms were four to eight miles from the bunker, a food supply expedition usually took all night. In the winter of 1945–46, the new *kolkhoz* system had not yet been established in Estonia, and the Forest Brothers could rely on their home farms or those of their relatives or friends to supply them with bread, butter, meat, flour, barley, milk, homemade cheese, eggs, potatoes, cabbage, and carrots.

During dark autumn nights and in winter snowfall or blizzards, the men brought food supplies from the farms to the bunker in knapsacks.

In some townships, overzealous Communists, Executive Committee members, and policemen would keep the farms suspected of helping the Forest Brothers under nighttime surveillance. The farm families were usually aware of being watched, and they put out prearranged warning signals for the Forest Brothers. The Forest Brothers stayed away from the farm whenever they saw the signals. If the coast was clear and the Forest Brothers were admitted into the farmhouse, the families would cover the windows with blankets, so that the lights in the windows late at night would not attract attention.

In the summertime, when the Forest Brothers lived in sheds or in well-camouflaged tents in the forest, they changed location frequently. Wearing women's clothing and head scarves, they lent a hand with the farm chores during the day or on moonlit nights: hauling manure, making hay, and gathering potatoes to repay the relatives and friends who had replenished their food supplies in the wintertime.

A Final Note

In early December of 1945, I left this group of Forest Brothers and was captured on a forest path under surveillance by the seven-man operative group led by MVD (later KGB) Lieutenant Uno Laht about five miles from the bunker.

My six companion Forest Brothers lived in these bunkers through the winter of 1945–46 until the spring. In the summer they moved from place to place, and in the autumn they selected a new location in another large forest to build new bunkers. In a raid on their bunkers on December 31, 1946, one Forest Brother was killed and four were captured. One Forest Brother evaded capture since he was away from the bunker during the raid, but he too was captured later. Of the five Forest Brothers who were captured and arrested, three perished in the inhuman conditions of Siberian forced labor camps, through harsh forced labor, hunger, cold, and lack of medical care.

— Olaf Tammark

Appendix B

This document represents excerpts of the bylaws of the Armed Resistance League (Relvastatud Võitluse Liit). The pages were obtained from KGB files on Ants the Terrible. They were obviously used as evidence of his anti-Soviet activities.

The Armed Resistance League Organization
The Organization "RVL"

The organization RVL is a voluntary, secret, and armed organization of national resistance to fight for the honor and independence of Estonia.

The Goals of the RVL Organization

1. To assemble capable individuals into an organized armed force for united military action
   a. in the event of widespread deportations or arrests;
   b. in the event of the widespread destruction or removal of the people's property;
   c. to wage an effective partisan war if hostilities begin;
   d. to defend a member or members of the RVL organization.
2. To carry out an ideological struggle
   a. by instilling faith in the restoration of Estonian independent statehood;
   b. by encouraging patriotic spirit and a feeling of solidarity;
   c. by increasing the people's spirit of resistance and by deepening contempt for the occupation authorities and their henchmen.
3. To wage battle with national traitors
   a. by finding out and exposing traitors and those collaborating with the occupation authorities;
   b. by bringing especially dangerous traitors to trial in the Security Court.
4. To carry out a united defense against the establishments of persecution run by the occupation authorities
   a. by providing material support for individual members as needed;

    b. by procuring hideouts for concealment;

    c. by obtaining as much reconnaissance information as possible, and forwarding it to individual members;

    d. by using, if the need arises, armed force in defense of individual members.

  5. To acquire military and political reconnaissance information.

  6. To bring about the economic and political disintegration of the powers of occupation.

The Structure of the RVL Organization

The activities of the RVL shall be led and managed by the commander of the organization. All members of the organization shall be subordinate to and accountable to him. The commander shall be accountable only to the representatives of the will of the people, i.e., to the legal government of Estonia.

The RVL Security Court

For the battle against internal and external traitors, the organization shall include a Security Court, which shall consist of three members appointed by the commander of the organization. The organization commander shall have no authority over the activities of the Security Court. The Court shall be accountable only to the legal government of Estonia. Cases shall be introduced to the Court by the organization commander or by an individual authorized by him.

The time and method of the execution of the verdict shall be determined by the organization commander.

The Member and Acquisition of Membership

Anyone wanting to fight for the honor and freedom of Estonia and prepared to faithfully and unconditionally fulfill the duties and tasks assigned to him as a member of the organization, and who does not have blood guilt against the Estonian people, can join the RVL.

A member of the RVL organization

  1. has resolute faith in the rebirth of a free and independent Estonia;

  2. is loyal to the principles and regulations of the organization.

The organization commander shall determine the procedure for the acceptance of each member.

Upon acceptance into the organization, the member shall take the following oath:

"As a loyal Estonian and member of the Armed Resistance League Organization, I pledge to dedicate all my physical and mental faculties to the fight for Estonian honor and freedom. While carrying out my duties, I pledge to act with responsibility and courage, without fear of giving my life for a better future for Estonia, following the example of our ancient heroes.

Betrayal and breaking of the oath will be severely punished."

Duties of the RVL Member

Every RVL member is bound by honor:
1. to be a credit to the RVL organization through his be-havior and attitude;
2. to obtain his own weapons and necessary equipment;
3. to support the organization materially within his means.

Every RVL member is obligated:
1. to be dutiful and disciplined;
2. to carry out, without resistance, all orders and instruc-tions, whereby the individual giving the orders shall be held responsible;
3. to hold fast to secrecy, knowing that the fate of the entire organization and many individuals depends on it;
4. to always step forth in the defense of one's companions in accordance with the principle: one for all and all for one.

Rights of the RVL Member

1. The RVL shall support each RVL member
   a. by supplying him with information;
   b. by giving him material assistance if needed;
   c. by supplying him with a hideout if he should come under persecution;
   d. by providing armed assistance.
2. The RVL member has the right to take revenge
   a. if an RVL member is murdered or apprehended by the establishments of persecution, then the organiza-tion shall take revenge on the guilty party;
   b. if other individuals must suffer or be punished through the fault of an RVL member, then the RVL member has the right to demand revenge and to require that the guilty party be brought before the Security Court for punishment.

Petition

Knowing the principles of the RVL, I wish to operate loyally according to them. Please accept me into the RVL under the following name:

Name
Year of birth
Education
Profession
Military rank
Activities during the occupations
Participation in battle
Participation in partisan activities
Special skills
Knowledge of foreign languages
Decision:

The Township Commander and His Duties

The township commander shall be designated by the commander of the RVL, and his duties shall be:

    a. to act as the local executor of the RVL commander's directives and instructions;

    b. to nurture a will to fight and a sense of solidarity and loyalty among the members of the organization;

    c. to nurture love of the fatherland and a conviction in the restoration of Estonian independent statehood among the members of the organization;

    d. to oversee the internal discipline of the township organization;

    e. to recruit members for the RVL organization;

    f. to carry out reconnaissance of military and political information;

    g. to organize assistance for members of the organization who are in trouble;

    h. to organize the acquisition of material and monetary reserves for the organization;

    i. to organize, if the need arises, military action to defend a member of the organization or in the event of widespread deportations.

The commander of the township organization is responsible for the security of all residents of the township who are members of the township organization or who are helping the RVL movement. For this reason, the township organization commander must be extremely careful and follow exactly all directives that are issued to ensure security.

Being designated as the commander of a township organization indicates the organization's great trust in that individual. Each commander of a township organization must be worthy of this trust.

No member of the organization should pay dearly for his faith in his commanders. To ensure this, each commander, if the need arises, must be willing to sacrifice himself for the honor of the organization and the security of his colleagues in the organization.

I.

The highest duty of every township organization commander is the creation of a strong township organization. A large township organization not only provides a larger armed force, but also allows for the acquisition of more comprehensive and detailed reconnaissance data. The township organization commander may recruit all men who meet the requirements set forth in the bylaws, and who own the trust of the township organization commander, or have the trust and recommendation of an organization member.

In the interests of the security of organization members, it is recommended that RVL members who are legally registered residents of the region must not know of each other's membership in the organization.

Those members who are non-legal residents or Forest Brothers may know each other. These individuals shall make up the armed force that is always on hand for a sudden call to action.

A membership applicant shall fill out the required form. The township organization commander shall send the second part of the form to the RVL commander.

In the event membership is denied, the township organization commander shall administer an oath of silence to the rejected candidate, also informing such person of the measures taken by the organization if the individual should reveal any of what he has heard.

If information or rumors are spread about the RVL, the township organization commander shall try to ascertain the source of the information and immediately inform the RVL commander.

The township organization commander shall supply a review of those men who, for any number of reasons, cannot currently be utilized as members of the organization, but who are probably willing to offer assistance. Such men shall form a reserve, from which new members may be recruited as the need arises.

II.

Successful operations by the organization are based on the acquisition of accurate political reconnaissance data. The organization must acquire information on the identity, activities, duties, and plans of the Communists as well as traitors.

The duty of the township organization commander is:

1. to acquire, within the borders of his township, the following information (including accurate addresses):
   a. on Communist Party members;
   b. on People's Defense Battalion members;
   c. on members of the Communist Youth League;
   d. on workers of the Executive Committee and Village Council;
   e. on other active or suspicious individuals.

The township organization shall make a note of all such individuals who formally hold any of these positions but do not operate in a manner that endangers the populace.

The township organization shall provide information on the reported and verified crimes and activities of more dangerous and active Communists.

Such information must be carefully investigated and verified. A special note must be made about activities that cannot be verified at present.

2. to acquire information on the activities and plans of the Communists:
   a. by working to obtain the information from a Communist. The following methods may be used: enticement; threats; guarantees of security and impunity for any individual who doubts the survival of Soviet authority; and alcohol (due to the human tendency to easily reveal secrets in a drunken state). Good results can also be achieved by using attractive and skilled women to obtain information from men, and vice versa. Acquisition of information from Communists is extremely risky, and great care must be taken in every case.
   b. by infiltrating RVL members or collaborators from the Communists perceived as trustworthy (for example, a worker, an employee, a new landowner or other individual) into Communist organizations, primarily into the Communist Party and People's Defense Battalions, so they can begin to provide regular information. These individuals shall get a certificate from the RVL stating that they have joined

the Communist organization at the RVL's orders, in order to prevent them from compromising themselves. Publicly, these individuals shall embrace Soviet attitudes. In order to ensure the security of these individuals, as well as the secrecy of the operation, the township organization commander may not provide any information to other township organization commanders about the individual nor the methods of reconnaissance being used.

Specific directives on how to operate in specific circumstances are impossible to provide. The latter methods are recommended because of their relative safety.

In any case, every township organization commander must exhibit initiative and creativity when putting together an efficient reconnaissance apparatus.

III.

The township organization commander shall acquire information on military units and their location, as well as military guardposts, fortifications, military structures (airfields, training fields, etc.), and warehouses in his district.

IV.

The township organization commander shall acquire information on the weaponry, ammunition, and battle gear existing in his district.

At the same time, each township organization commander shall attempt to ensure that each owner of a weapon shall protect his weapon and ammunition from damage and keep it in working order.

V.

It shall be the honor and duty of every township organization and its commander to help those RVL members in its district who have encountered difficulties and need support. For this purpose, the township organization commander shall collect necessary material and monetary reserves:

1. by obtaining and organizing support from patriotic and materially capable citizens on a voluntary basis. (Great care must be exercised in selecting these individuals; their names must be guarded with utmost secrecy. Under no circumstances must outsiders be told of the existence of the RVL.);

2. by forcibly acquiring (expropriating) state property.

The inviolability of private property must be strictly adhered to.

Accurate reports must be submitted on contributions, expropriation of state property, and operating expenses.

If it is not possible to assist a member in need of help, the township organization commander shall report on such circumstances and their causes to the RVL commander, who shall attempt to provide support in any way possible.

VI.

In accordance with the organization's bylaws, the organization members have the right to refuge and assistance if they come under persecution. To make this possible, every township organization commander must make plans for the concealment and feeding of an RVL member if the need arises. The township organization commander shall notify the RVL commander of how many individuals he is capable of hiding and supplying in his district, if the need should arise.

VII.

The township organization commander may use armed force on his own initiative in the defense of an RVL member and in the event of widespread deportations. In all other cases, the orders shall come from the RVL commander.

VIII.

The township organization commander shall submit a monthly report of his activities. He shall report special situations immediately.

Biographic Profiles

Audova, Leo: British spy. Fought in the Estonian Legion; captured by the British in 1945. After his release from prison, lived in England, where he joined the reconnaissance group prepared by Alfons Rebane. Captured in Estonia by the security apparatus; apparently executed.

Aunvere, Ants: Estonian Forest Brother. Born in 1916. Son of a Võrumaa county farmer. Joined the Forest Brother movement after the nationalization of his family farm, fighting until 1956, after which he worked in several areas of Estonia under an assumed name until he was arrested and sentenced to death in 1970.

Birk, Evi: Member of the resistance movement. Left Estonia in 1944, but soon returned to Estonia on behalf of émigré groups, also hoping to contact her fiancé, who had been left behind in Estonia. Imprisoned and sentenced to forced labor in Siberia. Currently retired; active public figure in Estonia.

Carr, Henry: British spy, "controller" of the SIS Northern Office. Born in 1891. Worked with intelligence service in 1919. Responsible for SIS activities in the Baltic States and the Ukraine during the postwar period. Died in 1988.

Hanko, Jüri: Schoolboy; member of the resistance movement. Arrested in 1944 by the NKVD and sentenced to Kolyma death camp. Survived; released in 1956; currently retired in Tartu.

Heeska, Johannes: Forest Brother. Farmer in Võrumaa County. Took part in the 1941 "summer war" against the Red army. Evaded German mobilization 1943–44. Hid from Soviet authorities 1944–1953. One of the most active members of the Forest Brothers unit led by Ants Aunvere. Arrested in 1953 and sent to Siberia. Released in 1970. Died in 1991.

Hellat, Toomas: A leader of the resistance movement. Born in 1920. Fled to Finland in 1940, returning to Estonia that same year under orders from Finnish intelligence. Returned to Finland in 1941. Member of the "Erna" unit; recipient of the Finnish Iron Cross. Joined German intelligence while maintaining contacts with the British, Swedes, and Finns. An organizer of the National Council. A leader of the Haukka-Tümmler reconnaissance group. Remained in Estonia in

1944, where he was imprisoned and sentenced to ten years in Siberia. Died in Estonia in 1987.

Ilp, Elmar: A Forest Brothers leader on Saaremaa Island. Born in 1919. Went into hiding during the German occupation. Imprisoned by Soviet authorities in 1945; escaped from prison. Alarmed Soviet authorities with his brutality and recklessness. Killed in battle in 1950.

Järlet, Eerich: Forest Brother in Läänemaa County. Member of RVL. Captured by the Soviet security apparatus and sentenced to death.

Käärmann, Alfred: Forest Brother from Võrumaa County. Served in the German army. Went into hiding after the arrest of his brother in 1944. Lost a hand during clash in 1945, but continued fighting until 1952, when he was captured by means of poisoned vodka. Imprisoned in Siberia until 1970; returned to and worked in Võrumaa County. Collected data about the resistance movement and recorded his own memoirs.

Kaljurand, Ants: One of Estonia's most well-known Forest Brothers; nicknamed "Ants the Terrible." Gained fame with his daring attacks and deception of the KGB. Captured by the KGB in 1949; sentenced to death and executed in 1951.

Karkman, Heino: British spy. Sent to Estonia on assignment in 1953; returned to England in 1955, relating his suspicions about the Estonian "Forest Brothers" to Alfons Rebane. Died under mysterious circumstances in Sweden in 1957.

Karotamm, Nikolai: Soviet Estonian puppet government figure; First Secretary of the Communist Party of Estonia 1944–1950. Born in Estonia in 1901; educated in the Soviet Union; returned to Estonia in 1940. Relieved of his post in 1950; worked subsequently in several positions as a scientist. Died in 1969.

Karuks, Endel: A Forest Brothers leader in Järvamaa County. Killed in a battle at Liigvalla in 1946. He was betrayed by a man named Ööbik, who approached him as he lay wounded during the battle. Karuks shot Ööbik to death and then took his own life.

Kask, Uno: KGB officer. Born in Pärnu City in 1918; served in the KGB from 1946. A leader of the "false Forest Brothers" movement in Estonia; later retired on government pension.

Keskküla, Jüri: Forest Brother; son of a Saaremaa Soviet activist. Joined the Red army in 1941; taken prisoner by the Germans. Upon discovering that his father had been killed in 1941 by the Saaremaa Forest Brothers, he voluntarily joined the German army out of fear. Returned to Estonia in 1944 and went into hiding with the Forest Brothers unit led by the man who had shot his father. After the unit was crushed, he hid out with his sweetheart until 1964, when he was discovered and arrested. Escaped punishment and lived near Tallinn at Saue.

Killar, Eeri: Forest Brother in Rõuge Parish of Võrumaa County. Hid out until 1949, when he was arrested and sent to Siberia. Subsequently returned. Currently lives in retirement in Urvaste.

Kirbits, Kalju: Estonian nationalist from Rõuge Parish of Võrumaa County. Digger by trade. Forcibly evacuated to Russia in 1941. Later worked in several parts of Estonia. Investigated the history of the Forest Brothers movement. Died in 1991.

Koovik, Haljand: A leader of the Võrumaa County Forest Brothers; known as the "Green General." Born in 1922. Son of a small farmer. Went into hiding in 1944. Killed in an ambush in 1949.

Kriisa, Lembit: Member of the resistance movement. Fled to Sweden during the second Soviet occupation, taking part in operations sending émigré agents to Estonia. Later, founder of a publishing house that has played an important role in preserving Estonian cultural history. Currently owner of Estonian bookstore in Stockholm.

Kumm, Boris: KGB chief in Estonia. Born in Pärnumaa County in 1897. Became People's Commissar of Security in 1941. Minister of State Security 1944–1950. Played leading role in carrying out deportations and suffocating the resistance movement in Estonia. Later retired on government pension; died in 1958.

Kuperjanov, Julius: Estonian military leader; lieutenant in the Estonian Army. Born in 1894. Gained fame by founding and commanding a partisan unit in the Estonian War of Independence. Killed in the battle of Paju in 1919.

Kurg, Friedrich: Major, Squadron Commander of the Tartu Cavalry Regiment. Born in Valgamaa County in 1898. Recipient of the Estonian Cross of Freedom for valor in the War of Independence. Leader of a Forest Brothers group in Ropka Township, fighting alongside his men in the liberation of Tartu on July 10, 1941. Commander of the *Omakaitse* units of southern Estonia. Estonian Volunteer Battalion Commander in 1942–44. As a Forest Brother leader, suffered grave injuries in an NKVD siege led by MVD Lieutenant Uno Laht and died by his own bullet on July 31, 1945.

Laidoner, Juhan: Estonian military and government leader. Born in 1884. Supreme Commander of Estonian forces in the War of Independence (1918–1920). Imprisoned by Soviet authorities in 1940 and deported to Russia, where he died in 1953.

Leetmaa, Meinhard: Born in Virumaa County in 1903. Second Lieutenant in Estonian army until 1940. 22nd Estonian Rifle Corps

232nd Rifle Regiment Company Commander in 1941. German prisoner of war, 1941–42. Member of Tartu *Omakaitse* 1942–43. Fought against Red Army as 2nd Estonian Border Guard Regiment III Battalion Commander in 1944. Lived in Estonia under false identity 1945–1956. Turned himself over to Soviet authorities during amnesty campaign in 1956. Emigrated to Germany in 1965.

Liiv, Valter: Forest Brother from Orava Township. Became active Forest Brother after the murder of his friends by local Party Secretary Sibul. Killed when someone betrayed him.

Lilleleht, Paul: Estonian military leader. Born in Pärnumaa County in 1893. Showed special courage in the War of Independence in battles against the German *Landeswehr*. Recipient of the Cross of Freedom. Led partisans in southern Estonia in 1941. Planner of the defense of Kilingi-Nõmme. Commander of the Estonian 6th Border Guard Regiment in 1944. Went into hiding in Estonia 1944–1949. Arrested and sent to Siberia, where he died in 1955.

Lipp, Heino: Commander of the Virumaa County Forest Brothers; nicknamed "Pargas." Born in 1910. Earned fame with his daring escapades. Killed in battle in 1949.

Loosaar, Eduard: Farmer from Orava Township. Mobilized into the German army in 1944; upon his release, mobilized into the Red army. Arrested in 1950 and sent to Siberia. Upon his return, lived and worked in his home area, writing an extensive summary of events in Orava Township.

Lukasevics, Janis: KGB general; a commander of anti-SIS operations in the Baltic States. Born in 1920. Joined the Latvian Communist Party in 1937; chief of Latvian KGB Counterintelligence after the war. Organizer of the "Red Web." Commander of KGB counterintelligence in England under assumed name 1972–1980. Died in 1988.

Lutt, Mihkel: Commander of a Forest Brothers unit in Võrumaa County, 1944–45. Captured and sentenced to death in 1946.

Maramaa, Ülo: Journalist and Estonian public figure; one of the leaders of the *Päästekomitee* (Committee to Save Estonia) created in 1940. Arrested by the NKVD in late 1940; executed on July 4, 1941.

Marnot, Oleg: Second Lieutenant in the "Erna" unit. Born in 1915. Estonian ski jumping champion. Fought as partisan in the summer of 1941 in Tartu. Brought by air to Finland and returned by parachute to northern Estonia as a member of the "Erna" unit. Killed in the battle at Kautla on July 31, 1941.

McKibbin, Alexander: A leader of British intelligence operations in the Baltics. Born in 1891. Businessman in Estonia before the war. Based in Helsinki in 1939; then in Stockholm. Established contacts between the resistance groups and the SIS. One of the leaders of operation "Jungle." Died in 1966.

Mõttus, Aksel: Estonian Forest Brother. Born in 1915 in Antsla, southern Estonia. Hid with his two brothers, and later with his father and sister for a total of twenty-three years in the forests of southern Estonia. Captured along with his brother in 1967; sentenced to ten years in prison for "banditism." Employed as hospital orderly after his release. In 1990, the Supreme Court of the Republic of Estonia refused to rehabilitate the Mõttus brothers.

Orasmaa, Johannes: Estonian military leader; general. Commander of the Estonian *Kaitseliit* (Defense League). Arrested after the occupation of Estonia in 1940; executed in 1941.

Päts, Konstantin: President of the Republic of Estonia; one of the best-known Estonian political figures. Deported to Russia with his family in the summer of 1940. Arrested in 1941. Died in 1956 near Kalinin in a psychoneurological hospital. Buried in local cemetery. His body was returned to Estonia for burial in 1990.

Paul, Peeter Mikhailovich: A KGB leader in Estonia. Fought in World War II on the Soviet side in the Estonian Rifle Corps. Coordinated KGB operations in several counties after World War II. Sentenced to death and executed by the Forest Brothers after the mass deportations of 1949.

Piho, Voldemar: Commander of a Forest Brothers unit in Võrumaa County. Born in 1919. Son of a farmer. Began to seek revenge after the murder of his mother by Soviet authorities. Killed in 1949.

Pitka, Johan: Estonian admiral. Born in 1872. A founder of the Estonian naval fleet. One of the chief organizers of Estonian defense forces during the War of Independence; commander of the Estonian fleet. Fled to Finland in 1940, where he sought support for the resistance movement in Estonia. Returned to Estonia in 1944, encouraging the spirit of resistance and making preparations for a partisan war. The battalion formed by Pitka played a significant role in the short-lived restoration of the Republic of Estonia in September 1944. According to some reports, he fell in battle; other information indicates that he poisoned himself in the woods late in 1944. Gravesite unknown.

Randmaa, Paul: A Forest Brothers commander in the Veriora district of Võrumaa County. Began seeking revenge after his father was killed by destruction battalions. Killed in battle in 1949.

Ranniste, Edgar: Forest Brother from Virumaa County. Led a Forest Brothers unit in 1941; later fought in the Estonian Legion. Returned to the forests in 1944. Arrested and sent to Siberia. Survived and returned to Estonia. An organizer of the League of Estonian Political Prisoners in 1989. Active researcher of recent Estonian history.

Raudvassar, Valdur: Member of the resistance movement. Born in 1941 in Võrumaa County. Sentenced to Siberia in 1961 for establishing an underground youth organization. After his release, he lived in many parts of Estonia, taking part in dissident movements. Currently a museum worker in Võru City; representative to the Congress of Estonia.

Rebane, Alfons: Estonian military leader; colonel. Born in 1912. Commanded a partisan unit in Virumaa County in 1941. Voluntary conscript in German army. Commander of Estonian "Eastern Battalion." First Estonian to receive the Knight's Cross in 1944. In 1945, as the commander of the Estonian Division regiment, he also received the Oak Leaves medal. Fled to the West, where he began establishing contacts with the resistance movement in Estonia. Chief of the Estonian section of operation "Jungle." Subsequently retired in Germany. Died in Augsburg, Germany in 1966.

Redlich, Endel: Leader of the *Relvastatud Võitluse Liit* (Armed Resistance League). Born in 1915. Son of a farmer in Läänemaa County. Went into hiding during the German occupation; formed the Armed Defense League in 1944. Killed in 1949.

Reinthal, Olev: Member of the Estonian resistance movement. Worked in the resistance group based in the Tartu Public Health Museum 1940–41. A leader of the uprising and liberation of Tartu. Active in the resistance to German occupation 1941–44. Subsequent fate unknown.

Roots, Jaan: Commander of the "Orion" Forest Brothers unit in Võrumaa County. Leader of a student secret organization in Võru Secondary School; after being discovered, was forced to go into hiding. His family was deported in 1949. Killed in 1952.

Saago, Richard: Member of the resistance movement. Born in 1914. An organizer of the Estonian National Council 1943–44. Fled to Sweden in 1944, returning to Estonia in 1946. Captured by the KGB; details of his fate are lacking.

Saaliste, Artur: Forest Brother. A leader of the *Omakaitse* in Läänemaa County. Went into hiding in 1944, later fighting alongside his brother until falling in battle in 1949.

Saaliste, Richard: A leader of the Armed Resistance League. Brother of Artur Saaliste. Born in 1916. Fought in battles to liberate Estonia in 1941. Officer in the Estonian Border Guard Regiment in 1944. Fled to Sweden in 1944. Returned to Estonia in 1946, where he joined the Armed Resistance League and fought in its ranks until falling in battle in 1949.

Salm, Heino: Police officer and regional historian. Took part in the capture of the last Estonian Forest Brothers as a policeman in the 1960s and '70s. Left the police force and worked as the director of the Valga City Museum, researching the history of the Forest Brothers movement in Estonia and using KGB archives materials in his research.

Schenkenberg, Ivo: Estonian partisan leader in the sixteenth century. Born ca. 1550. Organized a partisan unit of peasants in 1576 which played a significant role in the defense of Tallinn in 1577 during the Livonian War. Killed in battle against the Russians in 1579.

Särak, Voldemar: Member of the "Erna" unit in 1941. Active in the Haukka-Tümmler reconnaissance group 1943–44. Arrested in 1944; fled his trial with Harry Sepik. Fate unclear; some accounts say he fell in Estonia; some claim he was captured and sent to Siberia, where he was torn apart by dogs in an escape attempt. Harry Sepik was captured, but returned from Siberia and died in Estonia.

Silaraijs, Rudolph: Latvian military officer. Born in 1912. Leader of the Latvian section of operation "Jungle." Later a dry goods store manager in Canada, where he died in 1979.

Sisas, Eduard: Merited chekist. Born in 1898 in Võrumaa County. Worked as chekist in the 1920s and '30s in the Ukraine and the Crimea, where he led a false partisan movement 1941–44. Transferred to Estonia in 1944, where he led operations against the Armed Resistance League. Killed in Forest Brothers' ambush in 1949.

Susi, Arnold: Estonian government figure; member of the resistance movement 1941–44. Member of the Government formed by Jüri Uluots in September 1944. Arrested by the NKVD in 1944 and sent to prison in Siberia, where he met Aleksandr Solzhenitsyn and left a marked influence on the author's development. Returned to Estonia in the late 1950s. Solzhenitsyn edited his *Gulag Archipelago* in Susi's country home in Tartumaa County. Died in Estonia.

Täht, Karl: Forest Brother in Valgamaa County. Well known for his cold-bloodedness and sharpshooting ability. Killed in battle.

Talgre, Leo: A leader of the resistance movement. Born in 1919 in a family of Estonian Communists. After his parents left for Russia, he was raised by step-parents. Well educated. Fled to Finland in 1940, where he joined the "Erna" unit, returning to Estonia in 1941. One of the first Estonians to be honored with a Finnish Iron Cross for his activities in "Erna." Joined German intelligence, also maintaining contacts with the British and Finns. An organizer of the Haukka-

Tümmler group. Remained in Estonia in 1944; killed on February 24, 1944.

Tammark, Olaf: Born in Tartu in 1921. Served as volunteer in German Army, fighting in Demjansk in 1941–42 and on the Narva, Krivasoo, and Tartu fronts in 1944. Officer of the Estonian Division; adjutant to Major Friedrich Kurg, 46th Regiment II Battalion. Forest Brother in 1944–45. Arrested in the forests of Valgamaa County on December 8, 1945. Political prisoner in Siberian forced labor camps until 1954; released in accordance with the Adenauer–Malenkov Agreement; emigrated to West Germany. Settled in USA in 1958. Active member and leader of several Estonian émigré organizations. USA delegate to the Congress of Estonia. Retired, living in Tennessee.

Teder, Juhan: Estonian Forest Brother. Born in 1916. Farmer in Viljandimaa County. Volunteer in German army 1941–43; deserted in 1943 and fled to Finland. Smuggled back into Estonia as communications man for resistance movement. Failed to escape country after Estonia fell to the Red army in 1944. Arrested in 1944; sentenced to forced labor in Siberia. Released in 1956. Currently retired in Valga.

Tief, Otto: Estonian government figure; a leader of the resistance movement 1941–44. Hero of the War of Independence. Member of Smallholders Party in independent Estonia. Prime Minister in the Jüri Uluots government formed in September 1944. Arrested by the NKVD in 1944 and sent to Siberia. Survived and returned to Estonia, where he died.

Toomsalu, Auleid: Forest Brother in Võrumaa County. Joined Forest Brothers while fleeing arrest in 1946. Captured and sentenced to death by Soviet authorities in 1950.

Torma, August: Estonian government figure; ambassador of the Republic of Estonia to England. The Soviet government demanded his return in 1940, but Torma refused and continued representing the interests of the independent Estonian Republic in London. Thanks to Torma's efforts, Great Britain refused to recognize Estonia as part of the Soviet Union. Torma, sentenced to death *in absentia* in Estonia, died in the Free World.

Uluots, Jüri: Estonian government figure. Born in 1890. President and head of the last legal government of the Republic of Estonia 1939–1940. Went underground after the occupation of the country and escaped arrest. In 1941, as the Acting President in the absence of Konstantin Päts, who had been deported to Siberia, Uluots sent the German command a memorandum seeking to induce the German authorities to transfer power to the lawful government of the independent Republic of Estonia. Leader of national resistance movement

1941–1944. Proclaimed a new government of the republic in Tallinn in September 1944. Fled to Sweden, where he died in 1945.

Vaisserik, Arved: Resistance movement activist and local historian. Had contacts with the Haukka-Tümmler group. Imprisoned and sent to Siberia. Returned to Estonia. He has written a detailed autobiography and researched local history. Living in retirement in Aegviidu.

Velisalu, Endel: Soviet "partisan" in Estonia. Mobilized into the Red army in 1941 and sent into Estonia as a partisan. Interned in German prison camp. Located in the American zone at the war's end; repatriated to Russia. Arrested and sent to Siberia. Currently retired in Estonia.

Vellner, Harald: Estonian public figure and journalist. Fled to Finland in 1940, where he worked in coordinating the resistance movement in Estonia until 1944. Died in the West.

Zymantas, Stasys: Lithuanian scholar and political figure. Born in 1912. Lithuanian expert for the SIS. After the end of operation "Jungle," moved to the USA, where he died in 1973.

Bibliography

Archives of the KGB (AKGB), delo 25 819.

Bower, Tom. *The Red Web*, AKGB; 40–41.

Erilt, E. "Metsavennad," *Virumaa Teataja* (1990).

Gaspl, I. "Loks 'penidele'," *Kompromiss on välistatud* (1984).

Grisin, G. and Normet, A. "Lehed langevad," *Noorte Hääl*, (March 1957).

Grisin, G. and Normet, A. "Lehed langevad," *Noorte Hääl*, (April 1957).

Hando, August. *Leitnant Julius Kuperjanov. Partisanide löögivaimu kehastaja* (Tallinn, Eesti Raamat, 1936).

Hanko, Jüri. "Me olime noored, me tahtsime elada," *Kultuur ja Elu* (November, 1991).

Hanschmidt, A. and Mürk, V. "Alfons Rebase fiasko," 167-68.

Hanschmidt, A. and Mürk, V. "Alfons Rebase fiasko," *Kompromiss on välistatud* (1984).

Hanschmidt, A. *Nähtamatu duell* (Tallinn, Eesti Raamat, 1968), 49-50.

Heine, Eerik. "Metsavennad," *Eesti saatusaastad* (1964).

Järlik, R. "Veel kord 'Haanjamaa monumentidest'", *Edasi*, (January 26, 1988).

Jõgi, Ülo. "Erna grupi sünd ja tegevus," *Akadeemia*, Vol. IX (1990).

Kald, E. "Inimesed ilma inimlikkuseta," *Rahva Hääl* (September 17, 1968).

Kauri, Lembit. *Kirjutamata memuaare* (Tallinn, Eesti Raamat, 1989), 142-149.

Kits, Malev. *Haanjamaa monumendid* (Tallinn, Eesti Raamat, 1968).

Koit, Jakob. "Estnische Bauer als Krieger während der Kämpfe in Livland 1558-1611," *Annales Societatis Litterarum Estonicae in Svecia* (1966).

Kommunismiehitaja, (January 9, 1965).

Korsunski, M. "Eduard Sisase elu ja argipäevad," *Kompromiss on välistatud* (1984).

Kuznetsov, S., Kurilov, I., Netrbeski, B., Sigatsev, J. "Vooruzennoe natsionalistitseskoje podpolje v Estonii 1940-1950," *Isvestija VIII* (1990).

Lään, R. "Murrangulised aastad," *Harju Elu*, (February 4, 1988).

Laar, Mart. "Ernast Haukka-Tümmlerini," *Eesti Elu* (March, 1992).

Laar, Mart. "Vastupanuliikumine Eestis 1940-41," *Kultuur ja Elu*, Vols. X & XI (1991).

Laasi, E. "Lahing rahuajal," *Pilk* (July 1990).

Laasi, Evald. "Sissisõjast Eestis 1944-1953," *Looming* (November, 1989): 1521.

Leetmaa, Meinhard. *Sõjas ja ikestatud Eestis* (Stockholm, EMP, 1979) 226.

Letter to L. Siimaste, AEHS.

Lossman, Heino. "Kehra metsast Kautla soosaarele," *Eesti riik ja rahvas II Maailmasõjas* (1957): 67-69.

Mäeküngas, O. "Kui metsad varjasid vaenlasi," *Alati avangardis*, 237–38.

Memoirs collected from Põlvamaa expedition 1989, AEHS.

Memoirs from expedition to Vastseliina, 1989, AEHS.

Memoirs from expedtion to Virumaa 1990, AEHS.

Memoirs from Helme expedition, 1988, AEHS.

Memoirs from Leevi, AEHS.

Memoirs from Pikassilla, AEHS.

Memoirs from Sadala parish, AEHS.

Memoirs from Valgamaa expedition, 1989, AEHS.

Memoirs from Vändra, AEHS.

Memoirs from Vastseliina Parish, AEHS.

Memoirs of J.J., AEHS.

Memoirs of J.K., AEHS.

Memoirs of O.J., AEHS.

Memoirs of Kalju Aarop, AEHS.

Memoirs of Enn Ennuvere, AEHS.

Memoirs of K. Gailit, AEHS.

Memoirs of August Hatto, AEHS.

Memoirs of J. Heeska, AEHS.

Memoirs of Johannes Heeska (on videotape), AEHS.

Memoirs of Karl Helk (on videotape), AEHS.

Memoirs of E. Iher, AEHS.

Memoirs of Ü. Jõe, AEHS.

Memoirs of Ülo Jõgi (on videotape), AEHS.

Memoirs of A. Käärmann; Characteristics of Võrumaa Destruction Company, AEHS; AECP, f. 12, nim. 7, s.ü. 38.

Memoirs of E. Kask, AEHS

Memoirs of Kalev Kaur, AEHS.

Memoirs of former KGB-man, AEHS.

Memoirs of E. Killar, AEHS.

Memoirs of Kalju Kirbits, AEHS.

Memoirs of Taimi Kreitsberg, AEHS.

Memoirs of K. Kroon, AEHS.

Memoirs of E. Loosaar, AEHS.

Memoirs of E. Loosaar; Memoirs of A. Käärmann, AECP, f.1, n.3, s.358.

Memoirs of Edgar Mattiisen, AEHS.

Memoirs of A. Mõttus, AEHS.

Memoirs of H. Mõttus, AEHS.

Memoirs of Valter Pajumets, AEHS.

Memoirs of K. Raikna, AEHS.

Memoirs of Edgar Ranniste, AEHS.

Memoirs of Valdur Raudvassar, AEHS.

Memoirs of Valter Rull, AEHS.

Memoirs of H. Salm, AEHS.

Memoirs of A. Saulep, AEHS.

Memoirs of A. Susi, AEHS.

Memoirs of A. Talvi (on videotape), AEHS.

Memoirs of O. Tammark, AEHS.

Memoirs of Juhan Teder (on videotape), AEHS.

Memoirs of F. Tipner, AEHS.

Memoirs of Helle Ugur, AEHS.

Memoirs of Arved Vaisserik, AEHS.

Memoirs of Aksel Viisut, AEHS.

Memoirs sent to L. Siimaste, AEHS.

"Metsavendade rünnak Kiviõlile," *Eesti riik ja rahvas II Maailmasõjas* (1957): 121.

Mürk, V. "Lahing piirivalvekordoni juures," *Kompromiss on välistatud* (1984).

Muruoja, Marta. "Meenutades möödunut," *Vooremaa*, (April 3, 1990).

Noskov, J. "Jälitab Uno Vassmann," *Kompromiss on välistatud* (1984).

Oras, Ants. *Baltic Eclipse* (London, Victor Gollancz, 1948).

Parming, Tönu. "Population Changes in Estonia 1935-1970," *Populations Studies*, Vol. XXVI/1 (March 1972): 53-78.

"Provokaatorid püüdsid Eestis metsavendi," *Vaba Eesti Sõna*, (1967) 2.II.

Purre, Arnold. *Teine nõukogude okupatsioon*, 36; AECP, f.1, n.3, s.358.

Purre, Arnold. "Teine punane okupatsioon Eestis," *Eesti saatusaastad* (1964):33-35.

Rahva Hääl, (February 26, 1965).

Ranniste, Edgar. "Julgeoleku väeosa kuriteost Virumaal Undla vallas Udriku-Männiku külas 1945. aastal," *Kultuur ja Elu* (May, 1989).

Raudsepp, S. "Kas banditism või organiseeritud partisaniliikumine," *Vikerkaar XI* (1989)

Salm, H. "Orioni jõugu lõpp," *Aja pulss*, Vol. XXII (1986).

Salm, H. "Rännukaarel," *Koit*, (August 18, 1977).

Starinov, G. *Külalised taevast* (Tallinn, Eesti Raamat, 1990).

Taagepera, Rein, "Soviet Documentation of the Estonian Pro-Independence Guerrilla Movement 1945-1952," *Journal of Baltic Studies*, Vol. X, No. 2 (1979).

Taevere, D. and Mihhailov, R. *Agoonia* (Tallinn, Eesti Raamat, 1979), p. 144.

Taevere, Daniel. "Operatsija 'Okosko'," *Chekisto* (1970):126.

Taevere, Daniel. "Operatsioon 'Aknake'," *Rahva Hääl*, (December 16, 1967).

Tammark, Olaf. "Mehed koonduvad metsadesse," *Eesti saatusaastad 2* (1964):80-81.

Teras, A. "Vandeseltslased," *Kompromiss on välistatud* (Tallinn, Eesti Raamat, 1984).

Testimonies of German war prisoners, Estonian Archives in Lakewood, N.J.

Tõnismägi, H. "23 aastat tihnikus," *Rahva Hääl* (1990):27.X-3.XI.

Tõnismägi, H. "23 aastat tihnikus," *Rahva Hääl*, (October 27-November 3, 1990).

Uustalu, Evald. *For Freedom Only* (Toronto, Oma Press Ltd., 1977).

Uustalu, Evald. *The History of the Estonian People* (London, Boreas Publishing Co., 1952).

Uustalu, Evald. "The National Committee of the Estonian Republic," *Journal of Baltic Studies*, VII/3 (Fall 1976): 209-19.

Vainik, E. "Lugupeetud Sulev Raudsepp, Mart Laar ja teised," *Vikerkaar* (February 1990).

Zaitsev, L. "Po sledu volka," *Operatsija Sinii treugolnik* (1988):386-401.

The author also made extensive use of the files of the Archives of the Estonian Communist Party (AECP). Those files are listed below.

AECP, f.1, n.3, s.105.
AECP, f.1, n.3, s.108.
AECP, f.1, n.3, s.358.
AECP, f.1, n.4, t.246.
AECP, f.1, n.5, s.28.
AECP, f.1, n.14, s.87.
AECP, f.1, nim.14, s.87.
AECP, f.1, nim.2, s.105.
AECP, f.1, nim.26, 2.70.
AECP, f.1, nim.28, s.48.
AECP, f.1, nim.3, s.105.
AECP, f.1, nim.3, s.107.
AECP, f.10, n.3, s.2.
AECP, f.11, n.8, s.102.
AECP, f.12, n.7, s.38.
AECP, f.12, n.3, s.13
AECP, f. 12, nim. 7, s.ü. 38.
AECP, f.13, n.5, s.16.
AECP, f.13, n.5, s.2.
AECP, f.14, n.3, s.26.
AECP, f.14, n.3, s.27.
AECP, f.14, n.3, s.9.
AECP, f.14, n.3, t.26.
AECP, f.14, n.6, s.23.
AECP, f.14, n.6, s.85
AECP, f.15, n.5, s.15.
AECP, f. 15, n.5, s.184
AECP, f.18, n.4, t.6.
AECP, f.18, n.5, s.21.
AECP, f.18, nim.5, s.21.
AECP, f. 18, nim. 8, s.ü.5a.

Index